PORTRAIT OF A SOVIET SCHOOL UNDER GLASNOST

Also by James Muckle

A GUIDE TO THE SOVIET CURRICULUM: What the Russian Child is
    Taught in School
NIKOLAI LESKOV AND THE 'SPIRIT OF PROTESTANTISM'
RUSSIAN IN SCHOOLS (*editor*)
TURGENEV'S 'MUMU' (*with introduction, notes and vocabulary*)

Portrait of a Soviet School under Glasnost

James Muckle

Senior Lecturer in Education
University of Nottingham

St. Martin's Press   New York

All rights reserved. For information, write:
Scholarly and Reference Division,
St. Martin's Press, Inc., 175 Fifth Avenue,
New York, N.Y. 10010

First published in the United States of America in 1990

Printed in Hong Kong

ISBN 0–312–04748–7

Library of Congress Cataloging-in-Publication Data
Muckle, James Y.
Portrait of a Soviet school under glasnost / by James Muckle.
      p.   cm.
Includes bibliographical references.
ISBN 0–312–04748–7
1. Public schools—Russian S.F.S.R.—Moscow.   2. Public schools—
Russian S.F.S.R.—Leningrad.   3. Education—Russian S.F.S.R.—
Moscow.   4. Education—Russian S.F.S.R.—Leningrad.   I. Title.
LA832.M83   1990
370′.947—dc20   90–31927
                                                                          CIP

Contents

List of Plates

Introduction

This book arises from a period of three months spent teaching English in schools in Moscow and Leningrad in the autumn of 1988. One of its several purposes is to give a personal account of that experience, concentrating on the people who teach and learn in one of those schools. The teachers and pupils and their life and work are seen from the point of view of an English educationist, and there is behind almost everything in this book an implicit comparison with schools in England. It is, therefore, a 'case study' of one particular institution of a certain type, and it might be suspected that the case which is being studied is in some, most or even all ways not representative of the Soviet school. Fortunately, in the course of many years' study of the Soviet education system I have been able to visit about twenty-five different schools in five republics of the Union. This, together with many meetings with teachers and officials including a minister of education, and reading of the educational press and of official documents relating to schooling, enables me often enough, though doubtless not by any means always, to say what aspects of Moscow 'School No. 1937' are common to schools in general and which are peculiar to itself. The book is therefore offered to students of Comparative Education and Soviet Studies as an introduction to the Soviet school system. The notes are rather sparse, since I am presenting my own findings of a particular institution, but I have endeavoured to include in them recommendations for further reading both to students who understand Russian and to those who do not.

I taught in two schools, but this book describes only one of them. I spent considerably longer in Moscow than in Leningrad, and a portrait of two institutions, one of which I know very much better than the other, would scarcely have been satisfactory. Consequently I decided to concentrate on the Moscow school, while using material collected in Leningrad as a contrast or as corroboration to amplify the portrait. The book is not, however, meant to give a composite picture, and it should be quite clear which school is being described at any point. I am not quite sure why I have thinly disguised the Moscow school as 'School No. 1937', since I hope I say nothing to the discredit of those who work and study there, but none the less it seemed right to conceal its exact identity. '1937' is not its number, but it has a four-figure number which recently replaced the two-figure identifier that it has borne until now – and by which it will doubtless continue to be known unofficially, such is the power of custom and tradition! If there should be a Moscow school with that number, I humbly beg its pardon – it is *not the same* as my pseudonymous School Number 1937.

When I show my students of comparative education photographs of schools in other countries, I warn them to remember that as photographer I have chosen what pictures to take, and from what viewpoint to take them. The camera may not lie, but the person who holds it has his own presuppositions and prejudices. A knowledge of his background and experience helps to interpret his picture. Coming from what would have been considered thirty to forty years ago as an orthodox grammar school education, I studied Russian at two universities, Cambridge and Leeds. An interest in Russian literature and life has always been a major motivating feature in my career. I taught modern languages, most especially Russian, in two schools in Chichester and Leeds for fourteen years before becoming lecturer in education at Nottingham University. There I have been able to acquire knowledge of the Soviet education system; I am much less interested in its administration and management than in what goes on in schools and classrooms there.

It will be important for the reader a few years hence, whatever happens to the Soviet Union and its schools in the meanwhile, to understand exactly when it was that I taught in School 1937 and its Leningrad contemporary. It was September to December 1988. At that time the new openness of the press was having its full impact upon the Soviet people; a re-examination of the recent past was taking place as well as relatively free discussion of current issues. Even church affairs were being treated on television, often without hostile comment. Painting had been set free, cinema and theatre were blossoming – one of the most memorable evenings I spent in Moscow was at the Taganka Theatre seeing Yuriy Lyubimov's production of *Boris Godunov*, which seemed to me to be gripping, thought-provoking and true to Pushkin. Lyubimov had left the USSR a few years previously when this production, which cunningly stressed the complicity of the masses in the dubious events surrounding Boris's accession and his deposition, had been banned by the previous regime. In home affairs, there was nationalist unrest in various of the Union republics, especially Uzbekistan, Azerbaidjan and Estonia. The fearful earthquake in Armenia took place in early December (and was, curiously, relegated to second place in the television news bulletin that evening: viewers were kept in ignorance of the disaster for 23 minutes while the cameras showed Gorbachev's visit to the United Nations – not his speech, but his walkabout in New York). The Soviet Union was painfully withdrawing from Afghanistan. The sensational elections of early 1989 had not yet taken place, but were eagerly looked forward to. In education, reforms instituted in 1984 had all but broken down, and radical measures for progress were being suggested – see Chapter 6. Into this ferment, in October, the British Secretary of State for Education and Science came to see what was going on.

To say it was a great privilege to be allowed to teach in a Soviet school will doubtless sound like an unctuous and platitudinous cliché – I cannot help that! It is a thrill, after spending two-thirds of a lifetime studying a foreign language and culture, to be permitted to participate in the education of the youth of the country concerned. No longer do I feel like an observer, but more a participant in the process, however briefly I carried out the duties. I should like to thank the Central Bureau in London, especially Joan Hoggan, for encouraging me to go on the exchange and for making all the arrangements. In doing so I heartily recommend other teachers of Russian to take advantage of the exchange in future years. I thank also the newly constituted State Committee for Education of the USSR and the cultural relations section of the Ministry of Education of the RSFSR for admitting me to their schools. Thanks go also to colleagues and those who replaced me temporarily at Nottingham University, Anne Convery, Doreen Coyle and John Partington, without whose cooperation I could not have gone to the Soviet Union.

Most sincerely do I thank the children and young people in School No. 1937 (not forgetting the Leningrad youngsters too). If they had not been good-humoured, keen to learn and warm in the way they received me, I should not have wanted to write this book. Most of all, I thank my teaching colleagues for their kindness, patience, professionalism and frankness in discussion. While I was there, I joked about writing a book about them; they must have suspected it was not entirely a joke. I sincerely hope they find nothing in this book in any way undeservedly critical, and I am sure they will let me know if they do. They and their pupils have given me the most fascinating time of my professional life, and I shall always be grateful to them.

JM

1 Day of the Teacher
The Staff of the School and Their Work

ANNUAL FESTIVAL

'What lessons do you want me to prepare for tomorrow?'

'Oh, tomorrow. I must tell you about tomorrow. It will be chaos. Did you know that the first Sunday in October is called 'Teachers' Day'? . . . Well, on the Saturday before, the children turn it into a celebration. It will be interesting for you to see how awful our children can be.'

'Awful' is a word Marina Georgievna uses a good deal. She picked it up, apparently, on her sole exchange visit to America and uses it with American stress and intonation, yet in not quite the same way as a native speaker of English would. For her the word expresses mild disapproval. She is deputy head in charge of English at School No. 1937, a Moscow comprehensive school described in the official phrase as having 'intensified instruction in English'.

'Well, would you like to take the little ones at 8.30? Lesson 14, following on from the one you took today. Different children, but the same lesson. I think you still have the teacher's book and a copy of the textbook. And then the same lesson twice with two different sixth-year groups. I'll find out from Natasha what she wants you to do. There will be so much happening, you won't have a chance to do any more.'

At 8.15 on the Saturday morning, Saturday being a normal school day for most Soviet children, it is clear that something special is afoot. Many pupils arrive carrying bunches of flowers. There are more parents in evidence than usual. Several of the girls are wearing clean white pinafores with lace collars – a sure sign of an occasion – and some of the boys too are a little better turned out than usual. In the staff room a colourful poster has been pinned over the notice-board bearing greetings to all the teachers; a huge mock padlock of cardboard has been affixed to the doors of the cupboard in which registers and mark-books are kept. Music is playing in the corridors before school; and music over the public address system is another

1

characteristic of a Soviet festival. The children are a little more excited than usual, but lessons begin normally at 8.30.

A group of eight-year-olds come reasonably happily into the classroom, eager, it seems, for their fourteenth lesson of English. What they think when they see the English visitor standing at the teacher's desk, goodness knows. He is male – nearly all the teachers they have ever had or are likely to have are female. He – and whether they really understood this point is doubtful – speaks the language they are learning as his own. They probably know he understands their language, because they will have heard from their classmates that yesterday he had to explain the rules of a game to another group in Russian, which they never would have understood in English, since they know rather fewer than 50 words so far. Nevertheless, nearly all the lesson is conducted in the language they are learning.

'Stand up please. Get ready for the lesson. Good morning, boys and girls!'

This is what the book says they will be used to at the start. The greeting is acknowledged by a formal nod, since that is what the class has been brought up to do.

'Sit down please. Close your books.'

A gesture conveys the meaning for those who do not understand. I begin to ask their names and make a seating plan, since I need to know how to address them.

> What is your name?
> My name is Vika.
> What is *his* name?
> Her name is . . . . [laughter] His name is Alyosha.
> Is *her* name Katya?
> Yes, it is.
> Is *his* name Igor?
> No, he is not Igor. His name is Kolya.
> So, your name is Alyosha. Is that right?

Consternation. The book says they know 'right', but they clearly do not. This is sorted out in Russian.

> You are Alyosha, is that right?
> Yes, my name is Alyosha.

The children gobble up this uninteresting material. It flashes through my mind that interest and boredom cannot always be judged by absolute criteria. My student teachers in England occasionally apologise for giving a 'boring' lesson, when in fact the pupils have not been bored. On the contrary, they may have been given humdrum material, but because they felt they could master it, they sensed they were making progress and were not bored. Now this group of Moscow children who have been drilled to answer the question, 'What is your name?' in English, are actually meeting an Englishman, who is not merely being polite, but actually needs to know what their names are – and they can communicate that information (in, perhaps, a slightly stilted way) in *his* language. Genuine communication is taking place, which is what all the recent textbooks of language teaching say should be happening all the time. Nevertheless, the conversation now becomes more sophisticated and more artificial.

The teacher takes a pile of picture cards.

Is this a man or a woman?

Disaster. They do not know 'or'

Is this a man?
Yes, he is a man.
Is he a teacher?
No, he is not a teacher.
Good. What is he?
He is a vawker.
Yes, he is a *worker*, good.
Is this a man?
No she is a voomn.
Good, she is a woman. Say after me, *woman*.
OOman.
Woman.
Woman.
Everybody, say after me, *woman*.
Woman.
Worker.
Worker.
Oh, Dr Muckle, I am so sorry to interrupt the lesson. The parents are here, and would like to come in.
By all means.

English is switched off and we all become Russians for a minute or two. Four or five parents squeeze into the tiny room with flowers for the teacher. (They were not expecting me, but I get a carnation too.) They call upon three of their offspring to recite poems in praise of the teaching profession. In Soviet custom and practice it would not be considered sufficient simply to enter the room and offer good wishes all round. The occasion must have a feeling of slight formality, preferably with speechmaking (however briefly) and some ceremony. After the poetry, the flowers are presented, smiles, good wishes and thanks are exchanged in abundance, and then it is back to the voomn, the vawker and the like.

It is far from easy to plan a forty-five-minute lesson in a foreign language for eight-year-olds. Nevertheless, by constantly changing the activities, using pair-work, guessing games, whatever visual aids are at hand, and recordings of simple texts, the lesson passes happily and the children work and cooperate to the very end. They are set homework, though they are only eight years old and though it is Saturday. It is a simple listening exercise to a gramophone record they all have been given. I am glad to move to the sixth year (age 12–13) for the next two lessons, since teaching a foreign language in the very early stages, and to primary-age children, is a considerable effort, especially if the foreign language is being used as the medium of instruction. Expressing yourself simply in your native language is sometimes much more difficult than speaking a foreign one, which is why many native speakers of the languages taught in British schools regrettably speak English most of the time.

Later in the morning, it is announced that some ninth and tenth year pupils will be giving a short concert in the Assembly Hall. 'James – it will not be up to much' (a good colloquial English phrase, think I), says Marina, 'but do come and see it'.

In the event it turned out to be an enjoyable and very good-natured occasion. The hall is one of the most pleasant rooms in the building; it has a stage and curtains, which are suitable for concerts such as the one we were about to see, but which would be rather cramped and inconvenient for a full-scale dramatic performance. The pupils performed many songs in a folk style sung usually to guitars, some by individuals, some by groups. At one point the headmistress called out and requested a song she had heard the 'political song group' sing on a previous occasion. A fifteen-year-old boy, who, I remembered, had asked some rather risqué questions about AIDS and drugs in English schools the day before, took part with several classmates in a jokey sketch, the point of which was that teachers have a pretty rough time persuading us young people to take an interest in good music, art and literature; whatever they do, they won't turn us off our pop culture, but none the less, happy Teachers' Day! One boy of fifteen sang to a guitar in an, as yet, rather immature voice, but one which would clearly turn into a real Russian Orthodox Deacon's resonant bass. Is it something in the genes of the Russian nation that produces voices like this? The concert ended with a comic quartet on the theme of how hard they all have to work and what slave-drivers the staff are. It was all given and taken in extremely good part.

The teachers or those who were free to be present, were sitting at the front of the hall, behind a table laden with tea and cakes. The rest of the small audience sat dotted around the hall, classmates of the performers, a few parents and quite a number of former pupils who had come to wish their teachers well. What in the Soviet Union one quickly comes to regard as the inevitable speeches were made, but were short and to the point. A retired woman teacher who had served thirty-four years in the school was welcomed and heaped with praise and good wishes. The former *voenruk* (military training instructor) had also returned – both he and his successor spoke briefly and were given flowers. At about one o'clock, the staff retired to the home economics room, where – despite difficulties of shopping (the word *defitsit*, shortage, being as common in Moscow at this time as in wartime) – a sumptuous lunch was served. Because of current difficulties and the official disapproval of alcohol, not much of it was to be had, but the ladies placed the one small bottle of vodka between me and the two military training instructors – but it passed up and down the table quite a lot. There were a few more cheerful speeches and a great deal of banter and friendly chat, which went on till 3.30.

'Do you have a Teachers' Day in Britain?'

Perhaps we ought. The Soviet festival, apart from its purely pleasurable side, clearly enhances the prestige of the profession and must surely improve relations between pupils, parents and teachers.

TEACHERS: IDENTITY, TRAINING, LIFESTYLE

One major purpose of this book is to show the people who work in Moscow School No. 1937 against the background of that institution and its wider context. The teachers figure prominently throughout the book; but I begin with a sketch of the staff, or 'collective', as the Russians call it.

Over 85 per cent of the staff of School 1937 are women. Teaching has traditionally been regarded as a woman's job in the Soviet Union.

It is sometimes difficult to convince those who do not know the Soviet Union well that there is, compared with Western countries where women's emancipation and ideas of sexual equality in recent years have come to the fore, strong adherence to traditional notions of the roles of the two sexes. Wartime recollections of female officers and soldiers alongside men taking Berlin from the Nazis and peacetime scenes of women driving tractors and digging holes in the road are both accurate, but that does not mean that Soviet womenfolk are accepted as the equals of men in anything but theory. Teaching was always held to be a woman's job because of the low salary, but one of the reforms of education propounded in 1984 was to raise salaries by 30 per cent. An almost immediate consequence of this was an increase in the number of men entering the profession. It was said in 1988 that more than half the trainees on some initial training courses for mathematics and science were male. A second reason for the preponderance of women was the feeling among men that looking after children, bringing them up – to use the Russian word, *vospitat'* – was a task for women. Teaching children a subject could be a man's job, the pastoral side of a schoolteacher's work was not. The few men who do enter the profession are often promoted: a noticeably high proportion of inspectors, administrators and officials are male.

The new influx of men into the Soviet teaching profession has not reached School 1937 as yet. The six men on the staff were the music teacher, who was shared with another school, the art master, a history teacher, the boys' crafts teacher, a teacher of physical culture (as it is called in Russia) and the military training instructor, a Soviet Army major who was spending part of his retirement after forty years' service working at the school. The other thirty-eight staff were all women, and this proportion is fairly typical of the many other schools I have visited in European Russia.

The teachers in School 1937 represent the entire range of personality types which one might meet in the profession in other European countries. There are quiet and withdrawn teachers, and lively, extrovert types. There are those who dominate a class, and those who are relaxed with children. A few seem tense and slow to smile, many more fizz with life and humour. Some can rebuke a child quietly, others play hell so the whole school knows about it. Some merely get through the syllabus efficiently, while others can actually make the lessons interesting and explore the children's ideas and responses. Some are earnest, others lighthearted; most can be both. Many are outgoing and easy to get to know, a few are hard to relate to until you work at making their acquaintance. The majority show keen concern for the well-being and progress of their pupils have created an excellent atmosphere in School 1937; some even treat the children rather like nephews and nieces and are treated in return with trust and friendship, but without undesirable familiarity. The teachers would be recognised and accepted in any British staffroom as fellow professionals. They get on well with each other, though they are not unaware of the differences in their professional approach and skill. They have to work well together, especially in large departments like the English department, because the system requires team-work and eschews any tendency for teachers to hide away in classrooms unobserved by others.

Almost all the teachers are married to other professional people, all but the youngest with families. Their ages are from the youngest possible for a teacher immediately after training (22–23) to over sixty. This last sentence is not so banal as it appears at first glance, for there are some countries in Europe where it would not be so: in many parts of Germany there are simply no posts for newly trained young teachers. Moreover, retirement age for women in the USSR is fifty-five, but many choose to go on working into their sixties and seventies; for example, the headmistress of School 1937 was sixty-two.[1]

The majority of those teaching secondary-age children have been trained for four or five years after leaving school at seventeen, usually in a specialist teacher-training institution, where they have received what in British terms would be described as a graduate qualification in a specialist subject together with a teaching certificate.[2] In Russian terms, they have 'finished higher education'. All but one of the thirteen English teachers, for example, 'finished' the Moscow State Lenin Pedagogical Institute, which has a highly respected five-year course for English teachers and which is very hard to get into; the other had studied at the Maurice Thorez Institute, another famous specialist college for linguists, both teachers and interpreters. Courses for teachers of other subjects (such as Russian, mathematics, physics and history) have traditionally lasted four years, but are at present gradually being extended to five. The older teachers at School 1937 will of course have done school-based teaching practice during training, but this has been substantially extended since 1984 and every year of the courses now includes a period of it. Some teachers of subjects other than English have studied at universities, where most courses contain some slight instruction in teaching methodology, which is said to be intended to arouse interest in teaching as a career. The very youngest members of staff will have been sent to School 1937 on graduation without being given any choice, since all new graduates in any profession must accept *raspredelenie*, assignment to their first post. (After two years they may apply for a post of their own choice.) It is most unlikely that any of them would object to this particular posting.

Some of the older primary teachers will have trained either on four-year courses from age fifteen in pedagogical colleges or they will have completed full secondary education to age seventeen and then entered a two-year course at one of these colleges. Such institutions still exist in the 1980s, but the intention is to transfer all training of primary teachers to four-year courses in higher education establishments, thus creating what in Britain would be called an 'all-graduate' profession. Non-graduate teachers often upgrade their qualifications by correspondence or evening study.

It was difficult to estimate the stability of the staff, but my impression was that the middle-aged teachers had many of them been at School 1937 for a good long time. The head had been in post for seventeen years and other senior staff for considerable periods. At least one of the younger teachers was an old girl of the school; she had been rescued from another establishment where, thanks to the *raspredelenie*, she had unwillingly been teaching her second language, German. The morale on the staff appeared to be good, despite the poor building and resourcing, which will be described in Chapter 3.

The intellectual ability of these teachers is at least as high as one might expect from the staff of a good comprehensive school in Britain. They have, after all, gained entry to higher education against serious competition, and have survived a demanding course well enough not to have been assigned to a distant outpost of the Russian Republic (or even further!). Many of them show artistic and intellectual interests inside and outside their own subjects; theatre tickets and news of interesting art exhibitions are passed around along with information about such domestic matters as if and where sugar can be bought this month. Senior pupils gave the quality of the staff as a main reason for liking the school: 'The teachers here are civilised' – the word used was *kul'turnyy*, which implies both good education and civilised behaviour. Clearly, teachers who are themselves motivated by intellectual interests are likely to be able to motivate children. A few, but not many, of the teachers had been able to travel abroad.

The head of English had taught briefly in an American school on an exchange. No other teacher of English had visited an English-speaking country at the time of my visit, though shortly afterwards several pupils and two more teachers went on an exchange to America.

The political affiliation of the teachers is typical for Soviet schools. The Headmistress was a Party member, as was the head of English and certain other members of the staff. Overall, about 25 per cent of the teaching profession are Communists, that is, members of the Party.[3] The Party may be joined from the age of eighteen, and it is important to remember that it is an élite and that admission to it is no easy matter. Very few enter at this early age; the average age of entry in 1973 was twenty-seven.[4] Teachers younger than twenty-eight would mostly be members of the Komsomol, the Young Communist League. At the time of my visit, the future role of the Komsomol in schools and outside was a matter for earnest and heated discussion, as will be seen in Chapter 7. As is obvious from a 1984 document from the Central Committee of the Party and the Council of Ministers, the official organs of government and Party consider it important for teachers to work in 'a healthy moral and psychological climate', to be well 'informed on domestic and international issues' and for the best of them to join the Communist Party.[5]

CONDITIONS OF EMPLOYMENT: WORKING PRACTICES

Young Soviet teachers are expected on entry to the profession to teach eighteen forty-five-minute lessons a week. After gaining experience they may teach more lessons, and for the extra they are paid. If they run an official school club, their teaching load will be lightened. Pastoral responsibilities, such as being a class tutor, attract small extra payments; teachers of mathematics, who have more exercises to correct than others, are paid extra for the marking. Lessons begin at half past eight in the morning and continue until three at the latest. The school is open six days a week, but teachers teach only five. At School 1937 Monday was the free day for all of the English department (in some other Soviet schools every member of the same department has a different free day). Occasionally the day off is forfeited for in-service training. School holidays are short, except perhaps for the summer break of three months. Again, these are often holidays for the pupils, but not for the teachers. If a public holiday, such as International Women's day on 8 March, falls on a Sunday, no day off is given in exchange. In 1988 the November Revolutionary Holiday fell on a Monday, and it appeared that we should have Saturday to Wednesday off inclusive. However, on Saturday 5 November many of the pupils were in school 'on duty' to clean and repair the building supervised by staff, most teachers were there too writing reports and completing administrative tasks since it was the end of the first quarter of the year. Monday 7 November would have been free for the English staff anyway, and on Wednesday 9 we assembled for inservice training. A four-day holiday, therefore, amounted to one day only for the English department. On the other hand, we gained an extra Saturday off after Constitution Day (Friday) in October. Nevertheless, the New Year holiday is less than a fortnight, and the short spring break often finds the teachers at school while the pupils are away. The three-month summer break looks long, but examinations eat into it at one end and administration at the other. Soviet teachers work a long year, it cannot be denied.

The documentation and reports which they have to prepare on their work and on the progress of pupils differ in style from that expected in countries such as Britain, and there is something perhaps a little more bureaucratic about the way it is done. The 'diaries' carried everywhere by the pupils, in which they write what homework has been set and in which all marks are recorded, also contain space for quarterly reports. These are mainly for the marks awarded (see Chapter 2 for an explanation of the system); there is no space for any comment other than this. A certificate of exactly similar type may be provided on a sheet of paper no bigger than A5 size: it is headed 'Ministry of Education of the RSFSR. Notification of marks for knowledge and conduct'. The provision of such documents is doubtless much easier than the type of continuous prose expected on English school reports. On the other hand, I have in my possession a sheet of paper on which class tutors are required to provide thirty-one separate pieces of statistical information for the school director. These include the number of pupils in the class passing the course for that quarter (i.e. receiving satisfactory marks in all subjects), how many have received all excellent marks, how many good and excellent, how many failed through sickness; details are asked for on membership of youth organisations (see Chapter 7), the marks for conduct and diligence of these pupils, how many belong to clubs and societies and the library, whether their homes have been visited, how many are 'pedagogically neglected' or come from problem families.

There are even spaces for records of how many talks the teacher has given on road safety. The last three spaces on the questionnaire say: 'Plan of upbringing work', 'Work with parents' and 'Syllabuses completed', but there is no space on the sheet for more than a tick or yes/no answer.

Working practices must vary from school to school, but in No. 1937 teachers were centred very much upon their teaching room and did not often come to the staff-room. This was probably the most striking difference between the social habits of the Moscow teachers and their British counterparts. It seemed to be explained by the fact that the staff room contained nothing but three desks, two upright chairs, four armchairs, a wash-basin and mirror, three or four empty shelves, a cupboard for mark-books and registers, many notice-boards and a telephone. It was also a passage-way for pupils on their way to a classroom, and others frequently came in without knocking in order to fetch the registers. In other words, it was quite unsuitable as a social centre. (However, in the Leningrad school in which I taught later, the teachers also rarely entered the staff-room, though it was comfortable and had none of these drawbacks.) The deputy heads had small rooms to which they could go, and I was given a desk in one of these. The other teachers would stay in their classrooms during the frequent breaks, maybe gathering in small groups to chat, or preparing the room for the next lesson. Working practices during lesson time differ in the important respect that teachers often visit each others' lessons when they are free to do so. Another difference is in the respect accorded to the bell. Marina Georgievna detested being late for a lesson; when the bell rang, panic and anxiety broke out until she (or I, or anyone else concerned) was in position in front of the class. This was shared by virtually all colleagues and many of the children too. On one occasion I was chatting to a large crowd of younger pupils in class 3 (age 9). When the bell rang, they did not use my presence as an excuse to continue, but *immediately* went to their desks. The conditioning to the sound of the bell, as with Pavlov's dogs, was too strong to be denied.

HOW TEACHERS MAINTAIN AND IMPROVE THEIR PROFESSIONAL SKILLS AND KNOWLEDGE

The Soviet system of the inservice training of teachers differs from British practice. The idea of Saturday morning courses for enthusiastic volunteers, teachers being seconded one half day a week for masters' degree courses, or vacation conferences for such members of a subject teaching association as wish to attend are all foreign to Soviet concepts of inservice training. What has in England recently come to be called the 'Baker Day', after the former Secretary of State for Education and Science of that name, is much closer to what they would expect to see. Inservice training in the Soviet Union – in *any* profession, including teaching – is compulsory, universal, thorough and regular. Moreover, the classroom is no secret garden from which the individual teacher may exclude all except him or herself and the pupils. 'Open' lessons, as they are called, lessons which are visited by inspectors and other fellow professionals, are relatively frequent in the Soviet school. This section outlines the various aspects of professional updating which go on, but concentrates on the activities of the 'methodological association' or subject department within the school and the interschool professional improvement days.

The work of individual teachers and of the department is closely monitored by the head teacher and more particularly the deputy heads of the school. This is not, however, seen purely as a senior person checking up on inferiors; part of the function of the leadership is to facilitate interchange of ideas and experience between members of a subject department. For instance, the head of English at School 1937 kept records to show the times she had visited colleagues' lessons and how often they visited each other. By 4 November, the end of the first quarter of the academic year, Marina Georgievna had visited twenty-six lessons. Younger and less experienced staff had been seen three or four times, yet she still declared she was not seeing them enough. Teachers signed the book to show that they had visited others' lessons and had been visited: these records showed that this happened between eight and twelve times every week. Marina also sent round a questionnaire to her department, explaining that she was trying to encourage the use of modern technical aids. They were asked to state how many times they had used the tape-recorder, slides, film-strips and records and for the names of the English songs they had taught the children. Marina described herself as a 'slave-driver': the slaves responded cheerfully enough, and I witnessed one near slapstick interview in which a senior teacher made up a fictitious answer to the questionnaire, to Marina's mixture of amusement and annoyance. If the technical equipment had been of better quality, the incentive to use it might have been greater.

An equally regular and systematic means of maintaining the

professional skills of the teaching staff is the meetings of the subject department or *metodicheskoe ob'edinenie*. The English department met monthly after lessons in School 1937, and as a visitor from England and a professional teacher-trainer I was invited to play a leading part in the meetings – both at School 1937 and at the Leningrad school where I taught later. In my Leningrad school, the elected chair of the *metodob'edinenie* was not the head of department; the whole of the meetings were held, for practice, in English. At School 1937 meetings were held partly in Russian, partly in English. In November 1988 they had asked me to speak about current language-teaching methodology in Britain and to give them some background for general interest on British television channels and various other matters of life in England; the meeting went on to discuss issues of concern in the Soviet system of education. Many of these points related to the forthcoming Congress of Workers in Education (see Chapter 6) and went far beyond the interests of the English department alone. The teachers disagreed about how much variety should be allowed in the school programmes of different pupils: this amounted to a discussion of how both equality and the development of talent could be ensured. The assessment of pupils was also causing some unease, and Marina particularly thought that end-of-year examinations would be relevant in the last two years of schooling, but that they might be a demotivating feature in the early years; at any rate they would have to be handled very sensitively. They discussed the role of the textbook in English-language instruction and concluded that they should not be bound to it hand and foot. At one point a teacher suggested streaming the English groups by ability. Since there is no Russian word for 'streaming', no-one was sure what she meant; when it did become clear, feelings ran very high – the vast majority felt dividing children by ability to be objectionable, humiliating and counter-productive. Finally, the discussion returned to the point at which it had started – allowing children to specialise (obviously very much in the air as a result of the rival 'conceptions' or 'ideas' of education which are described in Chapter 6). Some thought it was good, since forcing children to learn everything would not work, others said you had to know quite a lot before you could specialise, and yet others saw little contradiction in the two opposing views. At that point it all degenerated into chaos and we went home for tea.

Such meetings are for the exchange of ideas within the school; now we may look at interschool discussion and dissemination. All professional people in the Soviet Union at whatever level have compulsorily to attend refresher courses every five years throughout their career. It is not the purpose of this section to describe such courses, which are substantial and last about a month. There are, however, continuous professional updating ventures, and a day for heads of English in Moscow schools with a special profile in English will perhaps illustrate the preferred style. They are held in a school and children were involved. All eligible personnel were there, unless there was a good reason for absence. The day I attended was on 'developing cognitive activity in the language classroom'. The basic idea was that it was good to challenge pupils intellectually by the content of the English lesson as well as by the language being taught. After an hour's introduction the seventy-odd teachers present (all women bar two) divided into four 'brigades', each of which crammed into a classroom to watch two lessons with different groups. The first teacher who performed for my brigade used the theme of friendship. This eighth-class lesson began inauspiciously with a fairly obviously rehearsed stilted discussion in English of the friendship of Marx and Engels; next pupils described some famous friendships and invited their fellows to guess who the people were; the teacher read a simplified version of Somerset Maugham's 'A Friend in Need', which appeared to be well understood. Pupils then discussed the qualities required of a good friend and the weaknesses preventing friendship; they were invited to confess their own weaknesses and write them on (anonymous) cards; these were passed around and advice to the author was given. 'My weaknesses are laziness and rudeness.' 'I advise you do spend your leisure time like Karl Marx', said one pupil. 'He spent it reading books and studying mathematics.' Even the teacher's card was discussed with tact and wit – and she defended herself more vigorously than any of the pupils!

The second lesson was for the tenth class, and the theme was art. The board was covered with reproductions of old masters, including some English painters, which were discussed and described by the pupils. The most interesting part of the lesson was the last fifteen minutes. The ten pupils had divided into two groups, each of which had chosen one abstract painting from a collection of seven reproductions. This in itself was new, in that abstract art was scorned, even banned, in the USSR until a year or two ago. Each group had to speak about the painting without saying which of the seven it was: the feelings and impressions it aroused, the shapes and colours. There was some disagreement, and pupils, particularly the boys, began to argue with each other (in English, of course). The other group had to say which painting they thought was under discussion and to say why. This was extremely well done and obviously greatly enjoyed by all. After lunch the brigades met with the teachers concerned and discussed and criticised the lessons. This was done with generosity and good humour, but theoretical issues and disagreements were not sidestepped. Finally, all the brigades reported back to a plenary session.

Such days are held in different schools four times a year. It will not have escaped the reader's notice that eight members of the English department in the school visited had to mount demonstration lessons, which must have been an ordeal that not all of them would necessarily relish. There had clearly been an element of rehearsal in the preparations for the demonstration lessons, but the best parts of those lessons were equally obviously spontaneous. In any case, foreign language acquisition includes a great deal of rehearsal of the learners' linguistic repertoire. It does seem to me that this format for the professional development of teachers is a very fruitful one – and it is used in all subjects, not only English. It is carried out on school premises with the pupils present and essential to the exercise. It breaks down the wall of secrecy surrounding many teachers and their classrooms. It places the onus on practising teachers themselves, but the professional trainers too play the role they are best at, namely providing the background and the theory to what is going on. It gives concrete examples of good practice which participants can try out and adapt in their own classrooms if they feel so inclined. Dissemination of good ideas is likely to be more effective and more likely to lead to teachers changing and refining their teaching behaviour in consequence.

This day was for heads of department, but there were several occasions during my stay in both Moscow and Leningrad when the school was used for seminars and demonstration lessons for groups of staff who had come from other establishments.

SALARIES AND STATUS OF TEACHERS

The salaries paid to Soviet teachers are not princely, despite recent increases. Here we are in difficulties, as translating roubles into sterling is far from a simple matter. The rouble is a non-convertible currency and is likely to remain so for many years to come. Tourists are given one rouble and a few copecks to the pound. They are disgracefully rooked by this rate of exchange, as the rouble has a notional value of about fifteen pence on the international or indeed the black market. However, the average worker in the USSR receives a wage of about 200 roubles a month. In assessing the real value of salaries, it is necessary to know what can be bought for the sum received. Taking the spurious tourist rate as a yardstick, it can be said that in the USSR housing, gas, electricity and telephone are absurdly cheap, public transport about town is virtually free of charge (and long-distance transport is cheap), clothing is very expensive and food is on the dear side. Now for the salaries; the head of a school the size of No. 1937 may expect to receive 350 roubles a month, the deputies about 320. As for the rank and file, salaries depend on age and experience, the work done and so on, but I was able to make some estimate of what people were actually receiving after deduction of income tax, since I was briefly shown the payroll. Amounts for the month ranged from 127 to 250 roubles; the average seemed to be about 180 roubles. (Officially published figures for 1986 give the average salary for a worker in education as 156 roubles a month[6] which is a poorer reward than that received by any other professional people other than those working in culture, art and health and social services.) These sums, for September, were being handed out in cash late during the first week in October. It was explained that banking in the Soviet Union was in such a rudimentary state that it was far simpler to hand out cash than for cheques to be paid into teachers' bank accounts.

What is the status of school teachers in the Soviet Union? The answer depends on what is meant by status and how it can be assessed. One clear indicator of the value placed on the work of a profession by society is the salary offered for doing the work; as we have just seen, by this criterion the status of teachers in the Soviet Union is low. Nevertheless, most teachers receive training of a comparable standard to other more highly paid professions, and the intellectual quality of recruits is good.

Sociologists occasionally carry out enquiries into schoolchildren's perceptions of different professions. How much reliance can be placed on these surveys, the findings of which vary a good deal from place to place and from year to year and which are often based on rather small samples in cities possibly with special conditions, is somewhat doubtful. Nevertheless, secondary schoolteaching has been rated neither particularly high nor especially low (a fraction behind physicists and a hair's breadth behind engineers).[7] In a Leningrad inquiry published in 1973 it was striking that girls classed secondary schoolteaching as very much more 'attractive overall' (thirteenth out of forty) than boys did (twenty-third), but when asked to rate it for 'social prestige', both sexes rated the profession much more highly, placing it sixteenth (boys) and tenth (girls) out of forty. However, this put it behind all sorts of scientific, engineering and technological professions, while almost everything else the boys at least rated less attractive was a manual job. It is often assumed that children reflect their parents' prejudices in such matters. Maybe they do, yet it must be said, education is highly prized in the Soviet Union, and those who provide it – teachers – are, on the whole, treated with respect.

Soviet teachers can point to the words of Lenin to the effect that teachers should occupy a high position in the socialist state, much higher than in bourgeois society. They are regarded as important workers in Communist construction, since they train and, it is hoped, form the attitudes of the younger generation; progress ultimately may depend upon them. Lenin's wife, Nadezhda Krupskaya, was a teacher and educationist of distinction; the present First Secretary's wife, Raisa Maksimovna Gorbacheva, has been a teacher. Such facts do more than a little to maintain the status of the profession. Krupskaya's name is in fact used as the title of 225 awards which are conferred annually on outstanding teachers.[8] Other than by these, the Soviet State rewards excellence in the profession by orders, medals, badges and titles such as *zasluzhennyy uchitel'* ('honoured teacher', a title awarded by the Presidium of the Supreme Soviet of a Union republic for 'outstanding achievement in Communist education' – long and distinguished service in the profession), *narodnyy uchitel'* ('people's teacher') or by such distinctions as *otlichnik narodnogo obrazovaniya* ('exemplary worker in education').[9] These probably create more impression than the odd knighthood or MBE for a headteacher in Britain – and in any case British teachers often receive such honours for work outside the classroom or even outside the profession. Promotion is available to the status of *uchitel'-metodist* (teacher-methodologist). These are outstanding practising teachers who are regarded as the best in their local areas and who take a leading role in inservice training. Parents, to judge by public comment, expect teachers to educate children morally, and complain when poor work in this field is thought to lead to hooliganism and petty crime. Teachers lack the freedom at present – but this may change – to make certain professional choices which would be regarded as important in some other countries, such as the selection of text-books, syllabuses and teaching methods, but they do have sole responsibility for the examination and assessment of schoolchildren, and they can strongly influence the career chances of pupils and consequently are a force for parents to reckon with. Recent moves to 'democratise' society mean that the views of teachers on the conduct of public education are now taken much more seriously than ever before. Finally, Soviet parents hand over their children for many hours a day to this profession, and while they are not silent about poor quality in schools if they perceive it, they entrust them to the schools with a reasonably good grace.

2 The Children

Pupils of School No. 1937 and Their Parents

School No. 1937 is a neighbourhood comprehensive school, but because of the intensified programme in English it acts as a magnet, drawing children from further afield. It provides education for what may be considered a better class of pupil than the mass schools which run according to the standard general curriculum, and consequently it and the host of other schools like it attract complaints that they are bastions of privilege. Some have argued that they breach the comprehensive principle, that they are in fact selective schools, that they give their pupils advantages not available to children in other schools. They were said to enjoy better buildings than other schools, though in the case of School 1937, as we see in Chapter 3, this is certainly not true. Almost vitriolic articles in the Soviet press, during 1987 particularly, protested that the special English schools were being exploited by influential parents, who were bringing all sorts of sinister pressure to bear on head teachers to admit their children over the odds.[1] They were said sometimes to be having their sons and daughters delivered to the school in official cars. Their children were known sometimes as *dozvonochniki* from the Russian for 'to get through on the telephone', since this was how they had been admitted. They were said to be the type who would enumerate the members of their family as 'Mum, Dad, the chauffeur and I'.

ADMISSION: HOMES

There are many different types of schools with 'intensified instruction' or a 'special profile', to use two of the official phrases which move in and out of fashion. At one time they were familiarly known as *spetsshkoly*, 'special schools', a phrase now officially confined to establishments for the physically or mentally handicapped. They are, however, still sometimes referred to by this name, or as 'English schools', 'sports schools', 'physics schools', depending on the special profile offered. Inmates of these schools, especially the English schools, are very sensitive to charges of élitism. Despite the fact that opinion in Soviet education was in 1988 veering strongly to support for schools which developed the talents of the pupils in some particular direction and to greatly increasing their numbers, even the pupils at School 1937 were a little touchy on the subject. One afternoon after school what one might call an amateur talent contest was held between ours and the 'ordinary' school next door, and during one satirical song performed by the other school the special nature of 1937 was referred to. This did not go down well with the school wall newspaper (produced entirely by pupils), which felt the remarks to be very 'tactless' – particularly, perhaps, because School 1937 was roundly beaten in the contest. But was School 1937 for an 'élite'?

To answer this question authoritatively would require far more inside knowledge than a foreigner could expect to obtain in a visit of a month or two. Nevertheless, it was possible to discover some evidence, hearsay though much of it was. The nature of the building, described in Chapter 3, would be enough to put many prospective parents off, and to make them try to get their children into some other school of the same type if a special profile was what they wanted. But the Russian parent looks beyond the building and might not find that as discouraging as one might think. There is no entrance examination as such, and there seemed to be no desire on the part of the teachers to introduce any sort of entrance test. In the school where I taught in Leningrad, in contrast, the preference for some sort of entrance test was openly expressed. At School 1937 there was, however, an interview, the purpose of which was to establish motivation on the part of the parents – did they really want their children to go through a special programme in English with all that it entailed? Staff said that if parents themselves spoke English, this was a 'plus', but it was, of course, not essential. One imagines that the existence of an interview would discourage some parents, and that others with apparently unpromising children might be dissuaded at the meeting.

In England, of course, schools are not all 'equal', however that is understood. There the nature of the catchment area is felt to have a great influence on the quality of the school, in the rather doubtful belief that middle-class children are better academically and better behaved than working-class pupils. The catchment area of School 1937 was unquestionably proletarian, but how many of the children came from it? I have not consulted the school registers, but, by asking a certain number of children, I arrived at the conclusion that about a third of the pupils lived in the flats next to or within walking distance of the school, another third came not more than one stop on the metro, and the remainder travelled quite a distance – one pupil I spoke to travelled four stations on the metro and then had a bus journey. The school staff told me that relatively few of the pupils were from working class families, and that most had parents who belonged to the 'middle and lower-ranking intelligentsia'. The people I saw on a parents' evening appeared to be mostly from this section of society as far as one could tell, but then one expects this type of parent to be more assiduous in attendance on such occasions. The pupils of the 'ordinary' school next door looked rather 'rougher'!

As to whether highly influential people were getting their children into the school, a chance encounter presented one example. Once at the British Embassy I was interpreting between a British Member of Parliament and a senior official in a certain important Soviet ministry. I discovered that, by one of those coincidences that sometimes occur, I had been teaching this man's son that very morning in School 1937. Now, he had every bit as much right as anyone else to send his children to that school, however far away he lived (and he *did* live quite a long way away). But his reaction when he discovered my connection with the school was interesting: he urged, nay implored, me to take his son under my wing and give him special treatment and extra coaching. 'I am determined he'll do as well as he can at English. You see that I can't speak it, or you wouldn't have had to interpret for me.' In true Soviet style he promised to help me in certain ways in return. I was relieved to be leaving Moscow within a few days, since the contact promised to be overpowering.

PARENTS' EVENING

The journalist Hedrick Smith, in his fascinating account of life in the Soviet Union, paints an horrific picture of a parents' evening he attended as the father of two American children in a Moscow school.[2] It was a relief to attend a dissimilar occasion for the parents of tenth-class pupils in late September 1988. The young people had entered the class three weeks previously and this was the first such meeting between the parents and the form tutor. Seventeen parents (more than two thirds of them mothers) were assembled at the start, and several more came trickling in later. Many of the matters raised were those one would expect to hear aired in any school in any country.

The teacher, who addressed the parents as *'tovarishchi roditeli'* (comrade parents) began by giving a general run-down on the class and praised the pupils' public spirit and *esprit de corps*, but she bewailed the fact that they were not 'keyed up' to work hard for entry to higher education. There had been cases of skipping lessons and slight unpunctuality; to get into college they would have to use every minute.

Abruptly the subject changed to an administrative matter: children should arrive at school during the dirty weather in October with a change of shoes, or they would not be admitted to the building.

Back to higher education: the reference or *kharakteristika* written by the school would carry weight only if they could present evidence of 'public responsibility' on the part of the pupil. Not all were expected to be a moral leader, but the 'attitude to labour' was basic to a good reference. Here we have evidence, if it is needed, that Soviet education pays much more than lip-service to the notion of moral education and preparation for responsible citizenship. In the age of *glasnost'* the type of responsibility required is doubtless changing, but the need for it is not declining.

The class tutor then sought volunteers to serve on the 'parents' council'. She wanted fathers as well as mothers; many were the excuses offered! Eventually three women were press-ganged into service.

At this point Marina Georgievna came in to talk about the special requirements for the examinations in English at the end of the year. Pupils would have to show they could read, understand, analyse grammatically, summarise and discuss an unadapted passage from a British or American novel. They should if at all possible subscribe to the English edition of *Moscow News* which provided material for another part of the examination – discussion of current affairs. She apologised for the English textbook, which was thought duller than the ninth-class book, but warned that, dull or not, pupils should not skip their homework. 'All the teachers know how overloaded the children are, but we're doing as much as we can to cram the maximum into our classes. Tell your children to concentrate, not to waste time.' Unnecessary absence should be avoided, but in cases of illness parents should keep their children at home, but see they did some relevant reading.

When the class teacher took over again, an attendance register was passed round. This question of attendance cropped up yet again when another member of staff came in and complained of truanting from the UPK, the interschool centre at which labour training (see Chapter 5) is carried on. 'Why can't they report on absence every single time?' asked the parents. 'Because our pupils are full of tricks and cover up for each other with spurious excuses', was the response. Participation by the parents increased in the latter part of the meeting; there was an animated discussion about health, including a case of jaundice, and demands for a class outdoor expedition to be cancelled, since one of the teachers had caught a severe chill on an earlier trip. Here the tutor stoutly defended the children's desire to take part in outdoor pursuits, and strongly advised against the parents' desire to forbid it. There were protests about the attitude and professional behaviour of one of the teachers in class. The tutor stood up for her colleague (not entirely convincingly) on the grounds that she was new to the school and did not yet fit in with School 1937's way of doing things. On both these matters teacher and parents gave as good as they got. The general tone of the meeting was very friendly, but frank and not lacking in protest or argument.

These matters occupied an hour or more, after which consultations with individual parents were held.

Parents tended to be very much in evidence on a Saturday morning, especially towards the end of the quarter, when the approach of reports might have aroused some anxiety. Some days one could see as many as forty or fifty on the premises, mainly mothers, at different times. The staff-room notice-board bore the dates of three lectures for parents. The titles were: 'Helping children to learn', 'Helping children to love books and develop artistic and creative interests and abilities in the youngest children', and 'Care for the physical development of children and anti-alcohol education in the home'.

ETHNIC ORIGINS

The racial background of the children in School 1937 will not detain us long. Strange though it may seem in an inner city area of the capital of the multi-ethnic nation that the Soviet Union is, the children there were almost entirely Russian. This statement is based on the evidence of the names of the children I taught. I began every lesson with a new group by asking the first name of each child, so that

I would know how to address him or her. I recorded 282 names, 277 of them Russian. Of the other five, one was the daughter of a temporary immigrant from another East European country, and the others were from other Soviet nationalities. No doubt some of the children were Jewish, which counts as a separate nationality noted on the passport of adults in the USSR. There are also, of course, two major nationalities whose names are largely indistinguishable from Russian: the Ukrainians and Belorussians. These are, however, very close cousins of the Russians (or 'Great Russians') as their alternative historic names suggest: 'Little Russians' and 'White Russians' respectively. Furthermore, there is no reason why Uzbek, Lithuanian or Armenian parents should not give their children Russian first names, though on the whole, they do not. Allowing for all these caveats, the school must surely be considered racially homogeneous. These 282 children were divided equally between boys and girls. This point is worth mentioning, since in Russia certain subjects are regarded as being more appropriate to one sex or the other: thus one school with a special profile in mathematics is over 75 per cent boys.

It is interesting to look at the actual names. There are fashions in the naming of children, and it is to be assumed that parents choose names for a variety of reasons: to commemorate some historical, political or artistic (perhaps even a fictional) personage, to compliment a relative or merely because they like the sound. Russian names are a minefield. Nearly all are liable to be commuted to derivatives, and not even the Russians can always tell what the full form is. Slava, for example, usually assumed to be a diminutive of Mstislav, can be derived from fifty different names. N. A. Petrovskiy's dictionary of Russian personal names[3] has helped in compiling the next paragraph.

When asked their name, Russian children almost invariably give the derivative by which they are known among their friends. Of the 141 boys I taught in School 1937, fifteen were called Dima. Colleagues informed me categorically that this name is a form of Dmitriy, but Petrovskiy gives eighteen names from which it can be derived. If all my Dimas were Dmitriys, by adding the one Mitya (another form of Dmitriy), this name wins hands down. Almost as popular was Andrey (twelve boys). Serezha (Sergey), with eight, is not quite as popular as it was a few years ago when the authorities put out an appeal to parents to think of other names, since school classes were overflowing with Serezhas. The following names scored between seven and four: Sasha (Aleksandr), Slava, Maksim, Denis, Yura (Yuriy), Misha (Mikhail), Anton and Pavel (and its derivatives

Pasha and Pavlik). Those scoring three or two include some fine relics from Slavonic history: Igor, Kostya (Konstantin), Kolya (Nikolay), Oleg, Stas or Stasik (Stanislav), Vadim, Il'ya, Vova and Vladik (probably Vladimir), Vanya (Ivan), Vitaliy, Zhenya (Evgeniy) and Kirill. Some splendid traditional Russian names like Boris and Gleb, Ruslan and Vasya (Vasiliy) scored only one, along with Artem, Viktor, Alik (which could be derived from eleven different names), Fedor, Timur, Tolya, Marat, Petya, Leva, and the four non-Russian names Uyaz, Levan, El'brus and Taptyk. Among the girls Lena (Elena), Olya (Ol'ga), Natasha (Natal'ya) and Ira (Irina) were the most popular with sixteen, fourteen, eleven and ten respectively. Anya (Anna) and Katya (Katerina) got nine each; Masha (Mariya) seven, Tanya (Tat'yana) and Yuliya six, Vika (Viktoriya), Sveta (Svetlana) and Oskana four each, Valeriya, Marina and Kseniya three each, and two each for Vera, Dasha, Zhanna and Nastya. The singletons were: Aleksandra, Alla, Alina, Alisa, Gulya, Dar'ya, Dina, Zhenya, Zina, Lyuba, Lada, Lina, Marianna, Maya, Mila, Nadya, Polina, Rosita (a Bulgarian girl), Roma, Susanna, Lilya and Yaroslava. It is good to see so many Chekhov and Turgenev heroines represented here, and to note that these fine traditional names are still popular; this list also includes one or two interesting appropriations from classical as well as Russian history which appear to be becoming popular. But only one Lyudmila – assuming, indeed that the Mila listed here was derived from Lyudmila: it can come from a whole range of other less common names.

ABILITY AND GENERAL CULTURE

How able are the children in School 1937? Again, it is an impossible question to answer. Some indication is given in Chapter 9, in which I describe teaching English to every child in one particular year-group. The best are very able indeed, but there are only a very few of these really high fliers. One would expect most of the senior pupils (who have undergone some weeding out) to do well in higher education. Not all would get in, given the nature of the competition, and not a single one was applying for entry to a university as opposed to some other type of higher education. At the other end of the spectrum I met pupils who were having difficulty with their English and who clearly found it difficult to keep up. I never met anyone who was unable to read, nor the Russian equivalent of English pupils who have been learning French for four years and still do not know what *je* means. What impresses the visitor more than the ability of the pupils is the level of motivation, the interest in English and their desire to master it. This is despite the fact that nearly all the young people saw English as an accessory to their careers; not more than one pupil in the last year was considering studying English in higher education.

Another feature of the pupils was the level of what one might call their general culture. The seniors were intelligently aware of the world outside their school and their everyday lives. This includes the world of art and ideas: literature, music, painting. Show them a reproduction of a picture and they know how to comment on it – they are open to the arts in this sense. It is true they have their popular music, and will joke about the teachers' attempts to interest them in 'high' musical culture, but they are not hostile to high culture and will discuss it sensibly. I have both conducted and witnessed lessons in English in this and other schools which have centred on the arts, and been impressed by the way Russian pupils could respond in an articulate manner to art objects. The impressive thing is that they can do this when unprepared. In two English lessons with parallel groups in the tenth class (age 16–17) I used a set of art postcards, photographs taken as essays in colour, composition, humour, sentiment and so on. With only a minute or two to prepare, the pupils put on a most impressive performance. They clearly knew without being told that I was asking them to describe the pictures, to express their feelings, to assess and comment – and they went further, in one case most amusingly extrapolating a political significance from one card (see Chapter 10).

The ability to perform in this way must be the result of training and of a generally beneficial background. One imagines that these children do not only receive instruction at school, but perhaps that their parents occasionally take them to an art exhibition or a concert and – most importantly – talk to them about it afterwards. And every pupil at this level can do it; no one falls silent and opts out when this type of subject arises.

CLASSROOM RELATIONSHIPS

What are these children like to teach? Relationships between staff and pupils were excellent in School 1937. As an incomer I found it very easy indeed to strike up a good relationship with classes, and for this I have to thank the regular staff who had obviously built up an excellent atmosphere over the years. I did not feel I had to win the trust and confidence of the pupils – I had it as a matter of course. A fool would lose this confidence, of course, but a mighty great fool he would have to be. There were one or two cases of lack of confidence between staff and pupils in School 1937. One concerned a new, but experienced teacher who had run into trouble because she was unable to adapt herself to the era of *glasnost'*: she still demanded answers learned by rote from the book instead of teaching her classes to think out matters for themselves. In another case senior pupils had gone to the head in a body to ask that the teacher of the recently introduced subject 'Ethics and psychology of family life' should be replaced by another. The head was unable to accede to the request because the teacher they wanted was already heavily overburdened. The problem had arisen because of lack of trust in a teacher with a difficult personality.

Behaviour *in class* was excellent. Sometimes classes were talkative, but it was usually work-related talk. It is sometimes hard to get children to concentrate on others' contributions to class discussion because they are preparing their own oral presentations – in the belief that they are going to be assessed and awarded a mark on the strength of this presentation.

The marking system will inevitably crop up in numerous places in this book. Though the awarding of marks was abolished briefly in the 1920s, after the Revolution, the traditional system soon re-established itself, and although it has its challengers, there are many in the Soviet Union who cannot conceive of education carrying on without marks being awarded every lesson. Everything from primary school to university final exams is marked according to the same system; oral contributions in class, written homework, formal examinations. A mark of 5 is 'excellent', 4 is 'good', 3 'satisfactory' and 2 'unsatisfactory'. Lower marks are available in theory, but rarely awarded. It is not the marks themselves, but the fact that they are given very frequently and used constantly as a carrot and a stick in the classroom, which causes controversy. Some teachers in School 1937 were opponents of over-marking, and compromised by not awarding marks *publicly* for performance in class. According to the 1989 provisional statute on the secondary school (see Chapter 6), these numerical marks will not be awarded in the first two years of primary education. Surprisingly, teachers in my Leningrad school asked how on earth British teachers maintained motivation in class if they were not constantly awarding marks, yet these same teachers were surely capable of motivating children without extrinsic devices. Children would sometimes suggest to me that I should give marks in class, but on the whole, bearing in mind a decade and a half of teaching experience in British schools when it seemed incontrovertible that pupils should have the right to make as many mistakes as necessary when *learning* a subject (as opposed to being *tested* in it), I was unable to change the habits of a lifetime.

It was something of a relief to discover that the children were sometimes naughty; at first they were so well behaved in my lessons that I began to think something must have been wrong with them. The eighth classes (ages 14–15) were the most obviously 'adolescent' in behaviour, and there were occasions when a child needed a sharp rebuke. Schoolchildren all over the world will be tempted to test a new teacher, but the Russian children I had to deal with were never a serious problem. If on the odd occasion they felt they had been dealt with too seriously, they were able in a mature way to raise the matter with me and explain, apparently without resentment. Another aspect of the relative maturity of the pupils was their tact. I remember one incident in a ninth or tenth-class lesson in which I was describing the activities of young people in Britain; we had got slightly off the point and the question of football hooliganism arose. Thinking, apparently, that I might find the topic embarrassing, one boy who obviously regarded himself as a political leader in the group muttered under his breath in Russian: 'Comrades! Drop this subject.' He must have forgotten that I could speak Russian; I quickly made it clear that I was happy to answer their questions on this as on any other matter – but the conversation quickly petered out.

SOME ENCOUNTERS

Accounts by teachers of their experiences working with children are apt to include anecdotes about individuals which the author believes to be significant for one reason or another. If these authors are Soviet, the episodes may recount how some recalcitrant youth who was disruptive, individualistic, selfish and lacking in public spirit eventually saw the error of his ways and became a good young Communist who put the collective first.[4] The effect is the same as many third-rate films of the Stalin period. I was not at School 1937 for long enough to build extensive relationships with children, but the one or two incidents described here may illustrate both that young people are the same all over the world and that Russians are in certain ways special.

Sergey was small in stature and underdeveloped, looking considerably younger than his fifteen years. I first encountered him in a talk I was giving to a rather large group of pupils, when he was unruly and had to be quelled pretty smartly. He did not misbehave further in that or other lessons, and when I met him in a corridor a day or two later and taxed him jokingly with his behaviour, he replied with perfect good humour that it was a consequence of his 'hot-blooded temperament'. Besides, he protested, he hadn't started the trouble, he was the one who got caught. The excuse will be familiar to anyone who has ever taught in a school anywhere. However, further conversation brought to light the fact that he felt out of place in School 1937 and wished to leave at the end of the year and train in a vocational school as a motor mechanic. Some days later I was told that Sergey's mother had rung the school and would be sending me some theatre tickets. When I arrived at the theatre, one of the central Moscow houses, for the Saturday matinée in the studio, I was surprised to be met at the door by Sergey. It transpired that his mother worked there on the direction side and that he spent most of his spare time helping. He showed me where to leave my coat, provided me with a programme, conducted me to my seat and engaged me in conversation till curtain-up; in the interval he reappeared, showed me back stage and entertained me until the play (John Osborne's *The Entertainer*) started again. After the show I was offered a cup of coffee – but I felt I had imposed enough, made an excuse and left. For the whole of this time I was looked after with great consideration and courtesy, but without being overwhelmed by Sergey's attention. His completely mature and natural behaviour never cracked for one moment. It was in total contrast with his raucous conduct in school, where he presumably did not want to be. His manner was, it should be mentioned, totally lacking in familiarity or 'greasing', or I should not have felt totally at ease as I did.

Vasya was aged fourteen and physically more mature than Sergey. When I had taken his class for the first time, he somehow discovered that I was keen on music, and he expressed the desire to organise a class excursion to the Glinka Museum of Musical Arts. Marina Georgievna told him to go ahead and make the arrangements; later the same morning he returned to my room and tried to get me to give him my telephone number (which I would not do), ostensibly so he could inform me of the arrangements for the visit. Then, to my astonishment, he informed me that he 'wanted to be my friend'. The directness of this statement so astounded me that I cannot remember what I said in reply, but the reader may be assured that I got rid of Vasya pretty quickly, I hope not unkindly. Now there is a cultural dislocation of understanding here, since Russian youngsters do actually propose friendship in a conventional phrase; whether a teenager can in Russian custom do this to a middle-aged man I rather doubt. For an adolescent boy to have a crush on a teacher is not all that unusual, but it is doubtful whether an English boy would have handled it as frankly as Vasya did. In my experience this was unique. The probable underlying reason for it, which I discovered from Marina, related to Vasya's home background: a one-parent family (the mother), a very much older sister, the household totally lacking in male presence. What Vasya wanted was a father, we strongly suspected. 'The trouble is,' said Marina, 'he needs a man to talk to, but he comes to school and we're all women here.' Vasya, I think, got over his crush; I had one or two sensible conversations with him in the corridors, but was unfortunately prevented from going on his excursion by a sudden attack of migraine.

The remaining incidents concern the social and political preoccupations of some of the pupils. Fellow Britons in Moscow at the same time who were teaching English in higher education institutes were of the opinion that students had been instructed never to approach them singly. When pupils at School 1937 came to me for my opinion on some politically related issue, they did so in pairs, but I always assumed it was because on the whole this is what children do. Two incidents spring to mind. One afternoon two tenth-class girls approached me with the introduction, 'Now there are no teachers here, you can tell us the truth: what do British teenagers really think of Soviet young people?' I did not wish to say that most of them probably never gave the matter a thought. The question and the manner in which it was put were far more interesting than any answer I could have given. It was clearly a matter of some importance to these girls how they were seen from abroad. How many British people care? It was not clear to me why the girls thought I might not answer the question frankly if a teacher was present.

A similar line was taken by two boys who came up to me after a question and answer session in class. One of their classmates had asked (and I think the question was probably intended seriously, though I tried to answer it not without humour), 'We have heard that in Britain you care more about animals than people. Is this true?' In my reply, I jokingly said that this was propaganda. The boys who came to me privately began, 'Speaking of propaganda . . .' What they wanted me to tell them in the absence of Soviet adults was whether it was true that unemployed people were dying of starvation in the streets of Britain, as they had been told. These boys were relieved to hear about the dole and supplementary benefit. It is interesting that some Soviet young people suspect so strongly that they are not always being told the truth about the West by their media. Their education has made them critical despite everything, even the horrors re-counted in Chapter 8.

DISCIPLINE

Behaviour out of class often left a very great deal to be desired. Staff did not seem to think that it was their responsibility to see that anything more than the most minimal order was maintained in corridors and outside. The din in the concourse areas during breaks was stupendous. Children dashed around madly. The little room in which I had my desk faced the windows of the boys' lavatories: doubtless these places were used for the intended purpose – that I could not see – but they were also certainly a centre for mischief, such as the throwing of water bombs out of the window. One day I followed a boy from the street to the school, and as he reached the main door he stubbed out his cigarette before entering. Now the pupils from the comprehensive near where I live in Nottingham do at least stop for a smoke a good quarter of a mile from the school, and they tend to hide in a dark corner behind the telephone box. Staff in Moscow do not seem to try very hard to prevent any of this behaviour. 'Yes, it's against the rules, but what can we do?'

Classroom monitors change weekly, and their duties are to prepare the room for the lessons, clean the board, check there is chalk, ventilate the room, hand the teacher a list of absentees, see the classroom is vacated after every lesson, clean and sweep up the classroom at the end of the day and 'hand over responsibility for the room to the duty class.' Every week one of the senior classes is 'duty class'. They are in evidence in the vestibule and passage-ways before school and in the breaks, but they do not seem to be 'looking after good order' (their ostensible purpose) in any but the most general way. Prefects, in the now outmoded British sense, they are not.

Dress, that is school uniform, is a relevant issue here. All Russian children wear the same uniform, whatever school they go to. (In some of the other republics the uniform differs from that in Russia.) For boys it is a navy blue suit, and the jacket may be in the style of a blazer or more like a tunic. Girls wear a brown dress, sometimes with a black pinafore (white on special festive occasions, when lace cuffs and trimmings are sometimes worn). Older girls prefer a separate skirt and jacket. Children who belong to the Pioneers (almost all in the age group) often wear the red neckerchief. I noticed, however, that a sizeable number of pupils did not wear official uniforms at all. On enquiry I discovered that this was against the rules, but the staff had not thought it serious enough to make an issue of it. There were no punks at School 1937 – but two of the most senior boys whom I taught, both of them highly respectable citizens, if extrovert and 'with-it' personalities, had had a go with some chemical substance in order to give their hair a mottled blond effect.

None of this amounts to any very serious misbehaviour, and it may be that my Moscow colleagues judged it wise to allow the children to let off steam in these ways without too much restraint. Serious offences such as vandalism or disruptive and dangerous behaviour are another matter. Academic misdeeds such as failure to do homework or skipping lessons, something of a plague in the senior classes, were also taken more seriously. I heard many children receive a telling off from the deputy heads – deafeningly by one of them, very quietly and discreetly by another. In general, teachers would say they had no effective sanctions. Children could be detained, if the home was informed about it. Extra work could be set. On one occasion in Leningrad the tenth class tutor had to deal with two boys caught playing cards under the bench during a biology lesson. 'What did you do to them?' I asked. 'There is nothing we can do. I said to them, "If you are so stupid you can't play cards in a lesson without being caught, don't do it!"' In the same school two other boys had vandalised the entrance hall: I found them in the head's study 'writing an explanation of their behaviour'.

Another part of these boys' punishment would certainly be the award of a mark of two for conduct at the end of the quarter. Two means 'unsatisfactory' and is regarded as a serious disgrace. In a school of six or seven hundred only a handful of pupils would receive two in any given quarter. It is not merely a matter of writing a figure on a piece of paper. An unsatisfactory mark for conduct might well affect a young person's chance of entry to college or to employment, or even of receiving a leaving certificate at all. Parents can be contacted, of course, and in Leningrad I was told that the parents who send their children to English language schools are more difficult to deal with than the ordinary – 'They are much simpler.' The last resort in disciplinary matters was taken extremely rarely, less than once a year, but it was held to be very effective indeed. This was a letter to the parents' workplace. It may seem odd, but trade union officials are expected to bring pressure to bear on the parents of recalcitrant schoolchildren, on the grounds that incompetent fathers and mothers are not fulfilling their duty to society.

SPARE TIME

In Chapter 11 the out-of-school activities open to the pupils will be described, but a few words about the way they spend their free time may be appropriate here. Senior pupils claim not to have much spare time. One said he worked at homework for three to four hours a day, six days a week, but others asserted that this must be an exaggeration: two hours would be nearer the average. They none the less felt that the work load was high, but believed it to be no higher than in other schools. In speaking to a dozen or more tenth-year boys and girls, an impressive list of activities emerged that they had given up in order to spend more time trying to get into higher education. Some of them had obviously been quite good at various sports from athletics to water polo, but had given them up for pressure of work. Many did, however, pursue sporting interests or cultural activities too: there was a singing group devoted to political folk music, for example. Extra coaching or attendance at preparatory classes organised by the college aimed at were common ways in which these pupils spent their afternoons. For instance, one boy who wanted to read Chinese in higher education was attending a 'School for young Orientalists', where he was not learning the language, but was finding out a good deal about Far Eastern countries. As for pure relaxation, many mentioned discos and dancing, frequenting the coffee bar in a 'house of culture', where film shows were also held. Younger pupils were often involved in the many activities run by the 'house of pioneers and schoolchildren'. The unit of purely social grouping for younger children is all the youngsters who live in one block of flats: 'the boys in our yard' constitute an informal club almost anywhere.

Holidays are often spent with the family in travel to the seaside or country; the Baltic, the Ukraine and the Black Sea were often mentioned in this context. Very many Moscow families, even those with a modest income, have a *dacha*, or country cottage, which is sometimes many miles away – or even many hundreds of miles. Distant relations in the country are visited; this or the dacha represent a totally different circle of friends and a complete change from Moscow. There are also many children who go to Pioneer camps in the summer, that is, to holiday camps run especially for children during the school holiday under the auspices of the Young Pioneer organisation. Younger children go as participants, older ones as helpers. Among the children in School 1937 there seemed to be a sharp division between those who were the Pioneer camp type of person and those who were not – a small majority of them were keen, and what they said they liked was the bathing, fresh air and fun, rather than the parades and flag-waving (which is a minor part anyway). Older children said they needed a rest from their parents, and helping at a Pioneer camp was the ideal way to get one. Why did they need a rest? 'They are always on at us about school when we are here, even if we are getting on all right! We get a bit tired of it.' One of the more thoughtful added: 'They need a rest from us too. They are always worried about us here, but at the camp they know we're looked after within certain limits.'

3 The Premises

The Working Environment for Pupils and Teachers

The school is situated on an attractive tree-lined street parallel with a busy railway goods line, which is partly concealed in a shallow cutting beyond a strip of park land. In the autumn, when I arrived, the leaves were still on the trees, but had turned to the striking colours so typical of European Russia. School No. 1937 is quite indistinguishable from its immediate neighbour, another secondary school, an apparently identical building constructed at the same time in the mid-1950s and standing a few yards away. It is hard to tell where the grounds of one school end and the other start. The pupils do not seem to mind, and colonise each others' extremely limited playground space for games of football, snowballing and informal merriment. The two buildings are surrounded on three sides by tall blocks of flats, with shops, offices and workshops at ground-floor level.

The buildings have no architectural merit or interest, except as standard schools of thirty-five years ago, but on a fine day they present a not unattractive aspect when approached from the road, since both are set among tall lime and birch trees of great age which thickly cover the ground. However, most pupils and visitors approach School No. 1937 not from the road in front, but from the busy street behind, where most of the buses and trolleybuses run and where the underground station is. 'When you come from the metro, cross to the middle of the street and walk along the park in the central reservation. Some of the people who live in those flats sometimes throw rubbish out of the window, and passers-by have been injured.' It sounds like the advice one might be given in the slum areas of any great city, yet – rightly or wrongly – one does not have any sense of being threatened. Poor and workaday the borough certainly is, yet I frequently wandered the streets after lessons or in free periods without apprehension.

The passenger emerging from the metro sees two main streets, both extremely broad as Moscow streets often are. At their intersection is a square with a very large and striking war memorial. Visible a few hundred yards down one street is part of a massive factory, which employs 50,000 people and makes cars, refrigerators and other consumer goods. Half a mile away along another street is the stadium of one of the most famous Moscow football clubs. The footpaths are crowded with shoppers, and the shops they patronise sell mainly food and clothing and resemble the standard establishments in all other parts of Moscow. Within a mile are to be found quite a good restaurant, a large bookshop singularly lacking in interesting books, a craft and hobby shop, and one selling alcoholic drinks strictly rationed to two bottles for each of the very numerous customers – on a *good* day, that is! Nearby is an ancient disused monastery, some of the surviving buildings of which are being restored. The cultural, educational and sporting interests of the population are served by the magnificently appointed Palace of Culture provided by the auto-mobile works, which is open to all, not only to its employees. The view of the Moscow River and of the South Eastern part of the city from the sports ground alongside is splendid. In short, the area may be 'proletarian' in character (in fact the name of the borough is *Proletarsky rayon*), but it is not unstimulating or lacking in effort to improve or preserve the environment.

From this direction the school is reached from the metro in two minutes by the park-like central reservation, which grants temporary safety from the feared falling objects. Sometimes pupils are to be seen here sweeping up leaves, rubbish or snow, depending on the season, as part of their specially organised civic duty, or 'socially useful labour' as it is called. Passing beneath a tall archway in the high-rise flats, the rear of the school comes into view. The visitor passes by a vast rubbish enclosure, which is never big enough for its contents, and makes his own way across the school territory, winding between a small area of hard standing used for sports, trees, broken-down sheds and more rubbish. Broken bottles often litter the way, presenting a hair-raising danger to the children, and despite the parties of pupils who seem to be perpetually clearing up in the school grounds as their contribution to socially useful labour, the land is never totally free of litter – and dangerous litter at that. 'It wouldn't have been like that in the 1960s', say the teachers. One day I passed a skip full of a great quantity of broken glass close to the school; where it had come from never became clear – the school windows seemed to be intact, at least. It appeared that it was not the pupils who were principally responsible for producing the rubbish, but the local drunks and hooligans.

At eight o'clock in the morning children of all ages are to be seen approaching the school building, the younger ones with their parents. Cheery greetings in English are cast in my direction as the front door is reached. One morning before eight we were unable to open this door with a key; the building had been used for local elections on the previous day and a stranger had obviously secured it. In a freezing blizzard we waited until someone's dad fetched a makeshift jemmy from next door and the deputy head broke in. There are three rows of swing doors to insulate the interior from the cold outside in winter; in good Russian style only one door in each row has been unlocked and the open doors do not face each other, so the crowd has to snake in. What would happen if a fire broke out when the school was full of children scarcely bears thinking about, but those who manage Soviet public buildings such as theatres, hotels and reataurants are disturbingly blind to the dangers of locked doors in places where large numbers of people congregate.

When entering the school for the first time, the visitor is struck by the sight of a large bust of Lenin which directly faces the front door. It must be said that after a few days, one ceases to notice it and takes it for granted. The ground floor vestibule in which it stands is spacious; on each side of the door are cloakrooms, the tiny canteen is at one end and the metalwork shop at the other. Three of the four floors above have an open area similarly spacious to the entrance vestibule, but on the upper storeys the space is surrounded with classrooms. This prodigal use of space in a building which is otherwise rather cramped is perhaps explained by the need for places where the 650 children can let off steam without going outside in the depths of winter. The first floor is used mainly by children of primary age and the open area of the second floor is the school museum – a professionally mounted display about the defence of Moscow during the Second World War which is designed to arouse and sustain patriotic feeling. The uppermost floor is the fourth, and it is occupied by a small workshop for the part-time technician (a recent former pupil who was not successful in gaining entry to the day-time course at the college of her choice so who is studying there in the evenings and earning a small salary here in the mornings), one or two classrooms, the domestic science room, and an attractive assembly hall which is used for concerts, ceremonies connected with the youth organisations and other gatherings. As this is an 'English' school, all the rooms have door plates in English: 'Gymnasium', 'Teachers' Room', 'Music', etc., but unfortunately some long past five-year plan produced notices reading 'Byology' and 'Assembley Hall'. The notice saying 'Third Floor' has been placed on the second, that is the third floor by the Russian system of numbering, not the English. Oddly, I quickly became so used to the errors that I believe I forgot ever to mention them to colleagues. One very quickly adjusts to the Russian variety of English and has to make a conscious effort to be accurate.

Apart from the bust of Lenin, the ground floor concourse area contains two things of interest. The first of these is a gallery of photographs of pupils, about thirty of them. The board on which they are mounted is about two or three feet square, and the standard of photography is good; in other words, the display is carefully and attractively presented and it is not vandalised. The pupils whose portraits appear are the *otlichniki*, those who have been awarded a run of excellent marks in the previous quarter. In schools in some other parts of the world the existence and maintenance of such a notice-board would be considered 'élitist', but in School 1937, as in most other Soviet schools, it is regarded as a constructive encouragement to hard work and consequent success. It illustrates the 'achievement-orientation' of the Soviet education system.

Another display board carries the *stengazeta*, or wall-newspaper. In a country where duplicating machines are rare and photocopying, in schools at least, nothing more than a dream, a school newspaper would be impossible. The solution is to produce one copy only of the paper and display it on the wall. School 1937's wall-newspaper is edited by two ninth-class pupils. It is attractively presented, with photographs, multicoloured lettering and borders and is written in a lively and sometimes quite amusing style. It therefore offers the young editors and writers some elementary experience in journalistic activity. Of course, views are sometimes immaturely expressed. It is usually tactful, but there was one instance during my stay at the school when some criticism of teachers was made in its columns, without, apparently, causing undue offence. As the visitor from abroad, I was the subject of one special issue, for which I was interviewed (in English) by two boys for about forty minutes and tape-recorded. They made the transcript and translation into Russian themselves, which must have been a considerable labour. The questions were intelligent and interesting points which arose during the interview were skilfully pursued. When the issue appeared, it was headed, 'Communication from the Komsomol Committee: establish reason for presence in the school of British citizen, male with fair, greying hair, speaks Russian with slight accent. Photograph attached.' The photograph had been taken by stealth and showed me apparently in dark glasses listening to the concert on Teachers' Day described in Chapter 1; it was later stolen from the wall-newspaper, whether by an admirer or by an enemy who wished to practise black magic on it I do not know.

With the possible exception of the hall, the entire building is unsuitable for its purpose, inconvenient and in many ways inadequate. It is necessary to stress this point, because in the year or two previous to my visit schools with intensified instruction in a foreign language, like School 1937, had been under severe attack in the press on the grounds that they often had premises much better than the normal schools and that they were consequently privileged in comparison with the mass establishments.[1] They were said to be concentrated in Moscow (and even here, within certain of the more well-heeled boroughs) and some other major cities. School 1937 is, of course, in Moscow, but not in a prosperous area.[2] Its worst problems are the lack of space and the poor equipment. The metalwork shop is cramped to the extent of looking unsafe. The sewing machines in the home economics room would have been the latest thing during the lifetime of most of the girls' grandmothers. (There is rigid sex differentiation in the craft teaching – metalwork is for boys and cookery for girls.) The gym is too small for a full class and the two changing rooms lack even a cold water tap at which pupils might have sluiced themselves down after a lesson. In the open air outside the school there is only one sports pitch; it has a hard surface and is intended for basketball, but is used for other team games too. Toilets throughout the building are well down to usual Soviet standards and would simply not be found acceptable in most Western countries; they scarcely conform to British hygiene regulations.

There is no properly equipped music or art room – merely two classrooms set aside for the subjects. The only items of musical equipment visible in the former are an upright piano of acceptable quality, some posters and a gramophone. There are no microcomputers and no computer room, and the now compulsory course in information technology in the last two years of schooling has to take place in another establishment, the vocational training centre (UPK) which is attended by senior pupils for their labour lessons too. Science labs contain minimum equipment. There are only enough classrooms for present needs, and when six-year-olds are admitted to school as they shortly must be, almost insuperable difficulties will arise. A school with a special profile in a modern language requires many small group rooms: School No. 1937 did not have these, and makeshift partitions had been erected, leaving a consequent problem for soundproofing. The resulting tiny rooms are, like everything else, cramped. The language rooms have record players and tape recorders, some of which work. In fact, the official syllabuses for all subjects contain lists of the minimum equipment and visual aids which all schools should possess;[3] to judge by comments in the educational press it is not always possible for every school to obtain these, though I have no reason to believe that School 1937 was short of what officialdom considered the essentials. About half the chalkboards (which in the Soviet Union are dark red rather than black) can only be written on with the greatest of difficulty; the chalk is of unbelievably poor quality. Projectors are a problem too – they are of antiquated design and unreliable performance. It would have been scarcely surprising if the English teachers had thought, 'Hang these contraptions; let's teach standing on our legs and forget them!' To judge by the cheerful displays, posters and pictures on the walls, what they seem to have said is: 'Blow this dreadful building; let us make the best of it and fling ourselves into the work, and take a real interest in the subjects we are teaching.'

Among the better equipped rooms were those used for primary teaching. One second-year class (age 8) had a room which was typical. A large portrait of Lenin was at the front, above a magnetic board, screen with overhead projector and a chalkboard which could be wholly or partly masked by curtains. At the back of the room were glass-fronted cupboards containing very modest displays of children's collections and craft work. At one side, some children's work in writing and drawing was rather untidily displayed, and there was an album with photos relating to a class excursion or celebration. Some boards at the side were the best kept: a display about Lenin (but does *anyone* look at displays about Lenin? Almost every classroom seems to have one) and another entitled 'Time, events, people'. Another very smart board was devoted to the organisation of the class section of the Octobrists (see Chapter 7).

Perhaps the worst disgrace at the time of my visit was the canteen. Its happiest feature was the personality of 'Aunty Nina', the manageress, who did her best in impossible circumstances and succeeded in keeping cheerful most of the time. It was a small L-shaped room with a servery by the entrance, three wash-basins let into the wall so customers could wash their hands on the spot and enough tables and benches for an absolute maximum of thirty-five people to eat at any one time – this in a school of 650 pupils. Since there is no set lunch time and pupils and staff are free at different times, and since many pupils spurn the food provided, the canteen can just about manage. The food is not cooked on the spot, but is brought in from a central distribution point; it is therefore always cold, except for the soup which Nina could keep on the gas. Nevertheless, the canteen had its good points, which can only be appreciated if the difficulty of shopping in the USSR is understood. Those who have not visited the country often do not understand that it can be extremely difficult to buy basic commodities like milk, cheese, sugar (hoarded, it was believed at the time, by those intending to distil bootleg vodka), fruit, meat and sausage. This is true even in Moscow, which is much better supplied than most other places; the problem is as much one of distribution as of supply – if one asks in a shop, '*Will* there be any milk today?' the likely answer is, 'If they deliver it.' But shops are not the only places where groceries can be obtained; sometimes goods which are not in the shops may be distributed at the workplace – industries with the greatest problems in recruiting workers are given the best supplies so they may lure potential employees into the factory by offering perquisites. Schools do not rate very highly in this respect, but I occasionally saw colleagues buying sausage and some-times meat from Nina in the canteen. She kept me supplied with milk, which the shops in the area where I lived seemed to sell only about one day in three. Fruit, cakes and pastries were also often on sale in the canteen.

The maintenance of the building and its cleaning was carried out by a small group of part-time cleaners who worked two hours a day and cleaned the concourses and lavatories, and by the children them-selves, who swept out the classrooms. Some time previously, I was told, a fearsome cleaning lady worked full-time (for a wretched 70 roubles a month) and ruled pupils and teachers with a rod of iron, chasing them around and discouraging untidy habits. Eventually this salary was recognised as being scarcely worth having, and from the departure of the cleaner concerned the school was serviced by part-timers. Keeping the school building clean can be described as socially useful labour; on the first day of the November Revolution-ary holiday a party of pupils gave the main foyer a thorough cleaning. This is a most unpopular duty, needless to say, but it can only be done when regiments of children are not trampling in and out. As autumn progressed another domestic chore was performed by the teachers – strips of paper were gummed over the gaps in the window frames to prevent draughts.

During my stay in the school great hilarity was caused by a message received from the education offices: the school had permission to buy a duplicating machine. The reaction of the staff was that it might as well have been allowed to buy a moon rocket for all the hope there was of finding one. But at least the episode indicated that money had been made available on this occasion at least. At regular intervals pupils would be seen arriving at school in the morning laden with bales of waste paper, in return for which the authorities would allow extra expenditure on library books and equipment.

This account of the school building, its contents and its surroundings must surely imply a desperate degree of underfunding. 7.2 per cent of the State budget is devoted to public education. An unsigned article in the journal *Narodnoe obrazovanie* (*Education*), emanating from the Ministry of Education of the RSFSR and entitled 'Financing: problems remain',[4] recommended as good practice that schools should try to obtain sponsorship from local industrial concerns, should sell the goods produced in the school garden or workshop. 'Have you seen our workshop?' asked Marina Georgievna. 'How could the children possibly make anything there anyone would want to buy?' The extent to which this is typical is discussed in the interview with the headmistress (Chapter 12); I have visited many Soviet schools, very few of which had deteriorated so much as No. 1937. My Leningrad school was very much better appointed in every way – not least the dining room, of which the pupils were still highly critical, as children always are. A poor building and equipment affects morale, creates inefficiency and proclaims a depressing message to pupils, teachers and parents alike – what can the quality of work be like in this dump? How can a society be said to value the work of its teachers or to be seeking the good of its children if it condemns them to work in wretched conditions? Yet this is not quite the way my colleagues saw it. Even the children, when asked about their school, would speak of the quality of the *teaching* they received – and the dedication and enthusiasm of most of the teachers was not in doubt. Despite the indigent, beggarly state of everything, it was still possible to do good work there. It must also be admitted that when a building becomes familiar to those who use it, it often seems cosy and congenial. If money had become available, it would probably not have been spent on such things as the dining room, but on something more directly affecting the work of the school: the poor facilities for physical education were perceived by the staff in this light. Nevertheless, teachers and children alike deserved something much better. When a local government election was held in the school building, the primary-age children were sent home and the ground and first-floor concourses were sealed off from us poor plebs who actually worked there. This, however, was not the biggest insult – that was the fact that all the office furniture installed for the day, desks for the returning clerks to sit at and so on, beautifully produced notices and slogans in red and white lettering, were of such a quality and newness as to make the drabness of their surroundings almost painful to us, who could only see them with difficulty through the screens set up to keep us out of the way. The lesson for the politicians elected is too obvious to need elaboration, but it can, happily, be said that the Soviet Union is now beginning to set less store by political show and more by social reality. More money is in fact promised for the schools. It is certainly needed.

4 The Story So Far

Where School No. 1937 Fits Into the System

Where had the children at School 1937 been before I met them, and how did they get there in the first place? What were they hoping and planning to do when they left? The purpose of this chapter is to provide a summary description of the Soviet education system[1] and supply some of the general background.

THE PRESCHOOL YEARS

Many Soviet children are entered in an institution from a very early age. The crèche (*yasli*), often organised by the mother's workplace, takes them from the age of three months, and the kindergarten (*detskiy sad*) from three; often these days the institution is known as a *yasli-sad* and caters for the whole age range from three months to six or seven years. Education is not compulsory until the age of six or seven, so the first decision the parents have to make is whether or not to send the child to a preschool establishment.

For several reasons the parents may have little choice. 92 per cent of women of working age are in employment. Salaries for both men and women are not high, reckoned by Western standards or by comparison with the cost of living in the Soviet Union, and most couples need two incomes. Soviet homes are not equipped with so many labour-saving devices as in other highly developed countries, shopping is stressful and very time-consuming; despite ideological assent to the idea of the equality of the sexes, many Soviet men expect their womenfolk to do all the housework and shopping. In coping with daily routines it is essential for parents to have their children looked after by others. That means, for the majority in the Russian republic at least, the crèche and kindergarten, which operate up to twelve hours a day and will keep children overnight if parents are away on business.

However, there are alternatives. The traditional upbringer of children in Russia is their grandmother, and until a few years ago she

44

was regarded by many young parents as a desirable alternative. But nowadays many Soviet grandmothers are refusing to carry out their traditional role; as more kindergarten places become available, they see no reason why they should accept the commitment. Children are, however, sometimes minded by friends or relations. Parents from the professional and intellectual classes who can arrange to work at home for some of the time may manage to look after children themselves. Parents may pay to have their children minded, or, of course, one parent, almost invariably the mother, can choose to take a break from working life in order to bring up the children, though many fear that career prospects may be severely damaged by this course of action.

The official attitude to preschool education, often indignantly asserted by kindergarten workers when they suspect others do not fully accept it, is that establishments with well-trained, caring staff are unquestionably the best place for young children to be during the day. They receive expert care, and, most important for a young member of a socialist society, they develop social relationships with their peers which are as significant as emotional relationships with their parents. Furthermore, the argument goes, even if they spend relatively little time with their parents, there is every likelihood that the quality of their relationship with mother and father will be enhanced, and the quality is what is important. But if all this is so, why should parents seek an alternative to preschool establishments?

They may do so simply because a place for their child is not available. Half the total age group in fact attends a preschool establishment, but in some large Russian towns this proportion can reach 90 per cent or even more; nevertheless, figures published in 1986/87 revealed that one and a half million more applications for preschool places were received than could be satisfied.[2] And despite the attitude that preschool is actually a better place to be than home and despite also the feeling that a mother owes the duty of labour to the state, there are many Soviet parents who do not wish to be deprived of the experience of bringing up their own children. Recent legislation making more generous arrangements for maternity leave and payment has proved very popular indeed, and many mothers are taking maximum advantage of it. (Women now have a right to partly paid leave for one year after the birth of a child and eighteen months unpaid leave.)[3] There are even a few parents who feel strongly that *they* wish to take responsibility for imparting values to their child, even going so far as to express it in terms of 'putting off the brain-washing as long as possible'. Needless to say, this view would be indignantly rejected by very many Soviet educators.

The overwhelming majority of children attending School 1937 – 75 per cent to 90 per cent had attended a kindergarten, and they clearly felt it was the 'normal' thing to do. The principal concern of these establishments is the general and moral development of the children and care for their physical well-being rather than formal instruction. Music, art, poetry and dance are all stressed; any visitor soon discovers that the children perform with great relish. Meals are provided four times during the long day. Medical advice is readily available. Parents pay fees on a sliding scale from 20 roubles a month to nothing, according to their income.

What is it like inside such an institution? Are children happy to go there? The point is made by sociologists that Soviet children are used to much closer contact with other relations, neighbours and friends than is customary in Western Europe or America, that they are taught to regard all friendly adults as 'uncle' and 'aunt', and that they are consequently not unwilling to be handed over by their parents to others for many hours a day. Visitors often comment favourably on the quiet atmosphere and the orderliness in comparison with nurseries or infants' schools elsewhere. The purposeful activity is also favourably noted, but it is thought to be very highly teacher-directed rather than child-centred.[4] In accordance with the principles of Soviet morality, great emphasis is placed on *collective* work and play. Soviet preschool children, by the end of their time in kindergarten, often show pleasing self-confidence in dealing with strangers.

COMPULSORY EDUCATION

One of the most controversial of the measures introduced by reforms of the school system in 1984 was the decision to lower the school starting age to six, though since 1988 educationists have been saying 'six or seven'. No matter that many Soviet children in certain republics had been in school at six for several years and that an earlier start is usual in almost every other European country except Sweden, the change from seven to six was quite vociferously opposed by a substantial minority of parents and educationists. Remarks are heard like 'Childhood is being cut short' or 'School is no place for six-year-olds'. (The most vociferous and unrepentant proponent of this view I have ever met was 'Aunty Nina', the kitchen lady at

School 1937.) This is strange in view of the high proportion of Soviet children who attend preschool establishments for many long hours a day as it is. Why is school sometimes regarded as 'no place' for them?

The answer is quite simply that the image of 'school' as it is perceived in the Soviet Union is of an extremely formal classroom atmosphere with much rote-learning and a very high factual content, almost entirely teacher-centred and making scant concession to the immature stage of development of the child. The work of Froebel was known in Russia in the 1870s, but such notions of early childhood education were too foreign to Russian practice to gain much currency. After the Revolution, in the 1920s, Russian schools experimented with methods based on the ideas of such as John Dewey and Helen Parkhurst, but – possibly again because these notions were simply too new and surprising in the Russian context – there was a return to so-called 'traditional' methods under Stalin. There was an objection to informal methods which was ideological: the authority of the teacher must not be called into question. Despite the possible attraction of a pedagogy which might involve children working cooperatively in groups, until very recently the reception classes in Soviet schools taught seven-year-olds in a very formal, though not necessarily ineffective, way. Everyone, parents and teachers alike, knows such methods to be totally inappropriate for teaching infants, which explains why they think 'school is no place for six-year-olds'. The introduction of compulsory schooling for children at the younger age has had to be accompanied by measures to sweeten the pill: the option of holding the first-year classes *in kindergartens* and the promise of much more appropriate treatment, premises and equipment for the reception classes in regular schools. This matter was being taken very seriously at School No. 1937 and was likely to cause them problems, as we shall see from Chapter 12.

Since 1986, then, (and in some republics for much longer than this) Soviet parents have been entering their children at six for primary education, which the expectation that they will stay in compulsory full-time schooling for eleven years. In towns and cities the school will almost certainly be an all-age, unstreamed, comprehensive, co-educational, primary-with-secondary school serving a set catchment area, and with a curriculum nationally decided which is taught using textbooks officially prescribed. There are about 140,000 such schools in the USSR.

As explained in Chapter 2, the parents of the children at School 1937 had taken advantage of the existence of schools with 'special profiles', to which parents from outside the normal catchment area may send their children. This school's special profile was, of course, English. These schools were once known as 'schools with a series of subjects taught in English', since at one time this was in fact done, but now their official title is 'schools with intensified instruction in English'. There are approaching 100 schools in Moscow with a stress on one foreign language or another, about 80 of them English. After leaving School 1937 I taught in a Leningrad school with one class following a special profile in Mandarin Chinese, and I have visited others at different times in five different republics of the Soviet Union with intensified instruction or special profiles in subjects as varied as mathematics, applied art, music, wood carving, sport and Russian. The boys and girls at School 1937 were there either because they lived close by, or because their parents had taken the initiative to enter them specifically at this school.[5] They would do this presumably because they believed some advantage would thereby accrue to their children, which is exactly why parents anywhere in the world select one school for their children rather than another.

The Soviet child arrives at school for the first time, perhaps passing through decorated streets after hearing festive messages on radio and television, on 1 September (the 'Day of Knowledge'), carrying flowers for the teacher. A short ceremony, usually held partly on the steps outside the school ends when the first school bell is ceremonially rung and older pupils take younger ones by the hand and lead them into their classrooms. The very first lesson in recent years has been a 'peace lesson', recalling in speeches, poetry and song the horrors of war and the need for world peace.[6] These rituals reflect the official values of the state and the importance attached to education, and they must inevitably serve to make a child's first day at school a memorable occasion.

In the first year of primary education at least the atmosphere and teaching methods will be less stiff than implied by the misgivings felt by opponents of school at six; for the remaining three years of primary education children will receive formal instruction in their native language and/or Russian, arithmetic, music, art, labour or PE, along with one lesson a week in the first two years entitled 'Acquaintance with the world around' (elementary geography, science and general social awareness) and in the last two a lesson of nature study. (Fuller details of the curriculum at all levels will be given in Chapter 5.) For most of this time the children will be taught by their class teacher; there are twenty weekly lessons in year one, rising to twenty-five in year four. A lesson traditionally lasts 45 minutes, though it is shorter for the six-year-olds. The 'daily regime' of instruction, though not of activities, in School 1937 is as follows:

8.30	Lesson 1
9.15	Break
9.25	Lesson 2
10.10	Long Break
10.30	Lesson 3
11.15	Long Break
11.35	Lesson 4
12.20	Break
12.30	Lesson 5
13.15	Break
13.25	Lesson 6
14.10	Break
14.15	Lesson 7
15.00	End of Lessons.

This applies to all classes, but the younger children will finish usually by 12.20. School operates Monday to Saturday. As many as 86,000 Soviet schools, including 1937, organise an 'extended day', by which pupils are looked after until their parents collect them or they can return home and be sure of being admitted. Where school buildings are not adequate to house all children of school age, a second shift operates. This arrangement may have to be introduced at No. 1937, but, needless to say, it is dreaded, since it creates as many administrative problems as it solves. No-one regards it as educationally satisfactory.

At the age of ten the Soviet child moves on to the secondary phase of education when he or she enters class 5 (by the new numbering). For most children this means no change of building, but that all subjects are now taught by specialists rather than by a class teacher.

A general course of study is followed in the first five years of secondary education; in School 1937 the intensified course in English is added to this. The first serious hurdle in terms of public examinations comes at the age of 15, when the children are tested in Russian and mathematics. This is done orally and in writing, and the examinations are carried out in school, conducted and assessed by the staff of the school.

Until a few years ago full-time formal schooling ended at fifteen for many children, and the eight-year course, as it then was, was known as 'incomplete' secondary education. As more resources for education became available the compulsory period was extended to ten years, but it was not until 1975 that the authorities were able to announce with confidence that every child starting school in that year would certainly complete ten years. Now, since 1986, eleven-year compulsory education is promised for all. Full-time education for the entire age group 15–17 is therefore a fairly recent innovation. What considerations has it brought in its wake?

Reading between the lines of the Soviet press, it seems clear that these years used to be seen by teachers as a finishing school for the rather more able pupil. It was at one time assumed that the others would take themselves off, if they decided to continue their full-time education, to another establishment, such as a vocational school of one sort or another. Some would leave school and continue their education part-time in evening classes. Those who stayed in the general school were expected to get on with an academic education, and to do it pretty well – regularly to get marks of 4 (good) and 5 (excellent), in other words. For a pupil to be awarded a 3, despite its designation as 'satisfactory', was seen as something of an insult. (The standard Soviet marking system is explained in Chapter 2.) When opportunities were extended, many more pupils chose to stay in the upper classes of the general schools, in the hope of gaining entry to higher education. Their expectations of employment in jobs carrying higher prestige were consequently raised. Meanwhile industry claimed to be experiencing a shortage of trained workers. School reforms promulgated in 1984 sought to remedy this situation, but have had very limited success.

Other types of establishment available at age fifteen include the PTU [*Professional'no-tekhnicheskoe uchilishche*] or vocational-technical college, which accepted students without an entrance examination at fifteen for a three-year course which partly continued general education but spent about 60 per cent of the time on specialist trade training. Recently a more advanced type of PTU has become very common (and indeed was intended to become universal) in which full secondary education was given as well as vocational training. These colleges are known as SPTUs – 'S' for secondary. The second main type was the secondary-specialist educational establishment, known as a *tekhnikum* or college (*uchilishche*), the former if the profile fell into the categories of industry, construction, transport, agriculture or economics, and the latter if it was educational, medical, musical, theatrical or the like. The training given in these establishments would be of an advanced level, though lower than that provided by higher education establishments, but of professional or semi-professional status. Thus they might train nurses and other health and leisure workers, kindergarten staff, agricultural technicians, toolmakers, and a variety of other workers. Until recently about 60 per cent of the pupils at age fifteen would continue in the general school, about 30 per cent in the PTU and about 10 per cent in secondary specialist education. This ratio varied considerably (in Leningrad very many more attended PTU), but in general it gives a reasonably accurate impression. Proposals since 1984 to change these proportions drastically and send 60 per cent to the SPTUs proved unpopular and the future of these vocational colleges is again under discussion.

In School 1937 the academic plan intended that about 25–30 per cent of pupils should leave at fifteen to enter the (S)PTU. I met a very few who said it was their firm intention to do this. However, the vast majority wished to go ahead and try for entry to a higher education establishment. I found only one pupil, probably the most able girl in the school, who wished to apply to read English, but even she did not feel confident enough to try to get into a university. Put off, most probably, by the stern competition, she was intending to try for a teacher-training college – the famous Lenin Pedagogical Institute, at which many of the teachers in School 1937 had trained and which certainly does not admit much second-rate material. The other pupils were seeking entry to various specialist colleges of higher education, according to the careers they wished to follow.

In the last two years of schools the academic content of the syllabuses followed increases if anything in seriousness. The curriculum followed is still a general one, and many pupils find the compulsion to follow courses in a wide range of subjects irksome. Optional courses account still for only a handful of weekly lessons, but they represent a slight opportunity to specialise in preparation for higher education.

The final leaving certificate examinations are more elaborate than those two years earlier. With the exception of some mathematics and Russian, they are oral, and by recent published regulations[7] six subjects are taken: mathematics, history and sociology and literature are compulsory (as is Russian language if the candidate is a native speaker of another language, as nearly half the Soviet population is). For entry to higher education, four or five subjects are offered, of which Russian language and literature must be one; the others are to be related for the course which the applicant wishes to follow. There is no clearing house for applications to several institutions, but for the most famous universities and institutes, entrance examinations are held (mainly oral, as ever), and by reason of the timing of these exams, two chances are possible. Candidates unsuccessful in both may be given a document to show third or further choices of institution what marks they achieved in the entrance examinations for their first or second choice.

HIGHER EDUCATION   ·

What may the pupils expect to find if they are successful in gaining entry to higher education? About 13 per cent of the age-group succeeds; more females than males. Many of the institutions are specialist colleges for one particular subject or group of specialisms; the emphasis in Soviet higher education is on training for employment rather than the disinterested pursuit of knowledge. Courses last four to six years, and students find the teaching approaches are similar to school work; they are characterised by a very high number of contact hours, gross lack of time for, and of belief in, independent study, and tight control of the curriculum, as in schools. Certain ideological subjects are compulsory, such as Marxist-Leninist theory and history of the Communist Party, and very often a foreign language and physical education too. Grants are relatively small and depend to some extent on the quality of the student's work; hostel accommodation (if the student is studying away from home) is very simple. Instruction continues for only thirty weeks, but administration and examinations occupy another twelve, leaving only ten weeks of the year free from organised learning. At the award of the final diploma, as we saw in Chapter 1 in relation to teachers, the student must accept direction into a post for two years – this may be anywhere in the Soviet Union, but again, motivation to work hard is increased because the best graduates are likely to be placed nearer home.

OVERVIEW

It is impossible for the foreigner to know the exact nature of the experience of schooling in the Soviet Union as it must appear to the Soviet young person. Which of us can really know what our own school days gave us – at least until the traditional forty years on, or until we have had the opportunity to compare with them something else, whatever that may be?

The present pupils in School 1937, having very likely been in a preschool establishment before that, have entered a school at the age of seven in which a closely defined and detailed body of knowledge is imparted. Until very recently, it would perhaps have been true to say that the school stressed the importance of the mastery of facts and was less concerned with discussion or argument, but by the autumn of 1988 many teachers – including the middle-aged ones who might reasonably be expected to have been conservative in their attitude – were trying to encourage independent thought and the mastery of concepts rather than mere facts. Unshakeable belief in the absolutely essential nature of hard work and academic success, is prominent in this school as in other Soviet schools. This ideal will be present in whatever higher education establishment the young people attend on leaving School 1937 at seventeen.

How far will *glasnost'* go? In Chapter 6 we shall see what would-be reformers have in mind. Even the reforms of 1984, which seem in 1989 to be conservative in spirit, call for creative thinking and an end to doctrinaire attitudes and stereotyped, ready-made opinions.[8] Pupils are now to be taught to think for themselves. Until very recently, at least, there have always been calls for correct political attitudes to be fostered in children. Educators brought up in the Western European tradition would suppose that teaching methods which encourage children to explore ideas more freely instead of making them learn conclusions off by heart would lead inevitably in many cases to the pupils making up their own mind on political matters instead of adopting the views their teachers believed to be 'correct'. The perhaps rather surprising conclusion I arrived at after my period of work there is that, in this very good school at least, the first priority was teaching the children to think for themselves, in the belief that this in the long run was in the best interests of Russia, the Soviet Union and the Communist Party.

5 The Curriculum
What Soviet Children Learn in School

One morning I was unexpectedly asked to conduct an English lesson with a senior class 10 group at School 1937.

'You will give' (this is Marina Georgievna's way of saying, 'Please would you give them') 'a lesson on recent changes in Soviet foreign policy.'

'But I don't know anything about it.'

'Don't worry, the children will tell you. They've prepared an article from *Moscow News* and you can ask them about it.'

It seems highly unlikely that any such exchange could have taken place a year or two earlier. For a foreigner to be sent to conduct a lesson on a politically ticklish subject such as this, even if a politically reliable member of the school staff were also present, would have been unthinkable. The use of *Moscow News* as discussion material is in itself significant, as this paper (which appears in Russian as well as a range of foreign languages) has proved itself as a flagship of openness and restructuring; short of using the British or American press, which was not at the time of this incident easily available in the USSR, *Moscow News* was the most suitable English-language material to provoke open discussion. It must also be said that in many English schools the reverse – a Soviet visitor taking a lesson on British government policy – might have been a little unlikely. Local and national politicians in Britain, as well as teachers themselves, are known to protest about real or imagined bias in teaching materials. Some who ought to know better appear to imagine that if school children read or if teachers teach from material of recognised bias, pupils are being 'brainwashed', being blissfully unaware that any competent teacher can use tendentious material in a critical way, and most pupils can be taught to be sceptical.

Nevertheless, all of this highlights the issue of the control of the curriculum. Who decides what the content of education should be? And since material can be taught in different ways, who decides or influences the manner in which that material is conveyed to the pupils? What are the unspoken, implicit, hidden messages which teachers convey through their lessons and through the customs and rituals of school life? This is an important matter in Soviet education, and this chapter is concerned primarily with the content of the education offered in School 1937, as in other Soviet establishments.

A noticeable feature of the conversation of many people in the Soviet Union used to be a tendency to say, 'Your facts are incorrect', or 'You are in possession of some incorrect information', when they really meant: 'I do not agree with your interpretation of the facts.' Soviet pupils and students were until recently not usually encouraged to explore ideas and discuss them, but to learn the 'correct' answers. Perhaps for this reason, the lesson on Soviet foreign policy was a disappointment, because the young people present were quite unable to handle certain abstract concepts, but tended to throw around words such as 'militarism' which they could not always define satisfactorily. The best they could do was that militarism meant possessing nuclear weapons. They did have a rational concept of the 'arms race'. While they were convinced Margaret Thatcher spoke purely for capitalists and Mikhail Gorbachev on the other hand for the working people of the whole world, they could not size up Ronald Reagan – since he had recently modified his hostile stance towards the Soviet Union, they did not think he could possibly be a conservative! In tune with an earlier Soviet stereotyped attitude, they seemed uneasily convinced that conflict between nations with different social systems was inevitable. Some pupils were sure that the present leadership was carrying out the wishes of the people; when I asked how the people influenced the leadership, the majority said the people had no influence at all. (This was before the sensational elections in the early part of 1989.) Open discussion of international politics was obviously something quite new to these young people, and they were unused to it; this is not to forget the fact that they were trying to carry on the discussion in a foreign language. Towards the end of the lesson the only Soviet colleague present, who had not so far intervened in any way in the lesson, became involved in the discussion. She was dismissive of an opinion put forward by a pupil on the grounds that it represented 'the old way of thinking; we don't believe that any more'. It would be a pity if *glasnost'* meant nothing more than learning off by heart a new series of orthodox opinions to replace the old, the things 'we don't believe any more'.

However, one feature of *glasnost'* is that disagreement between 'authorities' has become much more open and frequent in the Soviet media and society. Maybe the debate is still sometimes carried on in language which recalls the censorious and self-righteous bad old days. Maybe, as in this incident, the arguments now being conducted are designed to discover new 'correct' answers rather than to show that it is possible for intelligent people to hold differing opinions. It may be, however, that newer products of the Soviet education system may come to learn that books and teachers do not possess the correct answer to every question.

THE THEORY BEHIND THE CURRICULUM

Before discussing those elements of the curriculum which are special to School No. 1937 and others like it with a bias towards English, let us examine the content of education which *every* child in any Soviet school undergoes. There is a very large 'core' which all Soviet children from six to seventeen receive. First of all, it is important to understand a little about the theoretical basis of the Soviet curriculum. This is all the more important for the British, and most specifically the English reader, because the national curriculum which has very recently been imposed by legislation on England and Wales is strikingly lacking in an explicit theoretical basis. Subject areas to be included consist of English and mathematics as the most essential matters, the sciences also appear to be vital, and 'time must be found', as an earlier discussion document on the national curriculum put it, for certain other subjects. These other subjects were those which had little, or at least less, commercial application, like art and music – they appear to have little market value. There are many parents in the Soviet Union who share the prejudice of their British counterparts in believing that physics is more important than music, but Soviet curriculum philosophy actually combats this prejudice.[1]

Marx and Lenin being venerated in the USSR, educationists pay great attention to their relatively few statements on educational matters. Karl Marx held that children should learn about nature, man and society and the relationships between them, and Marxists believe that knowledge is indissolubly bound up with action. From this it might be expected that two important consequences should follow: that the whole of human knowledge should be tackled in a complex, integrated way rather than through separate lessons in chemistry, history, art, etc., and that Soviet education should have a strong practical bias. The first is not so, not yet, at least. The second is true in theory, since 'labour' education is compulsory throughout pre-school, primary and secondary education, and undergraduates are expected to contribute their labour to production and agricultural processes (by harvesting potatoes, for example). Moreover, 'polytechnical' (a word straight from Marx's writings) education, acquainting children with the various industrial skills of the artisan, is furthered by teachers explaining the practical industrial applications of material learnt, in chemistry, for example.

Marx, Lenin and their followers were critical of 'bourgeois' educational ideas, because they held that the property-owning classes maintained their hold over the proletariat either by denying them education or by controlling the content of the education they received. In Soviet curriculum philosophy, equality and justice have until very recently demanded that the content should be the same for all (though not, the theory books are careful to stress, *absolutely* identical). Central control of the curriculum is almost total. There is no question of individual schools or teachers being allowed to decide what subjects to teach or to draft their own syllabuses for core subjects; such freedom is regarded as 'bourgeois' – a clever trick enabling the dominant classes in society to control the masses by denying them access to the same knowledge as they themselves have. Soviet psychology, moreover, inclines strongly to the view that all, or very nearly all, children can be offered the same curriculum. Even children with special educational needs are helped as far as possible to follow the general syllabuses, sometimes in an extended period of years at school; the curriculum is not tailored to the child, but the child is helped to assimilate the curriculum.[2] All classes are mixed-ability classes. There is no word in Russian for 'mixed-ability', 'streaming' or 'homogeneous group tracking'. A teacher at School No. 1937 who was trying to advocate it was obliged to explain in other words what she meant; she received no support whatever, on the grounds that it would be inhumane to belittle children by discriminating in this way. The idea is not wholly without support among Soviet educators – a correspondent of the *Daily Mail* in 1989 uncovered a Soviet headmistress with a desire to stream classes.

What, though, is the content, the list of subjects, which all Soviet children should receive? By what criterion is it compiled? Ideas of man – nature – society are all very well, but what does that really mean when a curriculum planner is faced with the necessity of deciding what goes into a school timetable? There are two considerations which help here. First, there is the notion of the 'all-round harmonious development of personality' (Communist personality, it should be noted), and the need for 'a well-trained work-force of broad general culture'. These phrases recur constantly in standard works on the curriculum of Soviet schools, but they are now attacked in some Soviet quarters as 'outdated clichés'. Nevertheless, they are fine ideals in theory, at least, and they are not entirely unhelpful concepts when one is trying to understand the reasoning behind the Soviet curriculum. They unite the requirements of society with the rights of the individual to all-round education, so education is not purely an ego-trip for the pupil, nor should it be merely training for the national economy. No pupil can be allowed at any early age to specialise in the skills and knowledge which will make him, say, a good garage mechanic to the exclusion of all else. There are no classics graduates in Russia who say they never had a science lesson in their lives. Authority insists that all school subjects which are essential to the harmonious development of all-round personality should be compulsory, and all else may be optional.

Another principle is frequently quoted by Soviet educators: the 'unity of instruction with upbringing'. In other words moral and ethical education ('upbringing') cannot be separated from academic learning. If a child turns out to be a brilliant scholar but a self-centred cad, the system has failed. A great deal more will be said about this in Chapter 14, but for the moment it can be said that in the Soviet Union qualities thought desirable in the good citizen are fostered: they include being politically and socially active, showing respect for labour and knowledge of the world of work, love of the arts and natural beauty, Soviet patriotism, physical fitness, ethical behaviour, respect for the environment and public property, and knowledge of the rights and obligations of a citizen. It is scarcely necessary to say that teachers are less than one hundred per cent successful in inculcating moral values, and the system remains dissatisfied with its performance here; what is striking is the determination to succeed, and the conviction that this is vital to the curriculum.

THE CONTENT OF THE CURRICULUM. THE PRIMARY CLASSES

Since 1986, as we saw in Chapter 4, Soviet children have been starting compulsory schooling at six; it was seven prior to that. In School 1937 the youngest class is aged seven, since the school cannot yet accommodate six-year-olds. This is true of very many schools in the USSR; the children concerned receive their lessons at age six in the kindergarten building, but are taught by qualified school teachers. (The word 'teacher' is not correctly applied to kindergarten staff, who are known as *vospitateli*, upbringers.) About 50 per cent of Soviet children in general (the actual percentage is hard to establish accurately),[3] and in fact almost all the children who attend School No. 1937 and other schools in major cities, will have had five days a week of preschool education for several years before that, and probably long days too, so they will be well socialised into the ways of educational establishments and communal life with their fellows. To age ten they work mainly on language and mathematics, but with some art and music, physical education and the labour training (in the early stages simple crafts, paper work and modelling) which is compulsory to the end of schooling at age seventeen.

We shall not embark on a description of the complicated arrangements for children in non-Russian areas of the Soviet Union, since this is not relevant to the children in School 1937. It should, however, be remembered that about half of the Soviet population speaks a language other than Russian as its native tongue; there are about 130 such languages. Russian children learn to read their own language by the 'sound analytic-synthetic method', by which children are first taught to recognise the phonemes from which words are built up, then learn the shapes of the letters, and then read individual letters and also syllables consisting of a consonant followed by a vowel.[4] By the end of the first year of primary education they are expected to read aloud at a speed of thirty or forty words a minute. A good deal of formal Russian grammar is taught, even at primary level, and lessons contain periods of word building, simple sentence analysis, and a certain amount of more creative writing and response to poetry and stories. Primary mathematics contains the four basic operations performed upon natural numbers; the concepts of number and magnitude are introduced. The first priority is to develop skills of calculation, and arithmetical operations are related to real-life situations.

The music and art taught in primary classes is among the most adventurous work now done in the Soviet school. The subjects are often taught by real enthusiasts, not least in School 1937, who are responding to recent moves by educationists to free the subjects from rigidity and boredom, by working towards the aim of inducing the children to seek artistic and musical experience outside school. In art

Table 5.1   Model curriculum for schools with intensified instruction in English

Age of pupils	6	7	8	9	10	11	12	13	14	15	16
Class ('old' numbering)	–	1	2	3	4	5	6	7	8	9	10
Class (new numbering from 1990)	1	2	3	4	5	6	7	8	9	10	11
Russian language and literature	7	9	11	11	11	9	6	5	5	4	3
Mathematics	4	6	6	6	6	6	6	6	6	4/5	4
Principles of Information Science and Computer Technology	–	–	–	–	–	–	–	–	–	1	2
History	–	–	–	–	2	2	2	2	3	4	3
Principles of Soviet State and Law	–	–	–	–	–	–	–	–	1	–	–
Social Studies	–	–	–	–	–	–	–	–	–	0/2	2/1
Ethics and Psychology of Family Life	–	–	–	–	–	–	–	–	0/1	1/0	–
Acquaintance with the World Around	1	1	–	–	–	–	–	–	–	–	–
Nature Study	–	–	1	1	1	–	–	–	–	–	–
Geography	–	–	–	–	–	2	3	2	2	2/1	–
Biology	–	–	–	–	–	2	2	2	2	1	1/2
Physics	–	–	–	–	–	–	2	2	3	4/3	4
Astronomy	–	–	–	–	–	–	–	–	–	–	1
Chemistry	–	–	–	–	–	–	–	3	3/2	2	2
Technical Drawing	–	–	–	–	–	–	1	1	–	–	–
English	–	2	3	4	6	6	5	6	4	4	4
Art	2	1	1	1	1	1	1	–	–	–	–
Music	2	1	1	1	1	1	1	–	–	–	–
Physical Culture	2	2	2	2	2	2	2	2	2	2	2
Elementary Military Training (NVP)	–	–	–	–	–	–	–	–	–	–	2
Labour and Vocational Training	2	2	2	2	2	2	2	3	3	4	4
TOTAL	20	24	27	28	32	33	33	34	34	34	34
Options	–	–	1	1	2	–	1	1	1	2	2
Socially-useful Productive Labour	–	1	1	1	2	2	2	3	3	4	4
Labour Practice (in days)	–	–	–	–	10	10	10	16	16	20	–

lessons children work in a wide variety of media and produce many of their own paintings and models, but in music creative work in the sense of musical composition is rarely observed at present.

'Labour' lessons in the primary years are not unlike handicraft periods in schools in the West. The children make simple toys, decorative objects and simple household things, and often receive a good deal of help from their teachers. They make greetings cards for festivals; all of this introduces them to the use of simple tools such as scissors and materials like paper, cloth and cardboard. Some of their labour is tidying up the classroom and helping maintain the property; it is therefore useful and represents a saving in cost to the school – both of which are felt to be beneficial to the child in instilling a realisation of the worth of manual labour.

Moral education, as we shall see in Chapter 14, permeates the whole of the work done in the Soviet school, but there is one short course in the first two years of primary education which has aims which are distinctly moral: to acquaint children with social life and labour in Soviet society, to instil a considerate attitude to others and their work and property, to encourage love of *rodina*, which can mean either country or home area, and to foster a conservationist attitude to the environment. This is the course entitled 'Acquaintance with the World Around', which is centred round four topics: our house, our school, our town or village, our native country. The principal moral core of this course, apart from an explicit intention to instil confidence in the Party, is to develop a humane attitude to other people. Nature study in primary education relies heavily on observation of the changing seasons and the effects of this on weather, plants, wild creatures and human activities. The course includes work on the natural surroundings of the child's own area, the great variety of natural conditions in the Soviet Union, and finally some elementary health education – work on the human body and its health and fitness. This is also, needless to say, the theme of physical education, which is intended to have a sound theoretical core as well as practice of gymnastics, children's movement games and skiing, skating and

---

Note: Table 5.1 shows the curriculum which was planned for the school year 1990–91. More recent events have overtaken the plan (see Chapter 6), but nevertheless this table, if read according to the 'old' numbering, gives a good impression of the curriculum in the mid-1980s; if read according to the 'new' numbering of classes, illustrates what will doubtless be the situation in many schools until the differentiation promised by the latest provisional statutes can be introduced.

running (depending on the climate). Primary teachers are expected to incorporate bursts of physical activity into all lessons and to encourage energetic pursuits in the breaks.

SECONDARY CURRICULUM

The great majority of Soviet educators think very much in terms of traditional subject divisions, even at primary level. We shall see in Chapter 6 that an integrated programme is now proposed for the primary years. Nevertheless, there are, as we have seen, elements of Marxist theory which affirm the unity of all knowledge, and in the 1920s experiments with integrated curricula were carried out, only to be abandoned in favour of systematic instruction in separate subjects. This word 'systematic' almost became a slogan, a means to belittle 'project' or 'complex' methods of organising curricula. The debate is now beginning again, and in relation to the secondary level of education. As if recognising a contradiction, syllabuses from the 1980s highlight 'inter-subject links' as a means to breaking dowm barriers between curriculum areas. This is not enough for some educators, who see inter-subject links as a delusion, but for the moment, the secondary pupil faces a curriculum made up of separate subjects.

The secondary phase of schooling begins at age ten, and it should be remembered that at the present time the pupils of that age and older in School 1937 have had only three years of primary schooling, though as the new generation who started at six comes through, the position will be different. The table on page 60 displays the curriculum for the schools with intensified instruction in English; officially this was the plan for 1990–91, but many Soviet schools have largely adopted it already. (If proposals in Summer 1989 for a new school statute catch on, they will eventually be abandoning many details of it.) It differs in very few respects from the curriculum of ordinary schools; the differences will be explained later. The eleven columns, one for each class, refer to the situation as it will be when all children in the schools have started education at six, but until the early 1990s the majority of Soviet children will have experienced education from seven, of which one can receive an approximate impression by regarding columns 2 to 11 as representing the now obsolescent programme of the old classes 1 to 10.

The table shows that at ten history is introduced, at eleven geography and biology, at twelve physics and technical drawing. At thirteen, Soviet children have had their last music and art lessons, and they start chemistry. At fourteen maths and science are still going strong, history and labour education are increasing their share, and new subjects appear for the odd lesson per week: 'Principles of Soviet State and Law' and 'Ethics and Psychology of Family Life.' Labour and vocational education continues and gains an extra lesson at age thirteen; physical culture is followed throughout.

It would be impossible to describe the content of the syllabuses for all these subjects in any detail, but a general overview may prove useful. The history syllabus is considered to be of the greatest importance in instilling a Marxist-Leninist world view, and it is very extensive in its coverage. Thirty countries are touched upon, and it is certainly not parochial. Only the first year is episodic, and sets out to engage the pupils' emotional reactions to great events and times. The rest is serious and academic. The course sets out, not to teach children to discuss, but to instil conviction of the Communist Party's interpretation of history; since this has changed recently, the course and the textbooks are changing. A child who had attended industriously would have absorbed a great factual knowledge of world history, along with the interpretations; he would probably have been given far too much material to assimilate properly.

A similar breadth of content may be discerned in the geography syllabus. Its aims are among the most ambitious and intelligent of all subjects in the Soviet curriculum: to 'form ... respect for the traditions of the peoples of the world, ... to work out a sense of common purpose and responsibility in social and economic matters, along with a zealous concern for the natural resources of the homeland, pride in its economic success and responsibility for its developmental prospects'. The syllabus has moved away from old-fashioned catalogues of capes and bays towards concept-based and problem-solving work. The interest in world political systems and the means of production which it shows is not surprising for a Marxist-based course. Compared with current British practice, the Soviet geography teacher is well behind in field work and independent inquiry.

The curriculum has a heavy bias towards scientific study, both because of its possible practical industrial and commercial applications and because it is thought by Soviet educators to persuade children of the correctness of scientific materialism. There is tremendous emphasis on factual content: biology, botany and zoology involve the study of a wide range of plants and living creatures, not forgetting the human being; physics includes the structure of matter, motion, magnetism, electricity, thermal phenomena, and mechanics; in chemistry the organic and inorganic branches of the subject are kept separate and the major centres of interest are molecular theory, the periodic system of Mendeleev, the basic features of chemical reactions and chemical structure. Soviet teachers regard these syllabuses as overloaded; British teachers find them heavily teacher-directed and old-fashioned in their classifications into organic and inorganic, botany and zoology and so on. The need to develop in the child skills of observation, interpretation and problem solving are detectable in the syllabuses, but are perhaps not developed to the same extent as in the West. Soviet educationists are most dissatisfied with the biology course, as it seems to be less than satisfactory in helping children understand the theory of evolution, which is said to be its principal aim.

Labour training from age ten to fifteen is a problem for many Soviet schools. The subject is ideologically very important, because of the role of the working class and the importance attached to industrial production processes in Communist theory, as well as because it is thought to have desirable moral effects, such as when people have to work together in a team to produce an article. Throughout these middle years of education children develop a variety of skills and crafts – or at least, they do so if facilities exist. They work gradually towards the choice of one industrially or agriculturally useful job in which they are eventually, by the end of schooling, thoroughly trained – with the same proviso: if the facilities exist. In some fields there is strict segregation between boys and girls; the girls do cookery and sewing, the boys metalwork. This strikes few people as absurd, even when the girls concerned are hoping to go to college to study engineering. There are lessons of careers advice, 'professional orientation and choice of a career', as it is called. One lesson a week of technical drawing is compulsory for two years.

The newest syllabuses in music and art continue to be popular in the secondary classes where they are well taught, but at present they dwindle to nothing after three years. Literature is taught in Russian lessons, both Russian and world literature. Again, a very large number of works are covered, but the subject often appears to be popular with children, however dull the lessons – and they sometimes are very dull indeed. Russian language study continues to the age of fifteen, and although essay writing and discussion leading to the 'development of language' is an important part of this course, there is a very great deal of grammar, punctuation and morphology. Western traditionalists sometimes point to this aspect of the work with approval, but the truth is that Soviet educators complain bitterly that all the grammar-grind has very little effect on the children's ability to write accurately and punctuate correctly.[5]

Mathematics at this stage in secondary education consists of a thorough study of algebra and geometry for five years. The syllabuses of 1985 are still held to be rather full of material, but they are in fact much less so than earlier ones. It is when one talks to Soviet mathematics teachers that the difficulties of mixed-ability teaching in Soviet style (which is, basically, to teach the class as if it were a homogeneous fairly academic group) become obvious. The difficulties of enabling all children to keep up are considerable, and more work seems to have gone into the preparation of remedial materials here than in most other subjects.

Principles of Soviet Government and Law, a one-lesson-a-week course was intended, among other things, to combat ignorance of the law, which, it was believed, had led to avoidable crime. It contains some useful information about, for example, labour legislation, public and personal property and civil and family law. There is a great deal of moral teaching about the brotherly cooperation of Soviet nationalities, the concern of the Party for the well-being of all citizens, and suchlike. Ethics and Psychology of Family Life is a much criticised course designed to prepare young people for adult life, and specifically marriage. It deals with personal matters (though it has very little indeed to say about sexual relationships), and the pupils in School 1937 were, as mentioned elsewhere, dissatisfied with the way it had been taught by reason of the personality of the teacher. As one might expect, sensitivity is required in the successful presentation of the course.

Before considering the curriculum from age fifteen to seventeen, let us look at the differences up to this age for the children in the schools with intensified instruction in English, such as School 1937. The main one is the presence of English from age eight, and the relatively large time allocation given to this subject. In the ordinary schools the foreign language, which may be English, German, French or in a smaller number of cases another language such as Spanish, Italian, Chinese or Hindi, starts at age ten (class 5 by the new numbering), but in the last three years of schooling dwindles to a virtually useless one lesson a week. Teachers in these schools complain that children lose more than they learn at this stage; interestingly, in School 1937 there was a feeling that even more lessons than four per week would be better in the later years. In the early days of the existence of such schools other subjects were taught through the medium of English. I well remember in 1961 attending a lesson on the economic geography of Poland which was taught in English from a textbook written in English. This was discontinued ten or more years ago, since it was felt to retard progress in the other subject and to create a gulf between, say, students who had studied mathematics through the medium of English (and who were often ignorant of the correct Russian terms) and the rest. However, it is not entirely forbidden to use English in other subjects, and sometimes British or American history, geography or literature will be taught in English.

The only other difference between the 'English' schools and the 'mass' schools is the allocation of optional lessons. One or two lessons a week in the last five years is all that is offered to the children in the former, whereas in the ordinary schools children have two, three or four. The extra lessons of English are sometimes defended against attacks from those who see the schools with a special profile as privileged by saying that they are merely using the optional lessons for the special subject. This is not quite true now, as pupils at schools such as No. 1937 have a heavier programme in every year from class 2 onwards: two, three or four lessons more in each year than in normal schools.

Children enter the schools with an intensified programme in a language at six or seven, before anyone can know whether they are likely to have any particular aptitude for languages. With good teaching, of course, many with no particular gift do quite well, but there will be some who are advised to leave and go to another school instead. Some such pupils may have discovered an aptitude for some other subject in which a special profile is available in another school. Others may prefer to leave at fifteen and enter vocational education.

PUBLIC EXAMINATIONS

Yearly formal promotion exams were discontinued some years ago, but since 1987 they have been reinstituted on an experimental basis in the Russian republic from year three upwards. At the age of fifteen Soviet children take their first public examination. It does not resemble the English GCSE or Scottish O or S grade, as there are only four examinations: oral and written Russian and oral and written mathematics. The pupils in School 1937 and schools like it will also have to offer oral English. The questions, such as the 200 essay titles and the questions on Russian grammar and orthography are for the most part known in advance and are on sale in bookshops and at newspaper kiosks for months before the date of the exams. Obviously, the exact examples to be worked out in mathematics are not given, but they are chosen from the textbooks by the teachers, who conduct the examinations with their own children with a minimum of external moderation, sometimes none at all. Spontaneous conversation in a foreign language is only partly susceptible to rehearsal. The topics on which conversation will be held are, of course, known. This examination is not supposed to be used as an entrance test for the two senior classes of the secondary school, but it is undoubtedly sometimes used as such; in any case, the marks awarded are bound to be used when counselling pupils and their parents about their educational career after fifteen.[6] Some may leave and enter vocational college (PTU) or the more advanced secondary specialist colleges. The vast majority in School 1937 wished to stay on and try for entry to higher education.

THE LAST TWO YEARS

English is prominent in the curriculum of schools like No. 1937, with four weekly lessons. At this stage the course in Russian language has been completed, and the pupils study literature only. They continue with sciences and mathematics, adding computer technology and later astronomy. History increases in importance and social studies are added. Geography is dropped at the end of the penultimate year. Vocational and labour education increases to four weekly lessons. Physical education continues and elementary military training is compulsory for both sexes. The ethics and psychology course is completed by half way through the penultimate year.

Again, full details of all the syllabuses cannot possibly be given. In summary, however, the ideological importance of history, social studies and, interestingly, literature increases. The literature course in the penultimate class is concerned largely with classical Russian literature, though Shakespeare, Goethe and Balzac feature briefly; in the last year Soviet literature is studied. History is concerned with the last 150 years: general history (touching on West European countries,

America and Japan) starting with the Paris Commune, and Russian history from the decline of tsarism to the 1930s; in the last year the USSR since the 1930s is studied. The social studies course looks extremely indigestible on paper and is on a highly abstract level: capitalism, socialism, the Communist Party, Marxism-Leninism, dialectical materialism – all of this the pupils will need for their compulsory courses in higher education.

Mathematics moves on to solid geometry and calculus. The sciences are no less demanding, and indeed it may be asked whether it is wise to insist on all pupils of this age following courses of such advanced content in three sciences plus astronomy, and mathematics. The new course in computer studies, which its compilers say they have not got right yet, has proved highly successful and popular, despite the fact that the Soviet computer technology is lagging behind some other countries and the teachers complain bitterly about the micros they have in their classrooms – if, that is, they have any at all. School 1937 has none, and the pupils follow this course at the interschool production centre or UPK, where they also do their vocational training.

This vocational training has reached a faintly ridiculous point by the last year of school. In theory all the pupils should obtain a certificate by the time they leave school, which will qualify them to obtain work without further training and on full pay at a factory where the trade they have learned is plied. For pupils in the senior classes of a general, as opposed to vocational, school this will be a very low-level manual worker's qualification – one, in fact, which they are most unlikely ever to use, even if they fail to get in to a university or college. This raises the question as to why they need to obtain it, except for ideological reasons.[7] The children are not slow to ask this question, and they are about as keen to attend the lessons as they are to do their elementary military training.

In English the pupils at School 1937 are by this time pretty fluent. They will be able to converse freely on many subjects: everyday matters, politics, art. They can read fairly extensively (ten pages a week are set) and discuss what they have read in English. They will know virtually all of English grammar and have a vocabulary of 2200 items.

THE LEAVING EXAMINATION

Pupils take the final examination in six subjects (three of them compulsory: maths, Russian and history/social studies, though in 1988 the history exam was cancelled because of doubts about its ideological content in the age of 'restructuring'). These school examinations may be used for entry to higher education, but the entrance exams referred to in Chapter 4 are conducted by the institutions concerned. About the conduct of the examinations themselves, it is necessary to explain that except for Russian essay writing and some mathematics examinations, testing has traditionally been oral at all stages in the educational system up to final degree level. Since, as mentioned above, the questions in most subjects are set centrally and are known in advance, much teaching in many schools in the exam year consists of rehearsing acceptable answers to the questions.

Here we have the nub of the problem of curriculum. The content of education is not merely the ground which the syllabus says is to be covered; it depends too on the way that content is taught and the way pupils are expected to learn it. In Chapters 8, 9, and 10 we shall have a good deal to say about the way teaching and learning are conducted in School No. 1937.

6 *Glasnost, Perestroyka* and the School

Radical Reform in the School Today

In the Autumn of 1988 Soviet society was thoroughly launched into a period of change, one which was as astonishing to observers of the country from outside as it was to many Soviet citizens. Many on both sides of the borders could not quite come to terms with the innovations. Some Soviets were unable to cope with the new freedom of expression, and some Westerners were, in spite of themselves, still fighting the Cold War. What had brought about the new situation? What was its exact nature? Where does education figure in the changed social scene?

The Soviet Union has known no period in its seventy-year history to compare with the middle to late 1980s. The embattled early 1920s, when Russia was torn by civil war and under attack from eleven foreign nations, were culturally and educationally much more open than ever again until the 1980s, but these years soon gave way to Stalin's enforced industrialisation, collectivisation of agriculture and terror. Even more extreme suffering and hardship during the Second World War was followed by further oppression and terror until Stalin died; the country then opened up to some extent during the colourful, if eccentric rule of the somewhat unpredictable Nikita Khrushchev. His dismissal in 1964 led to two decades of what is now termed 'the period of stagnation' under Leonid Brezhnev and his two short-lived successors. Mikhail Sergeevich Gorbachev, when he took over in 1985, had to cope with massive problems which it will take decades to solve, if indeed they are soluble.

The principal problem is the economy, and from that many of the country's other serious deficiencies stem. For about sixty years the Soviet Union has had a centrally planned economy, which has centred on heavy industry rather than consumer goods; some critics argue that this is because it is easier to plan for heavy industry and get the figures right. Technology is backward by comparison with other leading nations, and productivity is low. Management is widely believed to be short on competence, communications are poor (the telephone system is lamentable and photocopying machines are virtually inaccessible) even when you know – this is no easy task – who it is you need to communicate with. Until the recent legalisation of 'co-operatives', thought by some to be a euphemism for private enterprise, the state has owned all manufacturing and service industries and half the agricultural enterprises – the rest are collectivised and run on socialist principles. The work force has a quite obvious tendency to idleness and, in the service industries, to insolence; the contents of the wage packet do not depend on the quality of the work done or even, it is widely asserted, on whether the employee bothers to turn up for work. The currency, the rouble, is non-convertible, which is to say it is almost worthless outside the borders of the USSR. The consequences of all this are that the Soviet Union is a difficult country to trade with, it cannot compete internationally with many far smaller countries, life for the individual consumer – that is, almost everybody – is hard because of shortages, inefficiency and (especially under Brezhnev) corruption, and inevitably dissatisfaction and disillusionment has set in. The political system has until very recently allowed little scope for protest and dissent. The country exists on the principle of leadership by the élite Communist Party, and for far too long the rank and file were expected merely to ratify, usually unanimously, the decisions of the leadership, whether national or local. A very great deal of power rested in the hands of Party officials, some of whom were unscrupulous, idle or corrupt. A British Member of Parliament reports asking Gorbachev who his opposition in the Soviet Union consisted of. His reply was, 'Everyone who isn't earning his salary.'[1] All regular visitors to the Soviet Union will have ideas as to what proportion of the population that comprises. It can be said with confidence that it would form an extremely small proportion of the staff of School 1937.

So much for the economy, but unless the economy is healthy, progress in most other fields will prove impossible. This applies equally to everything from the military machine to the education system. But the case of the education system is a special one, in that successful schools may well influence the economy for the better. It is often said that investment in education does not automatically improve the trade figures. In developing societies at least there is little unanimity about the exact nature of the interdependence of education and economic success. It can scarcely be doubted, however, that in an advanced industrial and technological society a well-trained work force at all levels is essential. Gorbachev has instituted policies which are intended to tackle the ills of all sectors of Soviet society, in the belief that economic reform on its own is unlikely to work. The three key words, which have become known – but not always understood – around the world are *perestroyka*: re-structuring and radical reorganisation of the way society is run; *glasnost'*: openness, publicity, free speech, discussing the difficulties of society in open language without the jargon, codes and pious platitudes of the 'period of stagnation'; and *demokratizatsiya*: democratisation, giving those who work in a particular concern or profession the responsibility for its success.

In the early years of Soviet Russia, when the new state took over education from the various agencies, some public, some private, which had run schools of all imaginable types before the Revolution, a highly experimental period ensued, at least in the main centres of population. In some schools the distinction in status between pupils and teachers was all but swept away, and authority – that of staff and also what has been called 'the authority of knowledge' – was keenly questioned. One still meets elderly people in the USSR who claim to have benefited from this approach. However, after generations of rigid authoritarian dogmatism on the part of all but the best teachers and mindless rote-learning by those pupils who wanted to succeed, these new ideas were all too much for most Soviet teachers and parents, and general relief was felt when Stalin reinstituted formal, or in Soviet educational jargon 'frontal', 'systematic' teaching at the beginning of the 1930s. From that time until the 1980s teaching changed relatively little. Syllabuses were crammed with factual content which was meant to be mastered, if that is the word, by heart. Acceptable interpretations of these facts was also taught by rote. There was a universal compulsory curriculum, schools have been run from the centre, and experimentation of any sort has been most carefully controlled. Reforms have come and gone: the length of compulsory schooling has increased from seven to eight and then ten years in Russia and most other republics and is now set to go to eleven. Various attempts have been made to provide a rational system of labour, polytechnical and prevocational education. Educators have also tried to devise means of encouraging excellence without infringing the comprehensive principle too much; the very existence of School 1937 is, of course, an example of this.

THE 1984 REFORMS

The present ferment began in 1984, though its origins can be traced back much further. In that year a discussion document on change in the school education system appeared. This was before Gorbachev succeeded to the highest office, but he was, in fact, chairman of the group which produced the report. After a few weeks of widespread discussion, in which a hundred and twenty million people are said to have taken part, the document was revised, though not radically, and a final version published as 'Guidelines for Reform of General and Vocational Schools' in April 1984.[2]

These 'Guidelines' and the reform they propounded represent the USSR before Gorbachev's succession to full power, before *perestroyka* and *glasnost'*. They are written in old-fashioned language, full of the opaque clichés, passwords, clap-trap and coded utterances which were necessary in the old style, and which many experienced Soviet readers automatically discount, but which none the less have established themselves in the thought processes of many Russians. Compulsory education was to be extended by one year, starting at six, the compulsory curriculum was revised and new, reformed syllabuses in all subjects were called for (a task which was under way in any case), they tried to ensure a secondary leaving certificate *and* prevocational education for all children, and they called a halt to further differentiation in the curriculum. They envisaged a doubling of the intake of vocational colleges (PTUs) at age fifteen, despite the obvious preference of the population for continuing with general education in the general schools at this age. They contained a great many pious hopes for the improvement of this, that and the other. They were received with some scepticism and suspicion in the Soviet Union, and foreign observers[3] regarded them as somewhat conservative.

I am not sure that this last judgement is correct. The proposed reforms had at least one feature of the greatest importance, and – if the 'Guidelines' meant what they said – could have had far-reaching effects. They called for major improvements in aesthetic education, and linked with this were demands for teachers of all subjects to develop creative attitudes in children. In another place it was stated, 'It is necessary to eradicate all manifestations of formalism . . . in instruction.' There is a reference in the 'Guidelines' to 'pupils' self-management'. It has to be admitted that this is wrapped up in a very great deal of talk about producing convinced communists, fostering the spirit of collectivism and protecting children (or teaching them to protect themselves, which is something different and preferable) from 'ideologically worthless, cheap and banal works of music, art and literature'. What is more, there was an obvious contradiction, in that independent learning was to be encouraged and dogmatic attitudes abolished, while children were none the less expected to learn 'correct' interpretations of the facts they were taught. Yet it must be said that, once all the linguistic and ideological lumber was cleared away from these statements, a very encouraging picture could be perceived.

The 1984 reform was soon to appear as something less than a total success and educators now speak of its 'collapse'. Schools began to implement the new curriculum and syllabuses and the start at age six. Practical difficulties beset other aspects of the reform, such as the improvement of labour training. There were bitter complaints from government about the slow pace of implementation and about obstruction from traditionalist sections of the teaching profession. Prevocational training in schools and the attempt to direct labour into occupations needed by the state by influencing the choice of training made by pupils had failed: young people were not usually entering the occupations for which they had been trained in school (that is, if they had in fact been trained for anything – the reform had not even succeeded in this). There was alleged to be a drop in standards of knowledge by higher education entrants. The schools were therefore seen to be failing both practically and academically. Traditionalists, but not only they, attacked the schools for moving at the pace of the average pupil instead of encouraging 'competitiveness of instruction'. This last characteristic was defined by one critic as 'creating technical designs . . . , solving scientific problems and [developing] the skill of managing. Giving out good marks merely for completing the standard assignments set for the whole class does not instil independence of thinking.'[4] Of course, there are always and everywhere people who believe that schools are going to the dogs, and that everybody but themselves is to blame. Dissatisfaction with education is almost a sign of civilisation. But it is clear that there was justification for disquiet in the Soviet Union in 1985–88, as the country did not yet seem to be getting the education system is needed and, perhaps, deserved.

Eventually a Plenum of the Central Committee of the Communist Party was devoted to education in February 1988. All the dissatisfaction and impatience of the past few years came out, and, perhaps to some surprise, Yegor Ligachev, who was scarcely regarded as a forward-looking member of the Party leadership, delivered a speech which positively encouraged innovative teaching, democratisation, restructuring and openness.[5] The Academy of Pedagogical Sciences of the USSR (known by its usual abbreviation APN, or more exactly APN SSSR: *Akademiya pedagogicheskikh nauk SSSR*) was threatened with real transformation – many academicians had been resisting changes in teaching method tooth and nail, opposing openness, democratisation and restructuring and failing to come to grips with the real problems of the system. Inertia and underfunding were criticised. Ligachev hinted at education in the general school (that is, not to transfer to the vocational college at fifteen) for all who wanted it until seventeen, the dropping of ineffectual efforts to incorporate job training into the general school, reorganisation of the vocational colleges (PTUs, which were not merely to provide workers for the local factory, but give proper prevocational training of broad relevance), there was to be less bureaucracy and paperwork in schools, more differentiation of curricula and a great expansion of 'special profiles'. Unrest among national minorities led to a subtly changed emphasis on the role of the Russian language, the teaching of which had for many years been naively regarded by Russians as a means to hold the Soviet Union together. (In the 1970s non-Russian parents were even being encouraged by the media to speak Russian to their preschool children at home.) While good Russian was essential for communication between Soviet nationalities, now native languages were to be encouraged.

It has never been true that Soviet teachers sat around waiting to be told what to do, and previous reforms of the system have either emerged from movements of opinion in the profession and in society, or else have failed because they did not have support among educators. All the present ideas about reforming teaching methods and considering the child as a first priority rather than asking how much information can conceivably be thrust down his neck have been around in the Soviet Union for many years now. Pressure for them has been gathering momentum among teachers and parents. They did not suddenly appear when Gorbachev announced the policy of *glasnost'*. The innovative work of certain outstanding teachers has been known to the public for some years. Parents of younger children and their teachers were queuing at the bookshops in 1983 for 400,000 copies of Shalva Amonashvili's book on child-centred teaching methods, and the authorities printed half a million copies of its sequel.[6] Their author is a Georgian professor of education and primary school teacher who has become a national figure and who coined the phrase 'pedagogy of cooperation' to encapsulate his philosophy of education. Another prominent teacher, whose name is frequently heard, is V. F. Shatalov, a mathematics and physics teacher from Donetsk. Rank-and-file teachers interested in innovation have set up 'Eureka' Creative Education Clubs, to visit and discuss each others' open lessons. Another significant development was the formation of the VNIK 'Shkola', or Provisional Scientific Research Collective on the School, a group of very prominent officials in public education authorised temporarily to look into creative teaching.[7]

In the August of 1988 there appeared in the educational press two draft documents with a similar short title, *Kontseptsiya obshchego srednego obrazovaniya* [The Idea of General Secondary Education], one of them[8] emanating from the APN, and the other[9] from the VNIK 'Shkola' (Provisional Scientific Research Collective on the School [*Vremennyy nauchno-issledovatel'skiy kollektiv 'Shkola'*]). The existence of rival bids for educational leadership, with the public being fairly obviously invited to choose between them, is in itself new, and this is not to mention the fact that other less official proposals were circulating in crudely duplicated form. We shall look at the two main documents in turn.

THE PROPOSALS OF THE APN

The APN 'Idea of General Secondary Education as the Fundamental and Unified System of Continuing Education' has a certain embattled air, betraying fairly obviously that its authors feel themselves to be threatened and that they seek to establish their credentials, both as leaders of educational thought and guardians of traditional values. They miss no opportunity to remind the reader of the 'achievements of Soviet education' (which are surely not in doubt). There is a strong air of rescuing the 1984 reform and making present practice seem to contain already most of the desired elements in the policy of the innovators. The language of the Idea contains all the clichés which doubtless make the traditionalists feel at home (the 'formation of a Marxist-Leninist world view', the necessity to improve history teaching in order to develop 'socialist consciousness' and literature as 'a powerful means of moral education'). However, the APN has clearly been moved forward a few steps, probably thanks to 'socialist competition' with the other think-tank.

The document opens with a call for the integration of schools and other educative social institutions, for humanisation – the intensification of attention to the personality of the individual as the 'highest value of society', for differentiation and individualisation – the creation of conditions for the free expression and development of the aptitudes of each pupil, and democratisation – opportunities for initiative and creativity of both pupils and teachers, and the participation of society in the running of education. Among a statement of well-known aims we find a new formulation: 'to create the conditions for the conscious self-determination of pupils, active self-assessment of their social needs' [actually – 'claims' or 'pretensions', *prityazaniya*]. On the curriculum, the Idea goes berserk: after advocating the development of 'national language-Russian bilingualism', daily physical education and art education, it appears to propose a plethora of new subjects – psychology, world culture, philosophy, economics, ecology – while warning against proliferation! Choice in education is seen as a good thing in itself, and is interpreted as a feature of democratisation: the APN points out that at primary level children should be able to choose what they draw pictures of and write about and which poems they learn by heart (this *is* actually new!) In lower secondary classes the options offer choices; in the last two years pupils should choose between PTUs (they are apparently intended to survive) and specialist classes or schools, in which the curriculum will consist of literature, history, art or world culture, social studies, maths, IT, PE, integrated science for humanities specialists, plus two or three specialist subjects. (Except for art, the suggestion about integrated science, a lack of one-and-a-half lessons of geography and one of a foreign language, this is almost exactly what they were going to get under the 1984 proposals.)

On the fraught topic of labour training, a great deal of tired and boring rhetoric is given another airing. Is there anything new here? Yes, for after affirming the status quo (general secondary schools do not [not 'should not'] usually give prevocational training, but where the conditions exist and the parents wish it, it should be allowed to do so – in other words, no-one is to be troubled by any changes) it sensibly recommends the establishment of a schools careers counselling service like those in many other countries.

In a section on the 'educational process' the APN comes to grips with a problem which obviously worries many Russians: the difference in readiness for school between six-year-olds. Delicate and deprived children should be dealt with in 'adaptation classes' (a new idea). The regular schools should provide help for physically and mentally handicapped children whose parents do not wish to place them in special schools, and for gifted children too. There should be 'state standards' of achievement; the parallel with recent developments in Britain suggests itself here. The foundation of a schools' psychological service is proposed. A call for the use in teaching of new technology is coupled with a warning about underrating well-tried traditional methods. Among a list of unsurprising characteristics of the modern teacher is a refreshing new one: 'Professional freedom, which is used for the perfecting of education and upbringing in the interests of children.' In-service and initial training should move in the direction of individualisation – tailoring such training to the individual's needs. A reliable system for supporting innovative teaching is said to be necessary; teaching salaries should be well above the average wage for the country, and teachers should be given grants for internal or overseas travel every two or three years.

This is not wholly lacking in imagination, and yet it is hard to resist the suspicion that it contains a strain of electioneering, of desire to please all the constituents. It is traditional in some ways, using the comfortable old jargon, it reassures by saying how much has been achieved in the past, but at the same time it manages to please the progressives by putting forward some child-centred ideas, by offering choice and some – but not too much innovation. Don't desert your old friends, the APN; and we'll press for travel grants and higher salaries for you!

THE IDEA OF EDUCATION AS CONCEIVED BY VNIK 'SHKOLA'

The VNIK 'Shkola' (the name means 'provisional research collective on "the school"') project is more radical, less jargon-ridden, more impatient with the past and less concerned to please its opponents. Nevertheless, it is far from trendy, and manages to maintain a dignified and not unduly polemical style throughout. Its authors are a large and influential group of people, many of whom are academicians or work for one or other of the APN's research institutes; they are therefore in competition with their colleagues, the authors of the

APN Idea of Education. VNIK 'Shkola' was timed to disband at the end of 1988, but its ideas have nevertheless entered the educational consciousness of the nation, and its members are far from defunct.

There are some very interesting and for the Soviet Union unusual ideas contained within this project. For instance, the earlier notion that the *state* was the principal agency to which the education system owed allegiance and which the education of the child should serve is rejected, and a restoration of the balance towards *society* (as opposed to the state) and the child itself is proposed. There is a stress upon development, democratisation, humanisation and realism in education. Constant development in the system is said to be what it needs rather than a great 'volcanic upheaval' every few years; realism means recognising what sort of reform is actually possible. Democratisation of the school means that it is to be open, and no longer run purely by what Marx, in a memorable phrase, called 'professional cretins'. The use of the word humanisation implies that the school should no longer be impersonal, but should 'turn towards the pupil and show confidence in him'.

The authors of the project call upon the school to act as a formative factor in economic and social progress and spiritual (i.e. in the Russian sense of inner moral and artistic) renewal. The school, they say, has been isolated – 'a left-luggage office for children' – and has consequently alienated children from the society it seeks to serve: this must be ended. The overall aim of the school to some extent recalls earlier formulations, but it is significantly different from them. It is 'to further the intellectual, moral, emotional and physical development of the personality, liberate its creative potential and shape a communist world-view based on general human values.' Old-fashioned phrases about the all-round development of communist personality are explicitly rejected. If this new emphasis is accepted, considerable re-writing of the textbooks will have to be undertaken. Even more innovative is the view of moral education. In the words of VNIK it has hitherto always been a series of demands addressed to the pupil, but now it should become 'a non-authoritarian, common, cooperative quest for a culture of behaviour', and be based on the idea of self-determination, the lack of compulsion and collective, purposeful direction. Even more rewriting becomes necessary here.

Many administrative matters with important educational implications are dealt with in the VNIK project. It would perhaps be truer to say that these are the administrative consequences of educational problems which it is sought to solve: for example, at what age should children start school? – six *or* seven, says VNIK 'Shkola', depending on school readiness. There should be open access and freedom of transfer to all schools and a right to remedial and accelerated teaching as necessary. Education should be decentralised, and local Soviets left to decide many issues as seems to them best. Central government must raise the proportion of national income spent on education (at present 7.2 per cent). The financial control of individual schools should be released from present restrictions and they should have the right to dispose of their own finances, moving 'from financial serfdom to economic independence'. This appears to be a suggested move towards what is in Britain termed 'local management of schools'.

The approach to labour education by VNIK is not entirely new, but it restates a position which is both politically and educationally orthodox in the Soviet setting. The labour foundation of the Soviet school, they say, has got mixed up with utilitarian work-training, which has become merely an addition to general education or an 'artificial professionalisation' of it. Labour, which should not exclude intellectual work, ought to be varied, purposeful, and have personal and social significance; it should involve the assimilation of the *principles* of a culture of labour, not be merely a collection of disconnected items. It should include voluntary social service, conservation work, participation in the work of governmental and social organisations, and should demonstrate the relation of school to real life. The labour content of the education given by the school should enable the child to conceive of working processes as an entity and should open to way for many-faceted harmonious development of the personality and healthy mental development.

In the lower secondary school the curriculum should be 75–80 per cent compulsory and the remainder consist of options. The upper secondary stage should be profoundly differentiated, and pupils encouraged to take different routes, including employment coupled with distance learning. The compulsory subjects in the last two years of school should be those of a general philosophical nature.

Teaching methods and attitudes come in for a great deal of enlightened discussion. VNIK states that naive faith in improved methodology as the cure for all ills must be forgotten: if this would work, children could just as well be taught by robots. The teacher must understand the child and stimulate children's interests. Knowledge, skills and habits are in themselves not enough – the personality must be developed – and to see education as nothing more than the imparting of information and delivery of explanations is insufficient. Spoon-feeding of factual content (what a Soviet educational journalist once memorably described as 'stuffing a goose with nuts') must end, and whereas the content of education should be a 'museum of human achievement' it should also be a workshop in which young people learn to acquire knowledge. The basic component of education is 'that which lies at the root of the growth and qualitative changes of man, what links him with ... the life of previous generations'. Teaching should be humanised in all subjects; science should be presented as 'a living process of seeking, discovery and invention'; the arts should be studied throughout the school career; PE should cease to be purely sport-oriented and become physical culture.

Syllabuses and teaching materials should be varied and subject to choice. The public should be able to influence curricula. Less 'frontal' teaching and more problem-solving, research and project methods should be employed. Assessment on the traditional five-point scale should reflect pupils' ability not merely to memorise facts, but to get knowledge for themselves, to solve problems and to achieve a rounded view of the world for themselves.

WHAT NOW?

It will come as no surprise that a substantial grouping in the teaching profession is opposed to radical change and resentful of the idea that such change is necessary. Improvement is one thing, revolution quite another. A contributor to a televised public debate chaired by the Minister, Gennadiy Yagodin (an advocate of restructuring and democratisation) on Teachers' Day, 2 October 1988, was loudly applauded by a section of the audience when he declared that democratisation and humanisation of the schools was not *perestroyka* (restructuring) but *pristroyka* (extension) of an existing sound structure. Even if many teachers such as these find reassurance in the idea that they are really doing quite well already, there are many others who are working for radical change in attitudes and practices. The profession was looking forward throughout the autumn of 1988 to a December congress of teachers at which these matters were to be debated. Elections were held in School 1937 to choose a representative to a borough congress at which in turn delegates would be elected to the All-Union Congress of teachers' trade unions. As is now usual, various candidates put themselves forward with a 'platform' – a statement of the policy they would adopt at the Congress. The election was held in School 1937 half an hour before school one morning and was keenly contested.

In the event this Congress seemed to come to no startling conclusions. At least the issues were debated. The conservatives had their say along with everyone else. Yagodin, however, received a great deal of moral support. As for the much criticised APN, complete restructuring has apparently been postponed for several years; vacancies as they arise are being filled by progressive educators, but no-one is being dismissed. As some critics are saying, 'These are the methods of the era of stagnation.' Did this mean a halt to radical change?

For a definite answer we shall have to wait and see. However, discussion has not ended and 1989 has brought some very significant developments. The immediate and most important result of the continued debate has been the confirmation by the State Committee for Education of four 'provisional statutes' for the secondary school, the vocational college, the secondary specialist school and the higher education establishment. The first of these was published in the *Teachers' Newspaper* in mid July,[10] in the hope that schools could get to work on it as early in the new academic year as possible. It is of the greatest interest for the future of the Soviet secondary school, even if the forces of inertia are doing their best to frustrate it. One correspondent to the press complains that his local education office is saying: 'The statute is only provisional – no-one has changed our instructions!'[11]

The principal features of this statute which announce significant change in the school include, first, acceptance of differentiation and choice in types of school and the curriculum they offer. The Soviet school is to be 'unified in fundamental conception, [but] varied in the content, forms, methods and organisation of instruction and upbringing'. Special profiles and elective subjects will figure prominently. Secondly, what must seem to the Soviets as a great deal of independence and freedom (within the law of education, of course) is envisaged, not merely for the individual republic or region, but for the individual school – in curriculum, disposal of financial resources, internal organisation (length of the working week, for example) and the ability to make legal agreements with other bodies. Children are to enter school at six or seven, according to their health and readiness, and primary teaching is envisaged as an integrated course, not as separate subjects. There will be multi-lateral syllabuses, considering the aptitudes and interests of the pupils, for the teacher to choose from in secondary education. Individual timetables both for the able and the backward are proposed.

The school will receive money from the state budget, but may raise additional sums by renting out its buildings, sports facilities, etc., selling the products of its workshops and gardens, giving adult education classes, providing courses for pupils in subjects not included in the national curriculum, and by raising funds from voluntary contributions from parents. Probably the most radical proposal is the election of a 'school council' (*sovet shkoly*) of teachers, pupils, parents and outside interests which, it seems, will have far-reaching freedom and responsibilities in the organisation and running of individual schools. Their powers would appear to be in many ways similar to those invested in English school governors by recent legislation, and the proposals have already aroused objections: 'How will some of these people know how a school should be run?' The presence of pupils on such bodies is a radical issue; one of the things they will have to discuss is financial rewards for good performance by the teaching staff. There is clearly enough meat here for Soviet teachers to chew on for many years to come, and how the provisional statute will work out in practice it is impossible to foresee.

In an interview[12] given at the time of the publication of this new provisional statute Yagodin made some trenchant points. On finance he declared that the State Committee was intending to go to the Supreme Soviet and ask for 10 to 12 per cent of the national budget to be spent on education. This is very optimistic, but the government can scarcely refuse a substantial rise in the present 7.2 per cent. In answer to cries from the republics of 'Why do we need an All-Union State Committee for Education?', he stated that such a body guaranteed the rights and freedoms of the citizen with regard to education. It is too easy, he added, for middle-ranking authority to complain about tyranny from above while being totally unready to share power with those below. When it was suggested that there was too much polarisation of attitudes between educators, when in fact the sides were not too far apart, he responded, 'The humane and the authoritarian school are incompatible. That is the essence of the conflict.' At meeting after meeting he had explained the State Committee's position to academicians and others of the opposing faction, but in the end the Congress 'upheld our position and the programme of action . . . There is no going back to the past for us'.

In all this ferment School 1937 has not been standing still. There is no reason why it should have any inordinate difficulty in recruiting parents and others onto any new school council. It will, however, have the greatest of difficulty in using its existing resources to generate extra income. It already has its own special profile (English), but unless it can employ an influx of new staff, it will, I anticipate, find itself short of the professional resources to offer much other curricular choice. But open to new ideas the staff certainly is. In the spring of 1989 meetings were held with a view to introducing Amonashvili's principles of primary teaching, the 'pedagogy of co-operation'. The school has a majority of restructurers on its staff and it seems most unlikely that they will be completely stopped in their tracks, unless something really disastrous happens at national level. The simple fact is that educational ideas, especially good ones, gather a certain momentum among good and thoughtful teachers. The recent debate has served to bring many such good ideas out into the light, publicise and – so, at least I believe from what I have seen – popularise them. The Soviet Union simply cannot continue to exist with a philosophy of education which seeks to do little more than prime children with facts – and imagined facts. It needs, and it knows it needs, imaginative and creative people who can reason and debate, and it needs divergent thinkers. In the restructuring of society they have plenty of problems on which to exercise and develop their creative talents.

7 Political Activity in the School

Readers from societies which are more politically apathetic than the Soviet Union may imagine that political aspects of the work of a school there are merely a matter of form. Perhaps, this misconception runs, the teachers ignore the obligatory ideological content of lessons, the pupils become immune to those parts of their textbooks and their lessons which convey a political message. Maybe assent to certain tenets of Communism becomes automatic, even unconscious. Opponents of Communism may even hope that the teaching of its doctrines could be counter-productive. After all, it is well known that the compulsory courses in Marxism-Leninism and history of the Party are unpopular in higher education and that students often attend without paying attention.[1] The act of Christian worship in British schools has, similarly, been cited as an example of unwise compulsion which, it is argued, has done no good to religion.

Disillusionment with the beliefs of Communism was no part of the visible life of School 1937 in Autumn 1988. That is not to say that there was no questioning of certain features of life which until very recently were sacred. One of these is the Komsomol, the Young Communist League. Current attitudes may best be illustrated by an incident in the theatre, which surprised me greatly when I witnessed it. The play was 'Under Section 206' by Vasiliy Belov, which was in repertoire at the Moscow Satire Theatre in Autumn 1988. It was a comedy about a pretentious young investigating magistrate who set out on a personal crusade to extirpate drunkenness and hooliganism in a remote part of rural Russia. Where common sense said he should leave well alone, he brought in the full power of the criminal code. In a crucial scene a local dignitary appeals to him: 'Are you a Party member?' Drawing himself up to his full height (and it must be admitted that the actor played the line for a laugh), he solemnly responds: 'I am a Young Communist!' At this the audience split its sides with laughter and applauded loudly. The same effect was achieved when I reenacted the scene at school and asked, 'Why is that funny?' When my colleagues had recovered their composure sufficiently to reply, they said, 'Because no-one takes the Komsomol seriously any more.'

It must seem incredible to many who experienced the days of Stalin and most of his successors that Soviet citizens could ever openly say such a thing about the Young Communist League. This organisation has for several generations been the guiding light of Soviet young people morally, politically, culturally and in every other way. Despite the fact that Soviet youth movements were to some extent at least modelled on the Scouting movement (sharing the motto 'Be prepared' and some of the same ethos), it can be likened to the Scouts and Guides only superficially.[2] Nor is it the Soviet equivalent of the Young Conservatives or the youth section of any British political party. On the contrary, it has always been an all-embracing national institution with a legally guaranteed monopoly of young people's loyalty. In many ways it has traditionally resembled a nonconformist church of the late nineteenth century, which provided not only religious observance, but cricket teams, literary and dramatic societies, social activities and leisure pursuits all imbued with the spirit of religion. In the case of the Komsomol, the uniting spirit was not religion, but a Marxist-Leninist worldview. Without being members young people would not gain entry to higher education, outside its aegis they could not band together to form anything even so innocent as a philatelists' club or a volleyball team. Young people are told the Komsomol has a great history; it was vital in the defence of the country against Hitler, and its formative influence in the years after the Revolution was not to be dismissed. 'If you want to understand the naive way we once regarded the Komsomol, you should read Nosov's *Neznayka*,' I was told. N. N. Nosov, the children's author, wrote several novels between 1954 and 1965 about Neznayka: *The Adventures of Neznayka and His Friends* was the first. It is set in a fantastic children's 'republic' of the future and, according to the *Soviet Literary Encyclopaedia* sets out to instil in its juvenile readers love of beauty and creative labour, as well as other standard virtues in the socialist canon.

There is no doubt, however, that the Komsomol is now in crisis. Young people will no longer accept its domination, its hierarchy inspires little respect, they will not vote tamely for approved candidates for the leadership, they question its right to prescribe moral precepts, they see no reason why they should not form their own groupings to follow an interest in anything from body-building to numismatics. In School No. 1937, out of about 210 eligible by age to join, only forty-two had done so by October 1988. 'A lot more will join', I was told. Why? 'Because their parents will tell them that it will help them to get into college.' And was that true? 'No, not any more; but the parents think it is.' A young member of staff who was in fact a keen member of the Komsomol, declared in the deputy head's room that the Komsomol should become purely a club for young people seriously interested in politics, and should cease to try to be a social, sporting, cultural, artistic and welfare organisation. The remark led to an animated discussion which lasted two hours.

The likeness of the Komsomol to a religious organisation, which I do not wish to push too far, may be further observed in the attitude of some members of the older generation to present discussion. Those *Komsomol* members who turned out to defend Moscow against the Nazis and who saw their friends killed in the process resent the expression of the view that the Komsomol is finished. As there are fundamentalist Christians who believe that the whole basis of their faith is undermined if the literal truth of one word of the Bible is questioned, in the same way do traditionalist Communists react to criticism, however slight, of the Komsomol. School 1937 has had to cope with such Party stalwarts who feel that the value of the sacrifices of 1941–45 is being called into question by pupils who do not show unswerving loyalty to the Komsomol. This attitude is, of course, a manifestation of the frame of mind which may be termed Stalinism: to demand faith in a set of principles, perhaps even a person or group of people, without regard to differentiation into essential and non-essential elements in those principles, a refusal to debate them, and the conviction that to question the smallest part of all this is to threaten the structure of the whole edifice. To use the religious analogy for the last time, it is like the Russian Orthodox Christian's view of Tradition: you either accept Tradition (singular, not 'traditions') as a whole, as it is, without selection or reservation, or you do not – in which case you are not Orthodox.

The pupils in School 1937 may have relatively little time for the Komsomol, but they are certainly keenly interested in political issues, as we shall see. In this study of the political life of the school, we shall look at the work of the youth organisations. I shall have something to say about the political content of lessons, and will describe the way political education of both pupils and staff is carried on outside the classroom.

THE YOUTH ORGANISATIONS

It is not an irrelevance to write of the youth organisations under the heading of 'political activity in the school', because they have explicit political aims. We are not speaking here of any 'hidden' curriculum: the ideological purpose of these bodies is overt and is taken very seriously. This point is further developed in Chapter 14, in which moral education is discussed. The Komsomol is under the direct control of the Party and in its turn guides the younger organisations. Nevertheless, one of the attractions of them is that many of the activities are run by the children or young people themselves, and they are controlled by adults at one remove; adults, of course, set the standards. Children aged approximately seven to ten, members of classes 1 to 3 at present, belong to the Octobrists, and are supposed to assent to the ethos of this organisation: they are preparing to become Pioneers, they love school and work hard, they respect their elders, they are 'upright and courageous, agile and knowledgeable', they are friendly, they read, draw, play and sing and they 'live cheerfully'. The Octobrists in each class are divided into detachments of five or six for purposes of friendly competition and for performing certain duties. These include keeping the room tidy, helping the teacher distribute materials, watering the pot-plants and seeing that the Octobrists in their group are tidily dressed. Every member of the group is intended to have a turn to act as leader during the year. The Octobrists are under the patronage of the older Pioneers, members of the All-Union Pioneer Organisation, who are aged ten to fifteen.

For all practical purposes it can be said that every Soviet school child of the appropriate age belongs to the Octobrists or the Pioneers. Entry to both organisations, especially the Pioneers, is something of a special occasion and is marked with due ceremony. Octobrists are received into membership within a few weeks of entering school. Eventually classes decide in which order their members will be received into the Pioneers, and especial honour accrues to those who are elected first. The ceremony for the School 1937 Pioneers took place not on the school premises, but in the Museum of the History of the Revolution, thus adding a further feeling of importance to the event, and making it memorable.

The principal aim of the Pioneer movement is to educate young people in the spirit of Communism and make them convinced fighters for the cause. This is, of course, not entirely a party political matter, since the ethos of Communism contains moral elements which many non-Communists would share. Pioneers are taught to have a social conscience and work for the good of the community, to work hard at school and help slower learners, to encourage good discipline at school, to take part in hobbies and cultural activities and to keep physically fit. Every school has a *pionerovozhatyy*, a Pioneer leader, whose task it is to organise the activities of the Pioneers within that school. What they do may best be illustrated by the following short sketch of Olga, who fulfilled this function in School 1937 in autumn 1988. She is seventeen years old and left school in the previous June. Needless to say, a member of the school staff is responsible for her supervision; in this case it is Irina Maksimovna, the teacher responsible for coordinating all extracurricular activities. Olga wishes to train as a primary teacher, but was unable to find a place at the Lenin Pedagogical Institute, since her marks in the entrance examination were one point short of the requirements. She intends eventually to train there as an evening student. The course will last five years instead of the four for full-time daytime study. One extra year does not seem enough to make up for part-time study, but the course will include no teaching practice: the work she does as Pioneer leader at School 1937 will count instead. She is not a former pupil of School 1937, and was sent here by arrangement with the department of the Pioneer House which deals with allocation of would-be leaders, as she thought that an 'English school' would be an interesting place to work in.

I asked about the aims of the work she did. She said it was general upbringing work and the organisation of out-of-school activities for the pupils. She works a thirty-six hour week and is present every day school is open: six days a week. A primary function is to coordinate the work of the Pioneer Council, which consists of two or three pupils from each class. They are responsible for organising the activities of the Pioneers, both day-to-day chores like picking up litter and longer-term projects of 'socially useful labour'. For example, Olga arranges visits to the nearby kindergarten, where Pioneers help look after the children. She arranges interschool and interclass contests of 'socialist competition'.[3] In conjunction with the teachers and the pupils' Komsomol committee she helps set up events such as the 'mathematics week', one of two subject weeks during this year. Such a project may seem to relate more to the academic work of the school, but the fact that it is regarded as part of the Pioneer Leader's sphere of influence reveals that the organisation is expected to permeate all aspects of the school.

Olga is a rank-and-file member of the Komsomol committee with no special powers, but she does contribute to their work, most of which is organised by the pupils themselves through their secretary and committee.

In an attempt to discover the range of her work, I asked exactly how she had spent the particular day on which I interviewed her. It began by receiving bundles of waste paper which the children were bringing in before school in order to raise money. Next, there was a meeting of the Pioneer Council to discuss who was to do what in relation to the impending initiation ceremony into the Pioneers. The Council also had to confirm the choices of the different classes as to which pupils were to be received first. Following this, Olga had to supervise a rehearsal for the 'Festival of the Little Red Star' – the reception ceremony for the new youngest members of the Octobrists, during which a Pioneer pins a red star badge to the Octobrist's lapel. This ceremony takes place shortly before the November Revolutionary holiday. It lasts about an hour, and involves the ceremonial aspects – parading with flags, speechmaking, the distribution of badges – and a concert of poetry and song.

After this, the leader had made herself available for individual consultations with Pioneers on routine matters. She had then gone out to the cinema to buy season tickets for a monthly series of films. About seventy children from the school Pioneer group had subscribed at minimal cost to the series of partly educational, partly entertainment films. She returned to the school for another rehearsal, this time of a 'solemn parade', which will be described below. Along with the meeting with me, it adds up to quite a busy six hours.

I took the opportunity to attend the solemn parade a few days later. The purpose of the parade was to mark the approach of the seventy-first anniversary of the October Revolution. All the Pioneers were present in the school hall, and were paraded in classes, lined up around three sides. They answered their class numbers loudly and proudly. There was a general air of organised chaos, a good deal of conversation and racket, but no unruliness. The children's behaviour, in fact, resembled that of Russian adults, who do not always keep totally silent on formal occasions. The colour was trooped; flags and some rather unmilitary marching were seen. The teacher in charge made a speech recalling the glories of the children's Komsomol predecessors in revolution and war. Class by class, poems were declaimed on such themes as friendship, honour, and patriotism. It cannot be said that either the speech or the poems were listened to by more than half the children. Nevertheless, there was colour, there was ceremony, there was action, and the children did not seem to be present against their will. What there did not seem to be, to British eyes, was solemnity; there was no levity, but the din and relaxed attitude belied the title of the parade.

Entry to the Komsomol itself is not a mere formality, and even before the present 'crisis', young people of fourteen to fifteen did not automatically join. Again, the role of the Komsomol is to further political and moral education, to foster resistance to bourgeois ideology and decadent life-styles, to encourage hard academic and physical work, to assist with careers advice and see that school leavers choose work necessary to the State. When a member leaves school, he receives a testimonial from the Komsomol outlining his achievement in these areas. The brief for Komsomol activity is so wide that opportunities for its work are legion, and it is again obvious, as with the organisations for younger children, that it permeates, or is meant to permeate every sphere of the school's activity.

What do older pupils of School 1937 feel about the Komsomol? I was told by some of them, and by no means a small disaffected group, that it had lost its importance as the centre of political activity for young people. 'It is not important to us any more.' 'It can help in some ways', I was told, and when I asked for an example – 'Well, it helped us get hold of and pay for some disco equipment for the Palace of Culture!' Did it help them to get into university? 'It used to help, once. That is far less so nowadays. To be a member gave you privileges. It meant prestige.' How many of their schoolfellows belong to the Komsomol? 'About two thirds.' This last answer was interesting, because I believed it was honestly offered: the truth as given by the staff is that only 20 per cent of those eligible belonged. The pupils were obviously unaware of the low figure, or perhaps they did not want me, a foreigner, to know. I do not think they were as devious as the latter explanation would suggest.

'You say the Komsomol has lost its importance as a focus of political education,' I asked. 'Are any of you interested in politics?' 'Yes, of course, we all are,' was the reply. 'No-one can possibly fail to be interested in politics; where matters of war and peace are concerned our survival depends on it.' This answer leads us into an account of the direct political education carried on in School No. 1937.

POLITICAL BRIEFINGS

The Russian word for this is *politinformatsiya*, and the system operates straightforwardly: a meeting of pupils is held with a senior teacher on Tuesday morning at which burning issues are discussed; later the same day that teacher reports to a gathering of colleagues and suggests to them the sort of things they might talk about with classes; on Thursday the pupils lead a short session with the rest of their class. How all this might have been carried on in the 'period of stagnation' (that is, the Brezhnev era) would not be too difficult to imagine even if one did not know that 'discussion' was conducted in an atmosphere of sanctimonious reverence for the latest doings of the Party or the most recent literary masterpiece of Leonid Ilich himself. How it was done in Stalin's day happily does not concern us either. In the autumn of 1988 things were much more relaxed.

Descriptions of typical sessions may help to illustrate how political briefing is carried on. Arriving in a blizzard at ten to eight one Tuesday, the meeting assembled in an empty classroom. The only teacher present was Marina Georgievna, a deputy head and Party member. Eleven boys and four girls attended, all from classes seven upwards. Marina began by checking which classes were represented and taking the pupils' names. Several days later, in private, some of these pupils assured me that attendance was voluntary. One boy stated that he attended because he had chosen (with his classmates' agreement but not at their election) to be a *politinformator*, political information representative; up to four pupils from his class usually came. As to the imbalance between boys and girls, the pupils commented that politics was more a matter for boys to become involved in. Girls, as one of them said, 'have more things to do'. Again here, we find standard attitudes in Soviet society reflected in the views of the schoolchildren: male domination of the higher reaches of the Party is proverbial in the Soviet Union.[4] We are, however, speaking of only one school, and it may be that in other places the females make the running politically speaking.

After the administration had been done, Marina invited the pupils to say what articles in the press had attracted their attention since last week. They made numerous suggestions, the first four of which all concerned recent Soviet history, three specifically during the Stalin period. They were an article in *Pravda* on 21 October 1988 on industrialisation under Soviet rule, one in *Moskovskaya pravda* on 24 October about Stalin himself, a story about a fifteen-year-old girl who had been sent to Siberia in 1929, and a piece about the Popular Front (Stalin's policy propounded in the mid-1930s which encouraged Communists in all countries to ally themselves with other parties and groups of all shades of opinion provided they were opposed to fascism). Marina expressed interest in all these suggestions. Her preferred mode of operation being more directly didactic and time being short she deferred discussion on these matters and turned to a sheaf of newspapers she had brought with her. In connection with these she raised a number of matters of more immediate contemporary concern. The first of these was the Law on Elections, which was printed in all the papers, and which gave Marina the opportunity to speak about the democratisation of Soviet society. She remarked that there had been many abuses and unsatisfactory practices in the past in relation to the way candidates were put forward and elected to government organs. There had been a campaign of criticism against some elected groups of legislators who were in office for no other reason than the prestige, who did not live in the constituency they represented and were not interested in its problems.

Interest also surrounded an interview with Gorbachev reprinted from the West German journal, *Der Spiegel*.[5] In view of the interest taken by Western newspapers, and not only the gutter press, in the private lives of public figures in entertainment and government, it may seem strange that the Soviet public knows little or nothing about its leaders as people. Marina made this very comment; she mentioned that Gorbachev had said that he enjoyed watching ice-hockey and going to the theatre, and read aloud his non-committal reply to the question as to which particular theatres he liked best. 'I go to many theatres ... I believe the most interesting play for us ... is *perestroyka* itself, ... a real drama, in which characters collide, in which new fights with old, in which consciousness is changed, radical change.' This provoked some discussion, one boy making the excellent point that perhaps Mr Gorbachev wished to avoid the errors of previous times when the casually expressed preferences of a leader were used unscrupulously to further the ends of some people and blight the careers of others. Marina turned to the more serious part of the interview and picked out several items. One passage related to *khozrasschet*, the economic accountability of Soviet industry and agriculture, and referred to the failure in some areas of rented farms to be any more efficient and productive than state or collective farms. She picked out a passage on conservatism in the bureaucracy and the nation in general; people were refusing to accept new technology and were indulging in the 'spirit of Luddism'. 'What ignorant savagery!' she commented; it is obviously a sore point for Gorbachev too! She further made reference to the equipping of Soviet industry; 90 per cent of the machinery is said to be worn out and obsolete. By this time the bell was about to ring for first lesson. 'That's the basic material: I wish you success!' And the pupils were sent forth into the wilderness to preach the gospel.

This eight o'clock meeting is followed up an hour or two later in a teachers' meeting in Marina's classroom in the long (twenty-minute) break. There is little time for anything more than a quick run-down on what took place at eight o'clock with the pupils, although in this one Marina added a few thoughts about topics to consider for the future (the principal one being the American Presidential Election, so events in other countries also figure in political briefings). Attendance is voluntary and very small (about seven was the most I saw), but despite the fact that Marina goes at it hammer and tongs, she does not have it all her own way, and discussion can be animated. The first time I attended or overheard the meeting, the subject was a speech by Gorbachev to journalists, in which he had mentioned that the press was giving the impression that there was far more opposition to restructuring than there in fact was. 'Please, please make this clear to the children, it is so important.' On another occasion, Marina devoted the few minutes with her colleagues to historical topics, which went back far further than the Soviet period in which the pupils seemed so interested. Again these were all based on articles in the press; the first was on history and its interpretation. Especially in the Soviet period, questions were raised as to issues of evidence and how it should be used. Historical facts in the Soviet Union have always hitherto been taught along with their acceptable interpretation, and it is doubtful whether any but the very best students understood that differing assessments of the same evidence were possible. Another press article had gone back to Peter the Great, Russia's first and greatest reformer, active c. 1699–1725. The obstruction and prejudice which the changes he instituted aroused were likened to the resistance to restructuring under Gorbachev. Even more interesting was a piece about Alexander Radischev (1749–1802), the radical writer who had been sent to Siberia for criticising the Russia of Catherine the Great. This had apparently suggested that the reason for his suicide was not, as usually stated, depression and fears that he might be imprisoned and exiled again, but disillusionment at the turn the French Revolution had taken from its libertarian beginnings to terror, oppression and imperial ambition. Obvious parallels with the Russian Revolution of 1917 were suggested.

It was even more illuminating to attend a pupils' political briefing meeting in the long break on a Friday morning, when those who had been present early on the Tuesday passed the message on to their classmates. I gave no warning of my approach; in fact I attended that particular session as I happened to be passing through the room by chance after giving a lesson in the adjoining classroom, and I believe my presence was noticed only by some of the pupils, though I did ask permission to remain. It was a senior (tenth) class, and out of over thirty pupils, fifteen or sixteen were present, plus the class tutor. Pupils later assured me that attendance was completely voluntary, and that the form teacher did not have to be there for it to be held. She did not conduct the meeting, and contributed to the discussion no more than many other pupils who were present. Three boys spoke for twelve or thirteen minutes in total about articles they had prepared and for the rest of the time there was animated discussion. They later told me that Marina Georgievna had suggested the topics to them, but that they did not necessarily feel obliged to accept her suggestions. Natal'ya Viktorovna, their form tutor, 'organised our discussion' but it would have gone on if she had not been there. The topics which aroused the greatest interest were, first, an article on Stalin from *Ogonyok*, a weekly magazine which was one of the front runners in the reform movement. Clearly the person of Stalin, who so dominated the lives of these young people's grandparents and the childhood of their parents too, was of major concern to them. Secondly, there was a heated argument about *perestroyka* which I could not follow. Questions afterwards elicited the explanation that they had been arguing about how restructuring should be carried through, not about whether it was a good thing or not. And how *should* it be managed, I asked? At this they became as vague as their parents might have been: the economic system needed to be changed, attitudes had to change, the quality of goods must be improved, and there ought to be goods in the shops for people to buy with their money. The boys, who, as I have said, made the running in the political field in School No. 1937, told me they wanted to initiate much more extended discussions on political matters such as this (again, always using articles from the press as the starting point, since this seems to be the standard formula). Many pupils were willing in principle, but it had not yet proved possible to find a time free from other activities.

Political comment was prominent in a satirical show performed in the school one afternoon in a meeting of one of the school clubs. In one sketch the difficulties schoolchildren have in thinking for themselves was amusingly represented when a 'typical pupil' was brought on stage with his arms and legs attached to strings like a marionette. He was set free, and when asked to express his opinion, was speechless – until the strings were re-attached.

POLITICAL EDUCATION IN LESSONS

Enough has been said to indicate that a goodly proportion of the pupils in School 1937 is keen to hear about and discuss matters which are in the broad sense political. It is necessary, however, to remind ourselves, if only briefly that political education has its place in the standard curriculum as well as in activities and briefings out of class.

A number of school subjects are regarded as crucial in forming political awareness and orthodox attitudes in schoolchildren. History and social studies are the leaders in this respect. Geography is another, and literature is similarly held to be important in the formation of a Marxist-Leninist worldview. Having said that, we are moving into the realm of moral education, with which political upbringing is intimately linked in the Soviet mind. What is important to understand is that the political content of lessons in the USSR and more particularly the requirement upon teachers to raise and teach about these matters is not a mere formality, but a practice which is observed conscientiously.

The textbooks do, of course, contain many sections and passages of a political nature. Needless to say, these can only be of general, not topical, interest. Now, it would be easy to find a number of choice extracts by which to mock the writers of Soviet textbooks. The following passage may serve as a reminder of the bad old Cold War days. It illustrates a particular type of old-style paranoia, and it is fair to remember that it was almost certainly written by someone who has never visited, and indeed never will visit, an English-speaking country. It is taken from a textbook for higher education which was being used in the Leningrad school where I taught. The teacher had selected this book not for its ideological content, but for its methodological excellence – which is not in doubt.

Unlike people living under socialism who are products of a

collective society, people in the West are brought up in a dog-eat-
dog society disguised under the mask of 'a society of free individuals'. Individualism, encouraged by centuries of capitalist existence cripples human beings and alienates them from one another.
The sick bourgeois society breeds non-communication and mutual
distrust among people, indifference to and disregard for one's
fellowmen [sic]. The philosophy of individualism (whose selfish
principle is: 'Everyone for himself and devil take the hindmost')
leads to misunderstanding between the young and the old, widens
the generation gap, contributes to the break-up of families with the
children often left to their own devices and the parents often
doomed to loneliness and misery at an old age [sic].[6]

This paragraph forms the introduction (in English) to a reading
passage from a novel by Sid Chaplin entitled, *The Watchers and the
Watched*, which some might think would have made a good title for a
book about the Soviet Union. What the outsider can never be sure
about is the subtext. Is this paragraph and others like it meant to be
taken at its face value? Is the writer trying to say something not only
about the evils of bourgeois society, but about other societies,
*an*other society? What is certain is that the children do not always
know what to make of passages like this. I was once or twice during
my stay in School No. 1937 pinned to the wall by pupils and told, 'The
teachers aren't here now, so tell us what England is really like!' So if
such passages are designed to be swallowed whole, they do not
achieve their purpose. It is a lesson for educators all over the world.

It is impossible to write at all satisfactorily about informal interven-
tions in lessons by teachers on political themes. Instigated by
unexpected questions or by points arising by chance, teachers in any
country will respond with unrehearsed contributions. I heard many
such incidents. It may be considered that my own presence in the
school contributed indirectly to informal political education, since I
occasionally strayed onto broadly political themes when asked, as
well as delivering little talks about life in England. However, the
heartening thing about these informal political discussions under
perestroyka in the school was that they were often in spirit very
similar to the type of discussion which might have been held in a
school in Western Europe. The disheartening thing is that sometimes
a new orthodoxy was expected of the children: new clichés for old.
Nevertheless, the pupils were very quickly latching on to the idea that
the new normality is for people to hold differing views, and not to
vote unanimously for the same policy.[7]

8 Learning in Class

What Lessons in the Soviet School Are Like

It scarcely needs saying that within any national education system teachers differ widely. The styles they adopt in the classroom result partly from their training and partly from their personality and the type of instruction they experienced when at school. Much has been made in Western countries of the difference between 'authoritarian' and 'progressive' teaching styles, and studies have discovered every imaginable point on the scale between the two extremes.[1] It is, none the less, possible to generalise about the manner most commonly adopted by teachers in Soviet classrooms. The fact that this is now likely to change under *glasnost'* does not alter the fact that there *is* a flavour which one experiences in a very great many Soviet classrooms, and that this flavour is different from that in many other countries. In this chapter I aim to characterise the dominant teaching style and say how I believe it will change in the future. I shall leave the matter of foreign language teaching to separate chapters, as this is a different matter and one of considerable interest for other reasons.

THE TRADITIONAL LESSON

I begin with a caricature. Thirty-eight boys and girls aged sixteen to seventeen are working in a room with their social studies teacher (a young man in his thirties). They are hunched over their textbooks as he announces the theme of the lesson: the Soviet State and the stages in its development, its main aim and objectives, the functions of the state, its origins, history and essence. They write the themes down as the teacher dictates them. They know that they must master the material somehow – or at least gain a satisfactory mark in the leaving examination – if they are to gain entry to university. Questions are directed by the teacher as the lesson proceeds. It is difficult to hear what the pupils are saying, since they are still poring over their textbooks and notebooks. It soon becomes clear that they are doing this in order to search for the answers to the teachers' questions, or to appear to be so doing. The questions are not designed to test the pupils' understanding, or ability to deduce answers, or – least of all! – to arouse their intellectual interest in the subject of the lesson; they merely coax the dutiful into finding the appropriate lines of the textbook in order to read them out aloud, sometimes at inordinate length. When explanations of such matters as the functions of the state, the differences between socialism and capitalism, or Marx's idea that the state would wither away are necessary, the teacher indulges in the purest abstractions, making little or no contact with the young people's experiences or knowledge of life. Few of the class participate in any way; all who do merely read aloud from the book in response to the questions. One girl on one occasion attempts a spontaneous answer, which is successful and is praised by the teacher; he is, however, unsuccessful in provoking any other thoughtful responses. At one point a television monitor shows a bust of Lenin while a short crackly recording of his voice is played. 'What conclusions can be drawn from Vladimir Il'ich's speech?' Silence. More silence. A girl then responds at high speed for several minutes, repeating the sense of the speech in similar, but not exactly the same words, which are in any case taken from the textbook. It is hard to believe that anything useful is being learned, or to avoid the conclusion that the youngsters would be better and more interestingly employed reading last week's *Radio Times* – or its equivalent *Govorit i pokazyvaet Moskva*.

I suppose I had better come clean and admit that I have been telling lies: this is no caricature, but a lesson I actually witnessed in 1980.[2] The good news is that a Soviet teacher-trainer who was also present was quite indignant at the tedious methodology: 'If he'd been one of my students I'd have given him a very poor mark indeed! And he kept the children two minutes after the bell! It's disgraceful – children are entitled to a break.' (The tedium and the overrunning seemed to be equally heinous offences, but I have to admit that every time I kept children for more than a few seconds after the bell in School 1937 I could hear her voice from the past reproaching me.) It is immensely reassuring that other Soviet educators find this type of pedagogic performance unsatisfactory, but it must be admitted that I had been manoeuvred into that classroom presumably because the school wanted to show the foreign visitor what they hoped would be a good lesson. It is very hard to find any redeeming features in the lesson at all: it did not stimulate, develop the pupils' cognitive abilities, help them to understand anything, interest or inform them.

It did not convey information efficiently, because the subject matter was quite beyond the majority of the class, and there was no attempt to make it accessible or palatable. The lesson was orderly and well disciplined, but in all other ways was a pedagogic calamity.

Before passing on to brighter things, let us hear another horror story. In a Russian literature lesson which I visited in 1984 the class of fifteen-year-olds were studying Maxim Gorky. (It is perhaps relevant to mention that, although the medium of instruction was Russian, the pupils were native speakers of another Soviet language.) Nothing by Gorky was read during the lesson, but his biography featured prominently, as did the titles of some of his works and some summary of their content. The style of this teacher (a middle-aged woman) was, like our social scientist above, catechistic: the pupils were conducted through the subject-matter by a series of questions, which they were expected to answer from memory. Many of these questions invited an expression of opinion or literary judgement, but it was quite clear that it was not the *children's* opinion or judgement that was being sought. The only acceptable answers were worded in a way which was obviously being rehearsed from lesson to lesson. In one case, a pupil was stumbling over an answer and the teacher, anxious to keep things moving, prompted him until he picked up the thread; she then continued in exact unison with the pupil for another ten or fifteen seconds! At one point Tolstoy's name was mentioned. 'We did him last year, but since his name has cropped up, we had better just revise Tolstoy.' And that great writer was 'revised' in the same arid and stupefyingly monotonous way. Later, Gorky's role in the theory of Soviet literature came up. A pupil tentatively described him as 'a representative of Socialist Realism'. This provoked an outburst of wrath of heroic proportions:

Teacher: What? What? What did you call Gorky?
Pupil: . . . a representative . . .
Teacher: [fuming] ??
Pupil: . . . the founder of Socialist Realism.
Teacher: [absolutely incensed by this time and scarcely mollified by the pupil's self-correction]: Yes, yes, the founder, the *founder*. He wasn't a representative, how can you talk such nonsense, why did you say that? He was the founder of Socialist Realism, *don't* you go saying he was a representative.

She worked off her aggression on this wretched pupil and then went back to boring everybody else silly. In answer to my tentative suggestion after the lesson that maybe it would be a good thing if pupils were allowed to answer in their own words and with their own ideas, she replied witheringly that of course that is exactly what they were doing. My immediate reaction was to think her a fool for trying to make me believe that, but perhaps she actually imagined that the children *were* expressing their own ideas. What were these children learning? That the study of literature is a branch of knowledge as exact as any of the natural sciences, in which factual details of a writer's biography and approved assessments of his work can be learned off by heart in order to demonstrate 'success' in mastering the subject. Maybe the children were grateful to this teacher for helping them to pass the examination. It was, however, a great pity that examination success and educational purposes were so much at variance. It was almost as great a pity that a teacher of such experience could feel it necessary to conduct a lesson in literature in such a manner, and without ever betraying the slightest fondness for the works of any author; or, one might add, any concern that the pupils should learn to value them. It is not surprising that a survey of Soviet arts teachers a few years ago discovered that more than half of them had no interest in the arts whatever, except for having to teach them.[3]

If one were to list the possible aims of a school lesson, they would be to convey information, to develop understanding, to foster the ability to deduce conclusions from evidence, to give the opportunity for aesthetic experience, to encourage discussion and debate, to give pleasure in intellectual activity, to foster creativity, to make pupils see the possibilities of all sorts of scientific and academic pursuits and to understand how practitioners in different fields work, to teach them how to learn and find out information for themselves and how to learn from the teacher, from books and resources of all sorts, and from each other. One might also add: to teach pupils to be critical of received ideas, from whatever source they are received. Not every lesson could conceivably work towards all these aims, but it is obvious that the two lessons described here matched very few of them; the first, it could be argued, came nowhere near achieving any of them, not even that of conveying information – which would appear to have been its only aim. The trouble with education in countries all over the world is that for centuries teachers and the public at large believed that its main, indeed its only, purpose was to convey information and to see that children learned it (off by heart if necessary). It would have been possible years ago to enter any school in England and see lessons of this type being taught. There are still people in Britain, some of them in high places, who resist the notion that schooling should do other than convey information. In the Soviet Union the content of syllabuses has been held to be overloaded with useless and unnecessary factual material for generations, but the problem has been to persuade the 'experts' to agree to leaving some of it out in favour of teaching concepts, ideas, debate and so on – or of persuading children to enjoy learning and appreciating the arts. The present uncertain state of the practice of education in the light of this particular controversy will be illustrated later. Meanwhile I intend to move out of the field of horror stories to describe two more Soviet lessons of the past in order to illustrate other aspects of the traditional concept of teaching which is now to be replaced or at least greatly modified.

Some British primary teachers may nevertheless think that the first of these lessons is in certain ways horrific. I witnessed it in 1980 in a kindergarten in Minsk, where six-year-olds were being prepared for formal schooling by occasional lessons in school style. It was a demonstration lesson, so perhaps some of its features were unusually exaggerated and perhaps also it had been partly rehearsed. If so, these two factors served to highlight the assumptions behind what went on. It was a thirty-minute reading lesson during which the children were learning to recognise a new letter of the printed alphabet, d. All the twenty children were seated at desks facing front, and they stayed behind them for the whole time. They raised their right forearm when indicating they could answer the teacher's question, but kept the elbow in contact with the desk. They invariably rose from their seats to address the teacher. (This is not insisted upon by teachers of senior classes, but the habit is so ingrained that I had occasional pupils in School 1937 who simply could not bring themselves to address me in class from a sitting position.) Most of the teaching was in whole-class style, though towards the end a few minutes were spent working individually. What some primary teachers will find unusual is that, although the children knew a mere handful of the letters of the Cyrillic alphabet and more than one of them were having some difficulty in pronouncing the Russian word for 'bicycle', they were also being drilled in the meaning of such words as 'sentence', 'syllable' and 'consonant'. Moreover, the teacher insisted, when she remembered, upon being given full-sentence answers. The lesson contained many exchanges like this:

1. Role-play in the kindergarten.

2. School 1937.

3. Junior English: a group at work.

4. 'What did you make of the maths homework?' A scene at break time.

5. Tenth-class pupils fascinated by the advertisements in the *West Derbyshire Recorder*.

6. The English department meets.

7. A 'solemn parade' of the Pioneers.

8. Aunty Nina gets dinner ready.

9. Absorbed in work at the Pioneer Palace.

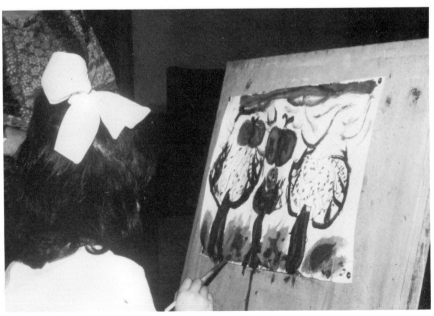

10. Coaching a youngster at the afternoon art school.

11. Senior pupils at work in the English classroom.

Teacher: What have we been doing?
Pupil: We have been making up sentences.
Teacher: What does our speech consist of?
Pupil: Sentences.
Teacher: Now give a proper answer.
Pupil: Our speech consists of sentences.

Or, after the reading of a short poem:

Teacher: What sound occurred most frequently in that poem?
Pupil: D occurred most often.
Teacher: What sort of a sound is d?
Pupil: D is a consonant.
Teacher: Why do you think d is a consonant?
Pupil: Because you can't sing it.
Teacher: Why else do you think d is a consonant?
Pupil: Because you pronounce it quickly and abruptly.

The content and vocabulary would be considered too advanced for English children of this age; it seems strange to be teaching so much technical information about language to children when they can recognise only a few letters of the alphabet. Moreover, the formality of the way the lesson is organised, its relative rigidity, the insistence upon certain rituals of seating, speaking, raising the hand and so on, all imply a concept of 'teaching' and 'lesson' which is alien to the primary school, certainly in Britain, America and numerous other Western countries.

As a final example, I recall an occasion which could be termed a lesson as a performance art. This was not a lesson in the strict sense of the word, but a rehearsed event, staged for my benefit as a visitor, not to deceive me, but to edify. The theme was 'Poetry and music of the Second World War', and the 'lesson' could with equal effect have been given as a recital in a theatre or similar building. The teacher was in charge of the linking commentary, and she called upon pupils to come to the front to recite poems or introduce recorded musical items. Together teacher and pupils had prepared and rehearsed the programme and they needed only an audience to complete the effect; this I supplied. Another occasion which contains elements of rehearsal is the 'peace lesson' with which every school year opens on 1 September.[4] Here again there are likely to be visitors, this time from the local community, there is an element of preparation in that individual pupils come ready to speak, recite or in some way contribute to the proceedings. The official briefing for this 'lesson' does in fact suggest that it may be given in a pioneer room, museum or 'memorial place' rather than a classroom.

These few examples from many experiences in Soviet classrooms before *glasnost'* got under way typify the traditions of schooling.[5] There is or was a strong emphasis on factual content, a reluctance to admit to controversy or uncertainty on any point, a consequent tendency to reduce aesthetic or what one might call philosophical subjects to a catalogue of stereotyped statements, little consideration of the child as recipient of all this, a strongly formal atmosphere, and stress on classroom rituals which amounts sometimes to turning the lesson into a ceremony. The subject matter most of all and the teacher in second place are firmly in control of all that happens. Children's ideas are accepted if they conform to teacher expectation, but are otherwise rarely explored. So at least it seems to the visitor, who is likely in the very nature of things to find the teacher on his or her best behaviour.

Until recently it was hard to be certain as to whether this critical view was shared by Soviet educationists, or whether it would be regarded by them as the calumny of a 'bourgeois falsifier'. Readers of this book will understand that I am expressing my own opinion, and that in any case one might expect there to be a wide range of opinion about these matters in the USSR too. However, I can state with confidence that there is a powerful section of educational opinion there which shares some of these views. In 1988 an article I had published on moves in Soviet music education was pirated from a British periodical, translated and republished with an introduction of the we-don't-quite-agree-with-all-of-this-but-like-it-even-so type in a Soviet teachers' journal received (if not read!) by all Soviet school music teachers.[6] I gritted my teeth and showed colleagues in School 1937 something else I had published[7] expressing similar views to those in this chapter, wondering what the reaction would be. The surest indication that they approved was that they passed on the article in question to senior pupils in the school to read.

THE SOVIET CLASSROOM TODAY

The tradition described could not possibly change overnight, even if all agreed that it should. Habits are ingrained, and even given a certain amount of good will, professional people find it hard to change the customs and assumptions of a lifetime. Could the literature teacher described above ever change? Maybe the social studies teacher was longing for a chance to get some discussion going, but was too afraid – as a Party member he was *obliged* to get the ideology right and could not afford to fall flat on his face in front of visitors. The primary teacher was obviously fond of her pupils and might have been willing to try another approach – if encouraged by her superiors. A leading inservice teacher-trainer stated to me in 1987 and again in 1988 that the system needed at least eight years for newly trained and emancipated young teachers to get into the schools and make any perceptible difference. The evidence from School 1937 was mixed, but it was clear that some of the experienced people were not only willing, but anxious to change. The remainder of this chapter can merely hint at the direction in which the school is going. The picture is a mixture, but one would expect practice to vary widely.

Russian language teaching would appear to be in crisis. On earlier visits I have witnessed some good lessons for various age-groups, with teachers using a variety of approach within the same lesson and not sticking rigidly to one single point from the syllabus for the whole time. Russian educators appear to believe firmly in an analytical, grammatical approach to their own language. Rules of grammar, rules of spelling and punctuation, parts of speech, gender and agreement – everything the foreigner has to learn when trying to master the language figures in the syllabuses for Russian children learning their own tongue. One wonders how Russian children would ever learn their own language without all this theoretical help, or how they managed to do it in the days before education was compulsory. Attempts have recently been made in England to reintroduce this sort of instruction into native language teaching; happily the Committee charged with compiling the national curriculum on English has resisted extreme pressure from governmental sources.[8] I say 'happily', because experience in Russia shows that all the parsing and clause analysis they get does not actually enable children to write good Russian.[9] The unfortunate thing is that, whereas in England the reaction to this situation is to say, 'Let's try something else', in Russia it is: 'Let's do even more clause analysis, parsing, theoretical grammar and so on.' Russian children have to suffer this to saturation point, and there are still strident complaints from teachers in higher education that undergraduates come to them unable to punctuate and spell.

A second-year (age eight) Russian class I observed bore many resemblances to the kindergarten lesson seen in Minsk many years previously. The formality was similar. 'Good-morning!' [after which the nod of acknowledgement from the class was rehearsed]. 'Tidy your work place, Sit down. Hands on the desk! But quietly!' Things relaxed as a ball was thrown around from child to child, and whoever was holding the ball gave the next letter of the alphabet in order. A few minutes of copy-book writing followed – copperplate loops and whorls were practised. Then the whole class wrote a short sentence into their books with accompanying commentary:

Pupil 1:   At the beginning of the sentence we write a capital letter.
Pupil 2:   In the middle we write the words separately.
Pupil 3:   At the end we place a full stop.

The main theme of the lesson was a point of spelling: the soft sign (a letter of the alphabet) when used as a mark of division between syllables. Other spelling matters were revised, so the lesson was not merely an exploration of this recondite matter alone. Spelling was practised by the whole class writing out together a few proverbs which included the words which are difficult to spell: for example, *Druz'ya poznayutsya v bede* (You discover your friends when you're in trouble). As this was done, the children talked through the process. 'We start with a capital letter. *Dru-*, *z-*, soft sign, *ya*, the soft sign divides a consonant from a vowel. We then . . . [etc.] Finally we write a full stop.' There was a break for a movement game – a song with actions. A written exercise followed which the pupils completed at their own speed. The teacher toured the room to help and correct, and finally showed a transparency of the right answers for pupils to correct their own work.

The last thing I should wish to suggest to the reader is that children in any country do not need drilling in the spelling and orthographical conventions of their own language. But should a wise teacher spend the best part of forty-five minutes with thirty-seven eight-year-olds on one spelling rule, with very little variety, without humour, and most of all without any reminder that the subject 'Russian' has other dimensions to it – poetry, stories, literature in particular? Yes, there were the proverbs, presented as they always are as examples of the unbounded common sense, wit and wisdom of the Russian people. But I have to say I have in other places seen much better Russian lessons in which grammar, orthography, vocabulary building, and imaginative response to literature and sometimes even music and art have been integrated into a coherent whole. This lesson resembled another Russian grammar lesson I saw in School 1937 with a much older class on 'word collocations and word building'. Again there was a great deal of dry theory, many technical terms, no attempt to make the material palatable or interesting and no humour. The syllabus for Russian contains a mountain of grammar, morphology, phonetics, graphics and syntax, and it also contains an element entitled 'development of connected language'. At the end of year eight this is all tested by means of a written essay and an oral examination concentrating almost exclusively on technical aspects of punctuation, spelling, declension of nouns, parts of speech and sentence analysis. By such instruments do Russian teachers try to enthuse Russian children with respect for their own language, the language which the great eighteenth-century polymath Mikhail Lomonosov said possessed 'the splendour of Spanish, the vivacity of French, the strength of German, the tenderness of Italian and the richness, brevity and vivid imagery of Greek and Latin'. Lessons like this fall far short of achieving that ideal!

I did, of course, visit other lessons for primary-age children in School 1937, which showed more variety and enthusiasm. There is, for example, a pleasing stress in Soviet education on the performing arts, and great use is made of puppet theatre 'productions' in developing children's language ability. A final point about the primary-age lessons is that the room in which they were conducted, which was the children's regular form-room, had a number of displays and notices on the walls, but very few of these were of the children's work in Russian or any other subject. Soviet teachers have yet to learn the possibilities of presenting such work; they do not appear to receive much training in this, and their professional skills lag far behind those of the British primary teacher.

A 'physical culture' lesson was no more encouraging. The facilities scarcely foster adventurous athletic activity, but what happened for the first twenty-five minutes of the lesson – that is, for most of it – did not make very good use of even what limited facilities they had. The seventh-class lesson began and continued in military style. The pupils formed up in a long row; 'From the right . . . *number!*' The largest boy then marched up to the teacher and announced, 'Comrade teacher of physical culture! Class 7b is ready for the lesson, total twenty-eight persons!' There was the usual crop of weeds sitting disconsolately around, having 'forgotten their kit' or whatever, but rather a large number – probably a quarter of the class. At least this relieved pressure on the small gym. The exercises then carried out consisted of walking round in a circle, running, and various other routine activities, the most demanding of which was pressups. Despite the forbidding opening, military discipline was not applied, and some of the children did not try very hard. The master was not even changed, and it was doubtful whether the pupils needed to be, as little they did seemed likely to break a sweat.

If the lessons described above were typical, then it would seem that the position is no better now than ten or twenty years ago – but, wait! Better news is to come. The trouble is – and this is no surprise to anyone in the teaching profession anywhere – that Soviet teachers have not found it easy to get away from heavy reliance on what they call the 'frontal' lesson. Seminars, discussions, presentations, topic work, group work, individual research and practical activities are all mentioned and to some extent recommended in recent methodological literature, but almost inevitably with the remark added that abandonment of standard lessons would be a mistake. This phrase 'standard lessons' is used in English translations of official reports to translate the one Russian word *uroki*, 'lessons'. It is as if the translator knew that British and Americans recognise the other things too as legitimate and usual ways of organising a lesson, but the Russians do not. Thus in recent versions of the syllabuses in science subjects, for example, teachers are instructed to allow more experiments to be carried out by pupils, as opposed to lecturing and demonstrating from the front bench. (Immediately a difficulty arises: how can this be done safely in a crowded school laboratory with thirty-seven or thirty-eight in the class?) In modern languages, the subject of the following chapters, pair work – children rehearsing dialogues and situations by talking to each other – were practised ten years ago, but strongly disapproved of in some quarters; now they are widely used.

I did witness much better native language and literature lessons in School 1937. Two in particular spring to mind, both with the fourth class, but different groups. One was on Pushkin's fairy tales *Tsar Saltan* and *The Golden Cockerel*. It was lively and enthusiastic, it included recitation, reading aloud, dramatic reenactment of scenes and discussion of moral issues arising from the stories, particularly the difficulty some people have in keeping promises and whether or not there was a positive hero in the tales. The teacher read the original tale on which the poem of *The Golden Cockerel* was based and asked the pupils to spot what Pushkin had changed. There was some dictation of notes on folk tales and biographical details about

Pushkin. A pastel illustration was passed around and duly admired. It was clear from the way homework was checked that the pupils had been free to choose which of the two tales to read and which parts to learn by heart. The other lesson was first described to me as a literature lesson and later as 'development of language'. It contained many elements of what would in Britain be called 'creative writing'. The teacher had brought in various items of folk art, mainly painted wooden ornaments and utensils for which Russia is famous. The class discussed why they looked specifically Russian. The teacher built on this to introduce the notion of the Russian spirit being conveyed through language, in song, tales, ancient epics (*byliny*), *chastushki* (short epigrammatic ditties in popular style), riddles and proverbs. Several children were asked to read aloud stories they had composed to illustrate Russian proverbs; these the teacher praised warmly and sometimes criticised gently. There was some recitation with percussion accompaniment provided by beating wooden spoons on the desk, the purpose of which was to highlight the rhythmic aspects of folk poetry and proverbs. One or two pupils performed *chastushki* to piano accompaniment (there was a piano in the room, so it seems legitimate to conclude that music is regularly used in the language and literature lessons). The teacher summed up the lesson to the class by saying how necessary it was to keep alive the wisdom and wit of the Russian people; it was perhaps not superior to that of other nations, but worth preserving none the less. These lessons both contained many 'progressive' features: a great deal of pupil participation, creativity, the relation of music, art and handicraft to literature, and the relation of high culture to folk culture.

The jewel in the crown of forward-looking Soviet education at present would seem to be the teaching of the arts: music and art in particular. In literature teaching the ideological side can much more easily get in the way, and it can become a branch of political and social studies. It can be, and still is sometimes, taught as in the lesson described in the first part of this chapter. As has been mentioned elsewhere in this book, one teacher in School 1937 has run into trouble with the parents for maintaining a rigid old-fashioned approach to literature. The school was lucky, however, to have teachers of art and music of a totally different calibre.

Soviet music education in the mass schools – not those for the specially gifted – has been revolutionised by the work of the composer and educationist Dmitriy Kabalevsky (1904–87). Long after the age when most people retire from active work in schools,

Kabalevsky compiled new aims for music education and a new syllabus, and over a period of ten years or more tried it out as a pilot scheme in schools, revised and published it.[10] Work in the field of art, which is in many ways comparable, has been done by the painter Boris Nemensky.[11] Kabalevsky has not lacked enemies, who reportedly intrigued long and assiduously against him, but I can say that I have not in recent years spoken to a Soviet school music teacher who did not support what he was doing. In a few words, what Kabalevsky did was to introduce entire new criteria into the argument. For example, a primary aim of school music teaching is that children should be stimulated to seek musical experience outside school and after they have left. Spontaneous emotional response to music is encouraged and welcomed in class. Aims of this sort contrast sharply with the limited objectives of the past – to learn the meaning of 'allegro' or the letter names of the lines and spaces on the treble staff. The lack of drilling in vocal exercises (without which some Soviet music teachers did not know how to fill the lesson time) was criticised in some quarters. The really encouraging aspect of all this is the enthusiasm it has engendered among all sections of the music teaching profession, including many of those one might have imagined were likely to be set in their ways.

One such was School 1937's music master, a man of sixty-one, of impressive appearance and character, with the great asset of a strong, rich baritone voice, and who was reputed to be a 'walrus' (that is, to bathe daily in the Moscow river whatever the outside temperature). The room in which he worked contained little evidence that it was a music room except for an upright piano and a record player; it was simply a classroom appropriated for music teaching. The fourth-class lesson I saw was nevertheless of high quality. A setting of words by Esenin – in fact amounting to a cantata – by the composer Sviridov was being studied. The children were learning to sing a strong melody from the second movement which they did in one and two parts. The record was played and allowed to continue for several minutes, but a number of listening tasks were set: does the tune of the song recur? Is it the same or different if you think you hear it again? How is it different? Are there any descriptive moments? Instrumentation, and the use of orchestra, chorus and soloists were discussed. The children's answers to the questions were good on the whole: the theme came back 'in a lower register', 'sounding threatening, somehow', 'much more slowly'. The descriptive moments gave much more difficulty, but eventually it was established that there was a blizzard, the twittering of birds and spring rain. The best features of the lesson were the willingness of the pupils to respond spontaneously to questioning, the fact that the teacher accepted every answer, even unwelcome ones, without slapping any child down, and most of all that the class listened with the greatest attention to the music. They had obviously been successfully taught that music was not background noise, but something important and meaningful which was meant to be attended to. Their singing too, incidentally, was coming on very nicely in response to the excellent model presented by their teacher.

The art teacher in School 1937 was a much younger man and a different personality entirely. He was a rather gruff and perhaps even slightly prickly character. As if to illustrate further that a very wide range of personality types can succeed in teaching, it must be said that the lessons of his which I visited were impressive in a quiet and unassuming way. He lamented the lack of a proper art room and equipment: how much better he said it would have been if the pupils had had proper easels like real artists instead of having to sit at desks exactly like a classroom for any other subject. The pupils were using a variety of media for their pictures of Russia centuries ago: water colours, wax crayons, pastels or coloured pencils. Churches, windmills and traditional secular architecture figured prominently. The teacher commented to me later that they needed to be put in touch with the history of their nation – what a pity it had been that at some stages since the Revolution the artistic achievements of the past had been deprecated. He toured the class, helping, supplying information, urging economic use of materials ('Be careful with those paints – someone has paid for those!') and harassing the idle (he parted two girls for 'not encouraging each other to work'). Praise was rare, but when it came it was given very warmly. I happened to be standing behind the teacher when he picked up one painting by an apparently unassuming small boy, and praised it, deservedly, for its imaginative qualities and the cheerful effect it created. He added further remarks about the way that pupil had developed in recent weeks. The boy was obviously absolutely delighted, but was too modest to show it openly; he sat positively purring with pleasure. Reserved and odd though the teacher's manner was, it was clear that this pupil at least greatly valued the praise he bestowed.

THE CLASSROOM ETHIC IN A STATE OF CHANGE

Twenty years ago it was possible to say that Soviet classroom teaching styles were what would have been considered in the West to be rigid, didactic, authoritarian and unlikely to produce a creative, adaptable and open-minded work force at any level. Ten years ago there was still heavy reliance on rote learning and filling children with factual information in the somewhat naive faith that to do so was all that was required. Assessment methods – mainly oral examinations in which the learned answers to questions known in advance were rehearsed – further encouraged this approach. But in the last decade more imaginative classroom practices have crept in, and they have done so in response to the realisation on the part of many Soviet educators that, while factual knowledge cannot be rejected, it is also important to foster the ability to learn for oneself, skills of discussion, creative methods of working and an understanding that knowledge is not immutably set in concrete for all time. These ideas would seem to have entered the Soviet educational consciousness through subjects like music, art, Russian language and foreign languages. There have been complaints from teachers of other subjects that teachers of music, for example, are spoiling the children for real teaching by encouraging them to express their own opinions (instead of listening to the 'correct' ones!) and spreading the dangerous notion that sitting behind desks with arms folded is not the ideal model for academic learning. Fifteen years ago one used to hear a similar view in England expressed by secondary teachers about primary schools.

The situation in School 1937 must surely be typical of that in many Soviet schools under *glasnost'*. Many of the teachers express a desire for change, and change is on the way in that school, particularly in the primary classes, where plans are being laid for radical reform. Some in the arts have already changed as far as they can, given resources and conditions. Some stick to former ways and resist change, whether from philosophical inclination or from inertia and inability to perceive the benefits. In the sciences the practical problems of laboratory space may in fact make drastic restructuring almost impossible, though if attitudes have changed, the more creative approach sought by educators may in part be realised. What is certain is that ten years from now (1989) studies of Soviet teaching method and classroom practice will arrive at very different conclusions from those of ten years ago.

9 English Lessons I

Visitors to the Soviet Union often express admiration for the foreign language skills of the people they meet. Sometimes they forget that the tourist who speaks no Russian is bound to meet mainly those who speak his language – scarcely a random sample of the population. Cocooned in a protective shell provided by Intourist or by some official organisation, it is easy to forget that one is insulated from many of the realities of life in the USSR, most particularly the need to speak Russian. Consequently the impression received is that the entire population consists of excellent linguists. What is the real situation?

All children in the Soviet education system study one foreign language, 50–60 per cent of them English. In the mass schools (unlike No. 1937) they start at the age of ten, but by the age of thirteen or fourteen the number of lessons a week has declined to a minimal one period. Without great motivation this can scarcely be regarded as very effective, yet research shows[1] that it forms a good basis for further study for those who go on to higher education. Motivation, however, is the key issue. There is, it seems certain, a favourable attitude among the general population to foreign language learning and a desire to air one's English when the opportunity presents itself. In schools like 1937 standards in English are high if only because the language is taught much more intensively there. Nevertheless, one meets a great many highly placed professional people who speak little or nothing of any foreign language. The general public is not exactly rich in people who can speak English well, but there are probably more who are prepared to try than there are those willing to try French in England, where that language is very widely taught.

The special position of English in schools such as No. 1937 justifies devoting extended treatment to it in this book. This and the following chapter look at the subject in some detail. The reader can find more general and theoretical accounts of language teaching in the Soviet Union elsewhere.[2] The purpose in these chapters is not to examine the methods used by Soviet teachers, but to look at children's and young people's performance in the foreign language classroom. How well could they actually speak English?

The style of English spoken by Russians is in itself interesting. Until very recently Soviet citizens have had hardly any opportunities to travel abroad, and even now such chances are rare. Only one of the teachers in School 1937 (the youngest) had studied abroad while an undergraduate. Apart from occasional foreign visitors, teachers spoke English mainly to each other and to the pupils. This in itself is excellent practice, but it means that Russian speakers of English develop a dialect which has certain features all its own. Even those who frequently meet foreigners, such as Intourist guides, have such ingrained speech habits that they do not break out of them. Some teachers at School 1937 would address the pupils as 'people'. 'Come along, people, it is time we started work.' They had problems with 'much', needing to be reminded that it is used mainly in the negative and interrogative ('Have you much to do?' 'No, not much' but 'I have a lot [not usually 'much'] to do today'). I was frequently asked – with perfectly polite intention – to do something in these terms: 'You will go and teach Natasha's class', rather than 'Will you go and teach. . . ?' Pupils would be told to 'look into' rather than 'at' their books; litter would be 'thrown' (i.e. dropped); children were told to 'take' their books or pens (i.e. get them out, open them, or pick them up). 'He is a pupil' was regarded as correct English for 'He goes to school' or 'He is a schoolboy'. There was widespread misunderstanding of such everyday words as 'breakfast', 'lunch' and 'dinner' (a minefield, of course, since their meaning varies considerably even within the British Isles). Most of these mistakes were explicable as direct translations from Russian. Even the authors of the official Soviet textbooks have no feeling for register in English and will perpetrate examples in a style similar to this: [a mother speaking to her son] 'Tom, you must find another favourite occupation. You devote far too much time to football.' Much of this could be remedied if professional Soviet linguists visited Britain or America for an extended period while still young and as students. Unfortunately – and this does not seem to apply to the teaching profession – the Russian who is totally insulated from real English develops an utterly irrational arrogance, to the extent of editing or even 'correcting' the English style of native speakers; this explains why certain translations of novels by Soviet or Russian authors read so oddly, even though they appear from the title page to have been translated by English native speakers. The fact is that the Russian editors sometimes really believe that they know better!

I quickly noticed that it was easy for my own English to become corrupted by the textbook Russlish spoken by all around me. This is partly a consequence of the need to use phraseology which the children understand, but it is partly also an example of the way in which anyone isolated in an alien linguistic community picks up the habits of his interlocutors.

Contacts with America appear to be far better developed than with Britain, and if real English is spoken, it tends to be American English. This matters little, except that some American teachers active in the Soviet Union adopt an aggressive stance and set out to extirpate what they see as unsatisfactory British variants, such as 'lift' for 'elevator'. The Russians, however, seem to understand this odd manifestation of linguistic prejudice, and they ignore it.

GENERAL PRINCIPLES

This, then, is the situation into which I came in the autumn of 1988. the children at School 1937 had been extremely well taught in English, but by Russian native speakers, though some had experienced short periods with American exchange teachers. They were taught both spoken and written English, with the stress on the spoken variety. They were studying from textbooks, some of which had been very recently revised,[3] but which none the less contained numerous linguistic deficiencies. These books contain a wide variety of materials: texts, dialogues, stories, many of them derived from English-language originals (Enid Blyton, *The Naughtiest Girl in School*, Kenneth Grahame, *The Wind In the Willows*, Gerald Durrell, and in senior classes Mark Twain, O. Henry, Arthur Hailey and so on), exercises, models for pair-work, grammar (in English – the teacher is to supply Russian explanations), vocabulary and expressions defined in English, pictures and suggestions for oral work. Gramophone records of much of this material were available, and children mostly had their own copies at home. Tape recorders were used, but slide and film-strip projectors were of poor quality and there were problems with blackout. The teachers had large collections of home-made visual aids, flashcards in particular. Homework was regularly set. The methods used can best be characterised as enlightened direct method: almost the entire lesson at all levels would be carried out in English, Russian was used to summarise knotty points of grammar or to translate unknown words, there was great stress on participation, on pupils making up their own dialogues and asking as well as answering questions, on English as a means of communication in the lesson as well as the subject of it. On the other hand, the children had heard hardly any first-hand accounts of life in any English-speaking country. But how did they behave in the classroom? How well could they perform in English, and how did they respond to teaching? It is the main purpose of this chapter and the next to answer these questions.

JUNIOR CLASSES

In Chapter 1 of this book I have attempted to give some slight impression of English for eight-year-olds. My experience with them was limited; it was enjoyable and instructive to work at this level, but I remain convinced that a much better job was done by their regular teacher, who shared their own native language and was more expert than I in the psychology and preferred learning styles of children of that age. However, even at the age of eight and after only a dozen lessons in English, it was still possible to carry on almost the entire lesson in English, provided one used only the limited vocabulary which they knew and was extremely careful about the introduction of anything fresh. A forty-five-minute lesson for eight-year-olds is, needless to say, far too long; twenty minutes at a time would be far preferable, but Soviet teachers are rigorous in dividing up the time into shorter periods and providing many different activities. Despite the fact that in Britain a decade or more ago primary-school French was discontinued, Soviet educators have succeeded, at least in schools like No. 1937, in their efforts with primary-age English – it is taught by well-trained specialists with apparently suitable materials, and the teaching is systematically organised nationwide and backed up by a good system of in-service training. There are moves to start even earlier: at School 1937 class 1, aged seven, do some English, mainly games and songs.

By class 4, two years later, pupils are already making significant progress with their English, and it is possible to communicate with them in a natural conversational style, provided the language is kept straightforward and delivered clearly. Pupils at this stage could understand and answer questions about short talks on such topics as how I had spent the Revolutionary holiday and respond by telling me what they had done. They could comment on pictures and answer such questions as 'What does this show?', 'What are the people doing?' 'Why are they there?' 'How do you know what time of year it is?' and so on – simple enough questions, but involving much more than monosyllabic conditioned responses. New words are explained in English, but the pupils feel happy when they take the point and can find and call out the Russian equivalent.

On several occasions during my stay in School 1937 I made tape recordings of lessons. These were unrehearsed and spontaneous, and possibly several of the children in a given class did not even realise that the tiny tape recorder was working. The resultant recordings are random examples of what children in the given classes could do. Here is a transcript of three and a quarter minutes of a lesson with a class 4 group. These children had been learning English for three lessons a week for two years. The textbook contained a short passage on the climate of the Soviet Union which was meant to serve as stimulus for oral work. I took the opportunity to speak instead about the climate of Britain in order to offer the chance for comparisons to be made.

J. M.:	[after the talk] Now, did you understand all that? *Vse ponyatno?*
Class:	Yes, yes.
J. M.:	Good, well see if you can answer these simple questions. Is Britain a big country?
Olga:	No, Britain is not a big country, it is a little country.
J. M.:	It's a little country, but tell me about the Soviet Union. Is that a big country? Is it a big country, Sergey?
Sergey:	Yes, the Soviet Union is a big country.
J. M.:	Yes, in fact it's the. . . ? It's the. . . ?
Sergey:	Large country.
J. M.:	Yes, you can say it's a large country, or it's the biggest country . . .
Sergey:	In the world.
J. M.:	In the world, right. In Britain is it often very cold?
Anya:	No, in Britain . . . very . . . not very cold.
J. M.:	It's not very cold, not often, because the sea is warm [refers to diagram on board] and the sea makes the country warm. What about the Soviet Union? Is it cold, Sergey, in the Soviet Union in winter?
Sergey:	Yes, it is cold in the Soviet Union in winter.
J. M.:	Good. That's right. What are the most beautiful seasons in England, in Britain? . . . Can you tell me, Natasha?
Natasha:	Summer is a beautiful season . . . in Britain.
J. M.:	Summer, you think . . . Well, I don't think so . . . I said

	there were two seasons which were very nice. Summer is often wet in Britain. Can you tell me what were the two seasons I mentioned?
Alesha:	I think that spring and autumn . . . the best . . . the best seasons in Great Britain.
J. M.:	Is autumn a beautiful season in the Soviet Union?
Katya:	Yes, it is a very beautiful season in the Soviet Union.
J. M.:	Why?
Katya:	Because there are a lot of nice . . . beautiful leaves on the ground.
J. M.:	Yes, and on the trees too. What colours can you see in autumn?
Dima:	A lot of . . . lots . . .
J. M.:	What colours?
Dima:	Ah. Red, yellow, orange.
J. M.:	Good, yes.
Dima:	There are lots of fruits and vegetables in autumn.
J. M.:	Yes, a lot of fruit and vegetables.
Natasha:	Yes. But it is very cold in autumn.
J. M.:	It can be very cold. Is it autumn now?
Lena:	Yes, it is autumn now, but it is cold as in winter.
J. M.:	As cold as in winter. Yes, good, so it's autumn now, but it's very cold. How many degrees is it today, do you know? It was minus ten yesterday; what is it today?
Anya:	Minus four.

Transcribed in this way, this does not perhaps seem remarkable. It is very simple, and there are some mistakes. But the experienced teacher of a foreign language will not have missed certain significant points. Not one word of Russian is used by a pupil. At least two-thirds of the group has contributed something to the conversation in this short time. Teachers who feel that talking to a class is often like extracting blood from a stone will notice that at more than one point the conversation takes a new turn because of a suggestion made by a pupil; even children as young as this *offer* topics of conversation (the fruit and vegetables, the comparison of autumn and winter) to the teacher. A transcript cannot show the good standard of pronunciation or the fact that, as the pupils became more used to me and the subject of the conversation, the answers came quickly and with little hesitation. The exercise was fairly unrealistic, in that the pupils were for the most part answering questions to which I, the questioner, knew the answers already and which would therefore not be considered 'communicative' by progressive modern language teachers, but I had the illusion none the less that we were all holding a reasonably intelligent conversation.

CLASS FIVE

Class five contains children of eleven and twelve. Experience of teaching classes at this level in School 1937 gave me some insight into aspects of the teaching and organisation of the school. On three consecutive days I taught six different fifth-class groups of ten and twelve pupils each. All six were progressing at identical speed through the syllabus,[4] and so I took lessons 11, 12 and 13 of Unit 2 of their textbook, which dealt with the comparison of adjectives. I first consulted the teachers' book,[5] which not only makes it clear what material is to be covered, but gives full suggested lesson plans.

It goes against the grain for many English teachers to follow a printed lesson plan line by line. However, could I do it any better than the book suggested? The plan was thorough and sound. The real trouble was that the material in the textbook was dull and lacking in any real human touches, any reference to life in an English-speaking country or any spark of humour. Moreover, it uncompromisingly taught 'as . . . as', but 'not *so* . . . as', being apparently unaware that 'not as . . . as. . . .' was equally correct, as well as making it easier for the children.

I racked my brains the evening before the first lesson for some way of bringing the material to life. I realised again how difficult it is to break away from a boring textbook which, however, contains everything the pupils need for their examinations; moreover, with no access to photocopying facilities or the opportunity to make visual aids, I was 'on my own'. The only solution for the first session appeared to be personal and sometimes even facetious, to ask the children's opinions and state my own – thus including some element of genuine communication.

The subject of the first lesson was comparisons and superlatives, which had already been introduced. A new structure was: 'It is the most . . . I have ever. . .', and the other was '(not) as/so . . . as.' As often is the case, the unexpected happened at the very start. When I began by asking two pupils to stand up and inviting the others to say whether Olga was bigger or smaller than Anya and the like, the eleven year olds for some reason found this hilarious and entered into the spirit of it with gusto. We compared the beauties of Leningrad and Suzdal, the ages of myself and themselves, the difficulty of mathematics and English, and the interest of *Tom Sawyer* and *War and Peace*. After the lesson I was amazed to be told by the regular teacher, who had been present, that it was a 'brilliant' lesson opening. Any English-trained teacher could have done the same, and would only do it anyway if he could not think of anything better. The incident illustrated that good old-fashioned non-communicative but unexpectedly amusing 'hup-two-three-four' drilling can work quite well.

The rest of the lesson contained fewer thrills. I told them the most interesting book I had ever read, the most beautiful music I had ever heard and the most exciting film I had ever seen. They responded likewise, and surprised me at the alacrity with which in pair work they composed dialogues on a basis of this not very exciting model:

> 'I was at the theatre yesterday and saw "Mary Poppins". Have you seen this play?'
> 'No, not yet'.
> 'That's a pity! It's the most exciting, the most colourful and the funniest play I have ever seen'.
> 'Well I hope my parents will get tickets soon. I'd like to see it very much'.

Some of the children managed to get an element of literary discussion into their creations. 'I was at the library yesterday and took out the book *Tom Sawyer*. Have you read this book?' 'Yes, I have, but I think it the most boring book I have ever read'.

Then the dreaded 'as . . . as'. The first group handled this quite well, but I had the feeling during my discussion with their teacher afterwards that she was suggesting I was not challenging the children enough or keeping them busy. Stung by the suggestion, I flung every bit of energy into the repeat performance with the second group. Failure ensued. Although the children were trying hard and I pulled every trick out of the bag – we did it in chorus, I put it on the board, we did it umpteen times, I explained it, we drilled it – in the end many of the pupils remained resolutely uninformed of the fact that while the metro is quicker *than* a horse, a crocodile (as one child put it) is not so slow *as* a tortoise. This time the audience of colleagues was entirely sympathetic. 'There's too much in that unit, and I only taught them "bigger than" yesterday', said their regular teacher.

A weakness in the officially planned programme, from which teachers in School 1937 were reluctant to diverge, now becomes obvious. The following lesson is the penultimate in the unit, before the test with which it finishes, but it is a passage for home reading which does not reinforce comparison of adjectives at all. Just when at least one of these classes needed more help (and the other certainly required consolidation) the topic was to change. The problem was, however, not mine, as next day I was asked to teach two different fifth-year groups and to test their home reading. The experience was again instructive.

The problem of interest and liveliness was the same as before – how to bring to life a text on the Olympic Games which the children had read for homework. It did contain some information of use and possible interest, and some jingoistic Muscovite propaganda: 'Moscow made the twenty-second Olympic Games a bright, beautiful and exciting festival of sport.' This in a book for children who were three years old at the time of the Moscow Olympics; and of course I was in a Moscow school – 270 million of the population of the Soviet Union do not live in Moscow! Yet it seemed almost impossible to break out of the confines of this didactic, tedious matter.

My solution was similar to that of the day before: to be personal, to seek genuine information from the pupils and give some myself – at least after we had dealt with the subject matter of the dreary text. This proved possible with the first group, which was so communicative and quick that I feared I would run out of material. I asked them about the sports they went in for or watched themselves. I discovered about their class football team and its record, who it played against; one boy was having fencing training five times a week after school; they told me good places to go swimming, some spoke of their figure-skating lessons and their fondness for skiing. I found some magazine pictures on sporting themes on a shelf in the room; they waxed eloquent about these. The official lesson plan had mentioned a film strip on the Olympic Games, but I decided to dispense with this, fearing difficulties with blackout and projector, and instead told the pupils about my own visit years before to the archaeological remains at Olympia, struggling hard to do it simply, and confining myself to a few facts like the running track being straight and covered in deep sand, the men in ancient Greece naked and covered in oil, and the bath tubs still to be seen in the dressing rooms. The final part of the lesson went back to the official plan – a short spelling test: competition, field, race, team, result, exciting. Success was almost total in this – 'field' was the only word which gave any difficulty.

Before the equivalent lesson with the parallel group, the teacher indicated to me that they had told her they found the text they were supposed to have read for homework difficult and had not, in fact, fully understood it. I decided on the spur of the moment to jettison my lesson plan and concentrate on the text itself: we read it, I questioned them closely to test comprehension, I invited them to tell me what it was they had not understood (without success). They seemed at least to have comprehended the outline and most of the details; though no-one could answer the question in the textbook 'what made the Moscow Olympic Games a bright and exciting festival of sport?' Nor could I, to be quite frank. We used the pictures again. Again, I asked them about the sports they liked, but they had little to say and perhaps were not particularly interested in sport. For the whole of this lesson it must be said that the children responded, and spoke English when asked to. But they were considerably more reticent and slower than any other group I had taken so far. There was no time for the spelling test or the talk on Olympia. I did not give up, but felt these children should not be overloaded and needed a lot of encouragement. There were some sad and passive faces in this group as if they knew or believed they were struggling. Was it right that they should be progressing through the syllabus at the same rate as the other groups? Had they in fact been 'setted'?

On the following day I was invited to teach the remaining two fifth-year groups for English. I planned a completely oral lesson, using some of the same material – the children's favourite sports, Olympia and the Olympic games – and asked them to talk about their holidays and how they spent them. In one way it was tough going with both these sets. They both contained a few lively and very intelligent children and a few that seemed to have been left behind. The rest looked at me with a slightly withdrawn gaze, as though they hoped I would not ask them any difficult questions. The lessons were hard work because, untypically, answers were short and slow in coming, and children were on the whole reluctant to volunteer answers. But there were no children who refused to speak when called upon, unless they really were lost. Their behaviour was exemplary. One or two had the friendly smiles of the less able child who knows he cannot do much, and is not particularly worried. And at the close of each lesson a stream of children brought me little presents – badges, postcards, etc. I am not usually rewarded in this way for giving a class in Britain.

I discussed this with the head of English. My first thought had been that the groups might in fact be setted. I am now convinced this is not the case. Apparently, there is a conscious attempt to allocate a mixture of achievement/ability to each group, so no teacher gets the dregs. The difference in performance is much more likely to be a result of the dynamics of the particular group and the professional and linguistic skill and the personalities of the teachers concerned. Whatever these remarks might appear to suggest to the contrary, I am sure that any British teacher of a modern language would feel that almost every child in these six groups was able to communicate, in however limited a way, and that all were cooperating. There was, however, a fairly wide range of ability represented. It may be that the absence of any bad behaviour suggests that no one was so far behind the rest as to be naughty out of despair, boredom or resentment.

A day or two later one of the teachers concerned showed me the marked homework essays from two of the six groups I had taught. The weakest read as follows:

My favourite kind of sport.

Many children like sport. Some like swimming, some wrestling, some running and others. Children like to ski and skate in winter and in summer like to play football, volley-ball and basket-ball. In summer children enjoy swimming.

My favourite kind of sports swimming and football. I go swim in the swimming pool. I usually take part in competitions. It is very interesting. It is pleaser to swim in clear water. After swim you usually fell fresh. Swim is good exercise for the body. You usually strong after swimming.

Football is very interesting sport. It is very difficult sport. People usually train hard. This sport have many fans. I enjoy playing sport, but I like to see the exciting match on TV too. Football players usually strong, healthy.

Sport give us a lot of joy. Many athletes have medals. They like to be a champion.

Sport is good exercise for everyone.

This work was marked 3 for content (satisfactory) and 2 for language (unsatisfactory). The best essay received 5 on both counts:

My favourite kind of sport is volley-ball. I like this kind of sport because it's very interesting, besides it is a very good exercise for body. People who go in for volley-ball are not afraid of cold or illnesses. If you want to play volley-ball well you must train hard. You must practise it. Practice makes perfect. If you play in a team you must be friendly and thoughtful of others. If your friend can't play volley-ball well, you must help him. You can practise volley-ball at the sports ground in a gym or at the stadiums. I go in for volley-ball. When I came to a gym where we play volley-ball first I could not play volley-boy at all. My friends and my coach halped me to become better. But of course I had to train a lot. I am fond of volley-ball. As for me, I think this is a best kind of sport. But I think that another kinds of sport are very good, too. There are many of them: tennis, gymnastics, football, basket-ball, figure-skating and many others. You can practise one of them. I think that all people must go in for sport. Sport makes people strong, cheerful and healthy.

These little essays typify some of the principal difficulties of learning English for a Russian. The most obvious is that of coming to terms with the definite and indefinite articles: knowing when to write 'a', 'the' and 'some' and when to leave them out. Even teachers are rarely perfect in this respect. The author of the weaker essay is also having difficulty with the present tense of the verb 'to be', which is usually omitted in Russian, and to some extent with 'have' which is expressed in a different way. Both compositions contain some trivial slips ('volley-boy', 'fell' for 'feel', 'pleaser' for 'pleasanter', 'halped'). There was one instance in each essay of an unnecessary correction inserted by the teacher. In the first 'very difficult sport' was corrected to 'kind of sport', the teacher being unaware that, in contrast with Russian usage, the word 'sport' can mean games in general or one particular athletic activity. In the second, 'at' in 'at the sports ground' was marked wrong. Many Russian teachers of English were very uneasy about the correct use of 'in' and 'at': I was asked time and again which was correct – 'in a lesson' or 'at a lesson', and the questioner often seemed unconvinced to hear that it scarcely mattered.

Perhaps the most interesting difference between these two compositions is the standpoint of the writers. The first had tried to describe, however simply, his personal feelings about swimming and football. He does mention the good effects of sport on the body and the mind, but the second author writes a good deal more about the 'moral' purpose of sport, which is stressed in Soviet education: the benefits of training, persistence and team-work and the physical and psychological results of athletic activity. The essay has discernible traces of the didactic tone of the standard Soviet textbook approach to *vospitanie*, as will be seen from Chapter 14.

Many might feel that to give the weaker essay an 'unsatisfactory' mark is rather harsh. After all, it communicates perfectly coherent messages in a language which is recognisably English. It would surely compare very favourably with the work of many much older British children who had been studying a foreign language for the same length of time – three years. The marking scheme applied is unyielding, and I was apt to find that I needed to adopt more flexible standards and reward children who had tried to write more adventurously but had gone wrong in the process. If this essay is the weakest, there can be little wrong with the teaching or the learning.

THE SIXTH CLASS

By the following year the children have grown even more confident in their use of spoken English. What follows is a transcript of a tape recording of the first few minutes of a lesson with a good sixth-year group, and it illustrates the quality of utterance of which these pupils were capable, remembering that they were unprepared, but operating with familiar material. I was taking them for the first lesson of a longer unit of instruction, which was concerned with theatre, cinema, television and leisure; by the end of it they were meant to be able to converse on related topics, to use a certain amount of new vocabulary and to handle participles in -ing. As an introduction to all this, I first announced that I would be asking each one of them to tell me two things they enjoyed doing, and then spoke briefly about my own hobbies, interests and spare-time activities. The purpose of this was to remind them of words and expressions they knew and to suggest things they could say to me when it was their turn.

J. M.: Now, somebody, please, tell me, tell the whole class what *you* enjoy doing after school or on a Sunday. Yes, Vika?

Vika: I enjoy reading adventure books and fantastic books [i.e. science fiction] and I enjoy playing the piano.

J. M.: Yes, you enjoy reading nature books [the recording shows I misheard her] and you enjoy playing what? I didn't hear.

Vika:	I enjoy playing the piano.
J. M.:	The piano, good. So you are a musician, you make music too. Right, Alla. What do you enjoy doing?
Alla:	I enjoy swimming and I enjoy playing with my friends.
J. M.:	Good . . . Who else enjoys sport? Stasik, tell us what you enjoy.
Stasik:	I enjoy volleyball, I enjoy swimming . . . and playing football.
J. M.:	Excellent . . . Yes?
Pupil:	I enjoy skiing . . . skis, and in winter I usually ski with my friends in the Park Kolomenskoe, and I enjoy swimming, and now, in . . . Saturdays I go to . . . *basseyn* [prompted by other children] . . . swimming pool.
J. M.:	Yes, *basseyn*, swimming pool, good. Alexey, what do you enjoy doing on a Saturday or a Sunday?
Alexey:	I enjoy . . . after school I enjoy football and play with my friends in the yard.
J. M.:	Football, and you play with your friends. Excellent. Anya?
Anya:	When we go to the Black Sea in . . . summer I enjoy swimming in the Black Sea. I also enjoy getting fives.
J. M.:	You enjoy. . . ? Oh, you enjoy getting fives at school; yes, who doesn't?
Pupil:	I enjoy skating and playing snowballs.
J. M.:	Yes, when it's snowing and the weather's cold . . . Who hasn't spoken yet? You haven't, have you. What's your name again, I've forgotten? Nastasya.
Nastasya:	I enjoy reading serious books and books about nature. I enjoy playing with my dogs and I enjoy playing badminton.
J. M.:	Good. You have some dogs, have you?
Nastasya:	Yes, three dogs.
J. M.:	Three dogs. That's very interesting. Good?
Pupil:	I enjoy going on hikes with competitions with my class and I enjoy gymnastics and swimming.
J. M.:	Swimming? Yes, good. Yes, Katya?
Katya:	I enjoy reading adventure books and I enjoy reading books about animals and I enjoy to see interesting films and I . . . and I . . . and I enjoy skiing, skating and swimming.

J. M.:	Skating . . .
Katya:	and I enjoy to play . . . to play . . . with my friends and to play with my cat.
J. M.:	Lots of things there. Oh, can I tell you one thing? We say 'I enjoy do*ing* something', 'I enjoy playing', it's better than saying 'I enjoy to play', which is not very good English. Who hasn't spoken yet?
Pupil:	I enjoy cooking suppers and dinners.
J. M.:	Excellent, so you enjoy cooking. Yes?
Pupil:	I enjoy dancing and singing.
J. M.:	Dancing and singing . . . Katya?
Katya:	I enjoy playing badminton. I enjoy running and playing [indecipherable] and I also enjoy . . . and in summer I also enjoy swimming.
J. M.:	Good. I didn't catch what sports you enjoyed. You said you enjoyed playing . . . volleyball? basketball?
Katya:	Pioneer ball.
J. M.:	Pioneer ball, ah, that's a game I don't know. Thank you very much, good. One more.
Pupil:	I enjoy riding a bicycle and I enjoy swimming and I enjoy cooking cakes.
J. M.:	Cakes, good. Now, Alexey.
Alexey:	I enjoy to drove by car because it is very interesting. In . . . this year I drove by car with our friends.
J. M.:	Yes? [I failed to catch the phrase 'by car' because of his strange intonation.] You did what, I didn't quite understand?
Alexey:	[crestfallen!] I enjoy.
J. M.:	Yes.
Alexey:	To drove.
J. M.:	?
	[Other children try to help.]
J. M.:	What is 'byka'?
Children:	*Mashinoy.*
J. M.:	Oh, ah, I see, yes. Right, Stasik, thank you.
Stasik:	I enjoy playing volleyball, basketball, football with my friends.
J. M.:	Yes.
Stasik:	I enjoy to go to the country too. I like to read adventure books very much.

This was the first five and a half minutes of the lesson. Many will find this unsurprising and workaday – it consists of the usual practice, endless repetition and rehearsal of everyday language that is necessary to the learner. It is repetitive, but some of the more able children can vary statements to some extent, using adverbs and adverb phrases. They do not all repeat what others have said, but explore the vocabulary they have relating to interests and leisure pursuits and use it to the full. Russian is resorted to only twice in five minutes. They appear to understand most of my interjections and respond to them. Communication breaks down twice, but is restored without much difficulty. The most striking feature, which is, of course, not obvious from the transcript, is the pace at which the conversation was taken and the willingness of the pupils to communicate. There was scarcely a gap at all; when a child did pause to think it is indicated by three dots in the text, but in fact most of the exchanges were at something approaching normal conversational speed in English. There was no case of stubborn refusal to say anything more than the minimum. In this connection it should be remembered that Russian children are brought up in all subjects to speak formally and at length; most of their tests and examinations are oral, and marks are given in class for oral performance.

Attentive readers will have noticed that I omitted to correct some of the pupils' mistakes in English. There are two reasons for this. The first is that, when teaching your own language, you tend to overlook errors which do not prevent comprehension; in other words, it is easy to forget that mistakes have been made. Secondly, the idea is gaining currency – and in fact has almost become conventional wisdom – that to be over-pedantic in the correction of mistakes in a foreign language is counter-productive. This applies particularly to putting right errors while the pupil is still speaking. I subscribe strongly to this view. Colleagues in School 1937 tended to agree with me, whereas those in the school in Leningrad where I taught later were at first much more difficult to persuade. They would constantly interrupt a child while speaking, leaving no opportunity for the pupil to notice and even correct his own mistakes (which many could in fact do), and sometimes their amendments were unnecessary (replacing one already correct phrase with another) or trivial. The hidden curriculum conveyed by the teachers was: 'I am not in the least interested in what you say, but I am neurotically obsessed with the way you say it.' The further message the pupils received was as clear as a bell: 'Every time I open my mouth this adult slaps me down.' It was scarcely surprising that the seventh class in that school spoke English no better than the sixth class at School 1937.

The syllabus for the sixth year does not list more than half a dozen major grammatical forms or structures (mainly the infinitive, gerund, and two types of participle). The pupils have to add 250 lexical items to their vocabulary and maintain those learned already, making a total of 1350 by the end of the year; this is extended by the mastery of two prefixes (mis- and dis-) and six suffixes (-ment, -ist, -ism, -ic, -al, and -ical). The impressive aspect of the work the teachers do with these children is the thoroughness with which the relatively limited material is consolidated, and the consequent fluency of the pupils in using the language they have been taught. In lessons such as the one a small part of which is transcribed above these children showed they could comprehend fairly extensive short talks lasting two or three minutes, including jokes and anecdotes, they could talk quite interestingly about their own hobbies as here, they could compose short dialogues in pairs on set themes and perform them, they were used to reading and discussing texts about three pages long. Most impressive of all was the fact that, young as they were, it was possible to communicate with them effectively in English – communicate both ways, not simply tell them things. This was true always provided the language was kept reasonably straightforward and suitable allowances made.

10 English Lessons II

In the senior classes the same principles of language instruction are continued. English is the language of the classroom, there is a stress on the spoken language and translation plays only a very small part in the work of the pupils. It is at this stage that the main linguistic advantage of attending a school like No. 1937 with intensified instruction in English becomes obvious: in the mass schools one lesson a week of English is all that is provided in each of the last three years. The lesson allocation in years seven to ten in School 1937 is $6+4+4+4$.

CLASSES 7 TO 9

By the seventh class adolescence is setting in, and it might be expected that resistance in one form or another to teaching might be perceptible. It is true that behaviour in class 8 was sometimes less than perfect, but it scarcely constituted disruption or a 'discipline problem' if an experienced teacher was in charge. Work at English vocabulary continues, adding 850 new items over the last four years of instruction, grammar works its way through the mysteries of modal verbs and the more complicated tenses, including conditionals and the subjunctive; the intellectual content of the texts for reading and discussion intensifies from year 8 onwards.

Work in class 7 resembles that in class 6 in many ways; I find that my lesson notes contain many of the same themes, but treated in a rather more sophisticated way. Pupils can take longer talks, including quite long lectures on life in England, preferably illustrated with slides, and they show by their questions (in English) that they have understood most of what they have heard. The subject of life in England is important to them, as the syllabus for the final years and consequently for the examinations contains the requirement that they should be able to converse about the political and economic systems, geographical features, historical events, youth organisations, education system, manners and customs, science, literature and the arts in English-speaking countries. In a way this is a wholly unreasonable requirement, since scarcely any of their teachers have been able to acquire this information. Soviet textbooks are written by people who are similarly ill-informed and who lack the knowledge, experience and understanding to present the English-speaking countries to Soviet children. A major contribution which a British or American visitor can make is to tell Soviet pupils about these things. I was frequently called upon to talk about youth organisations in Britain. The assumption seemed to be that there must somehow be something in Britain akin to the Komsomol (see Chapter 7). The cultural gap in this respect was almost unbridgeable, and my talk on Scouting, church youth clubs, Youth Hostels Association, Duke of Edinburgh's Award Scheme, school clubs and societies, teenage discos and the like would sometimes be followed by the reaction, 'But what about "informal" youth groupings?' (meaning the formerly illegal clubs outside the Komsomol). The nearest equivalents I could think of on the spur of the moment were pop group fan clubs and football hooligans.

It is possible to illustrate the high standard of English achieved in the last three years by accounts of the best of which pupils in these years were capable. In an eighth class group I once was asked to take a lesson (without preparation) on the general theme of ecology. Fortunately I had in my possession a beautiful poster supplied by the Information Department of the British Embassy entitled 'The Face of Britain'. It kept us interested for half an hour or so; I did most of the talking, but the class was able to contribute some ideas about whether the Electricity Board should be allowed to build a hydro-electric station on the Scottish loch portrayed. When asked to follow up this lesson a day or two later, I hit upon the idea of a rather sophisticated role-play. First I showed slides of my own house in Nottingham, of the estate where it is situated and of the surrounding open area. I explained that a builder had applied for permission to build 350 houses on a piece of green belt nearby, but had been refused. A rough map was drawn on the board, the English law about green belts and planning permission explained, and I announced that we would briefly enact the inevitable public inquiry into the builders' appeal against the refusal of planning permission. The group of twelve pupils was divided into builders, local residents and county council representatives; briefing amounting to no more than half a side of A4 in my handwriting was given to each section. After five or ten minutes of preparation in the classroom, during which each small group planned its campaign, we spent twenty minutes on the debate. The performance of the pupils was remarkable. They fully entered into the spirit of the role-play and argued their respective cases with some relish. It was not necessary to intervene to see that each participant made some contribution; the pupils passed the baton to each other, so everyone had a fair chance to speak. This they are obviously trained to do (and I can only remember one class I taught where an over-talkative child attempted to monopolise the conversation). Despite the inevitable bias in my briefing towards the local residents, the best of the argument was had by the 'builders'; these wicked capitalists produced arguments which demolished the others' case quite effectively. Apart from the obvious ability of the pupils concerned, the success of the activity was explained by the teacher as a consequence of the teenagers' keen interest in matters of conservation, which have come to the fore in the Soviet Union relatively recently.

Another series of lessons in class 8 concerned the subject of humour. At the first of these I was present and participated, but it was led by the usual teacher. The text for reading was the story from Jerome K. Jerome (Chapter 8 of *Three Men in a Boat*) of how Herr Slossenn Boschen is tricked into singing a tragic German song to an audience which has been told it is the funniest ditty ever composed. This incensed the Russian eighth-formers, who unanimously found the joke an extremely bad one because it must have hurt Herr Slossenn Boschen's feelings greatly. In vain did I point out that the audience was made by far the bigger fools of; that was no excuse. They remained similarly sceptical of my assertion that in English culture it was (and possibly still is) permissible to make fun of the Germans in a way that one would treat no other nationality. The vigour with which they defended their position in English suggested that in the following lesson, for which I was responsible, a moderately theoretical approach might be fruitful. This indeed proved to be the case. In preparation I asked the pupils for homework to prepare to tell a funny story. Not all were willing to do so when it came to the point, but I did not insist, and they all produced something in the end. This formed the basic material for the lesson – the retelling and correction of the stories. However, more interesting probably is the fact that it was possible to discuss the type of humour in each story: word play, character, slapstick, satire, and to assess its target and its quality. Again, no one switched off when the discussion became abstract. Russian pupils expect their language teaching to have some intellectual content.

Ninth-class pupils have passed the hurdle of the first public examination at fifteen, they have resisted any pressure there might be

to leave and continue their education in another type of establishment, and it can be assumed that they are fairly serious in their desire
to go on to higher education in two years' time. English will still
figure in that higher education, but for very nearly all the pupils of
School 1937 it will not be the main component. My own contact as a
teacher with the ninth classes was limited, but it will be obvious from
these accounts of work with class 8 that the next year must be even
more flexible in their command of English. It was possible to
communicate with them through the medium of English while
experiencing the feeling that it was almost like talking to English
people. This is, of course, an illusion in many respects – we know, for
example, that their active vocabulary consists of only 1900–2000
words – but pupils have sufficient experience of the language to
handle efficiently any everyday situation and to discuss many issues of
general importance: political, social, personal and intellectual. In
Chapter 3 I refer to having been interviewed at length in English by
two ninth-form boys for the school newspaper. They were doubtless
among the best and most serious-minded pupils, but the quality of the
questioning would have been scarcely more searching if they had
been using their native language.

TENTH-CLASS ENGLISH

In the early days of my stay in School 1937 I was impressed by the
keenness and ability of the tenth-class pupils, and on occasions
decided to try them out with some totally unprepared activity, not
knowing whether or not they had ever done such a thing before. The
teaching style for English in School 1937 was, it must be said,
somewhat book-bound – enlightened and civilised, but nevertheless
very dependent on the official textbooks and readers. A certain
uneasiness was detectable if I gave any sign of wishing to depart from
the set syllabus; this was certainly not due to any fear that I might
stray into the discussion of politically impermissible topics, but rather
a feeling that the pupils' exam results might suffer. The tenth class
studied from textbooks which have been very little revised in ten or
fifteen years.[1] Reading passages relied heavily on twentieth-century
American story writers such as Mark Twain and O. Henry, and the
book for 'home reading' – ten pages a week was set for discussion in
class – was Arthur Hailey's 1960 novel *The Final Diagnosis* in a
slightly abridged version. The sort of novel one might read while

waiting for a train scarcely caught the imagination of these young people (who, of course, had to struggle through it collecting useful words rather than read for pleasure), and a certain degree of boredom with it could be discerned.

One morning I decided to use a collection of art postcards which I had bought a few days before leaving for Moscow, in the hope that they would prove useful as teaching material. This hope was well realised, as the following transcript, made from a tape recording of the lesson, shows. Getting learners to describe a picture in order to develop their vocabulary and fluency is, of course, a favourite activity of teachers of foreign languages, but I hoped these pupils would be able to do a little more than that. I wished to try an experiment – to see whether any aesthetic education they had received enabled them to comment on and speculate about an art object. The lesson was delivered in two parallel groups in consecutive teaching periods. I attempted to record both lessons on tape, but failed to obtain a recording of the first; this was a pity, as the pupils performed as well as those in the second group. In the transcript below of the second of these lessons, taken with the group believed by the teacher of both to be marginally more able, I have edited nothing which the pupils said, leaving all their mistakes and hesitations, so that the reader may judge the standard of their spoken English when given only a very little time to prepare. Some of my own contributions have been shortened for reasons of space.

There were fourteen pupils in the group, nine girls and five boys. After checking their names, I introduced the subject of photography.

J. M.:	Do any of you take photographs?
Pupils:	*Chto?*
J. M.:	[mimicking] *Chto? chto?* We're supposed to be talking English now! Do any of you take photographs? Who has a camera? One, two . . . five. Tell me what you take photographs of.
Lena:	To tell the truth I take photos rather rarely, because I don't think I'm very good at it, but when I take photographs I used to photo my family and friends.
J. M.:	Right, so family and friends. Boris, did you say you had a camera? What do you take photographs of?
Boris:	You see, I usually take . . . friends [indecipherable] or episodes from my own life.
J. M.:	Episodes from your own life . . . for example? [laugh-

ter]. What did you last take a photograph of?

Boris:	You see, we were working in our [campus?] and I climbed their house... [?]
J. M.:	[puzzled!] Yes? To the top of the block of flats?
Boris:	No, the stairs. And when I was jumping down [more laughter] my camera [?]ed.
J. M.:	[mystified] So you took a photo to remember that event and Lena takes them to remember people. What do you take them for, Peter?
Peter:	To tell the truth, I am not very fond of taking photos, but if I do, I take photos of my friends or my family.
J. M.:	How many of you take a camera when you go on holiday?
Ira:	I think that we take people and places and everything that surrounds us that we want to remember and not to forget.
J. M.:	What is the most interesting or dramatic photo that you have ever seen? Mitya?
Mitya:	I think the most dramatic photo I have ever seen is ... was the photo of ... you see, I am the fan of Dynamo Kiev, and the most dramatic photo I have ever seen was the photo of the last goal of ... which was kicked ... by them in the final match with [?].
Zhenya:	You see, not long ago I was in the exhibition of the international photo in ... near ... on Komsomolosky prospekt and there I saw the most dramatic photograph of a dying of AIDS man.
J. M.:	A man who was dying of AIDS. Yes, photos like that can be not pleasant, but dramatic ... Anyone else seen a dramatic or interesting photograph?
Slava:	You see, this photograph concerns football as well and – you see – I watched the world football champion last year and during the last game between the team of the Federative Republic of Germany and Argentina, there were taken a great number of photos, and I enjoyed one of them most of all. It was the photo of Diego Maradona jumping with joy when he realised that they became world champions.
J. M.:	Yes, Lena?
Lena:	You see, last year Nastya and I were lucky to be in a Soviet-American camp and we took rather many photos

	there, and I think that the most dramatic photo was taken on the day when our American friends had to leave and we were not sure that we will meet again and that's why everyone was crying. These photos were very dramatic and sincere.
J. M.:	[corrected a mistake: rather many/rather a lot] Well, can a photograph be a work of art?
Pupils:	Of course.
J. M.:	Of course. I've got some photographs here and I'm going to give each desk one photograph and ask you to tell me what you think of it as a photograph, what you think is interesting, the mood the photographer is trying to conjure up, or we would say, evoke, er . . . and tell us about the photograph. I'll give you the card like that, don't let anybody else see it . . . Either or both of you describe it to the rest of the group, and the rest of you may ask them questions about it. [A short time was given for preparation.] Now tell us about it. [The picture shows a bicycle leaning against a mature tree in a field, in evening light, with a line of Scotch pine out of focus in the background.]
Ira:	You see, it's interesting . . . In the first place it is interesting to know that this picture attracts and . . . because, when you look at it, you smile . . . the thing is that you don't understand what the author wanted to tell us.
J. M.:	Not the author, but . . . what do you call the. . . ?
Pupils:	[confusion] Painter . . . Photograph . . . Man who made the photo . . . Artist.
J. M.:	You could say the artist, but what do you call a man who takes photographs?
Pupil:	The cameraman.
J. M.:	The cameraman . . . would be for a television camera or a film . . . The photographer.
Ira:	What the photographer wanted to tell us about. So that I think that the general tone of this photo is humorous.
J. M.:	Humorous?
Ira:	In the first place we can see the tree and the bicycle near it.
J. M.:	Right, so there's a tree and a bicycle beside it, yes.

Ira:	Beside it. And, er, the action takes place in the evening because we can see that the sun is setting.
J. M.:	The sun is setting. Now you said: 'The action takes place'. What action is there?
Ira:	There is no action, no real action . . . [interrupted]
J. M.:	What do you think, Anya?
Anya:	You see, it's rather hard for me to speak about this picture, er . . . I don't think it's humorous.
J. M.:	You don't think it's humorous?
Anya:	I don't think so, and . . . er . . . I can't speak about any action here, because we can see only one . . . er . . . we can see a bicycle which is standing and we can see a man whose bicycle it . . .
Pupil:	We can suggest that . . .
Anya:	We can see only the bicycle, and I don't think what the photographer wanted to say.
J. M.:	Right, just stop there for a moment. Listen, you've heard it's got a bicycle, it's got a tree, it's a landscape. Ask some questions to the people over there about the picture and try and find more about it.
Vanya:	Does the action take place in the countryside?
Anya:	Yes.
J. M.:	Yes, well you said, 'the action takes place?' Is it set I think you would perhaps say, is it set in the country-side? Yes. Some more questions.
Natasha:	Can we see people?
Anya:	No, we can't see any people.
J. M.:	Some more questions, someone on the back row?
Peter:	Is it a landscape?
Girls:	Yes.
	No.
	Why not?
J. M.:	Well, yes, in a way it probably is.
Anya:	Yes, I think that it is a landscape.
Tanya:	When was the picture, the photo taken? I mean, in summer, or in spring or. . . ?
Lena:	You see, it was taken in summer and it was taken in the evening, as I have said already . . .
Pupil:	Is the picture bright and picturesque or it's rather gloomy and sad?
J. M.:	Yes, what's the mood?

Lena: It's hard to say. It's evening, and the colours are not bright.

J. M.:   Well, let's show it to them, let's show it to everybody. Why do you think the photographer took that photograph? Has anybody got an idea? Lena?

Lena: I think the photographer took this photograph because I think that the colours are really unusual here when we look at the trees . . .

J. M.:   Yes, you like the colour?

Lena: I like the colour very much. The colour of the ground and of the trees which are in the background. There is something green and yellow in the same time, and I think that really the photographer liked those colours . . .

J. M.:   Yes. Why has he put the bicycle in it?

Anya II: For contrast, I think.

J. M.:   Contrast with what . . . or between what?

Anya II: Contrast between nature, the evening, [indecipherable] and the bicycle, the bicycle is a product [mispronounced] . . .

J. M.:   A what?

Anya II: A product.

J. M.:   A product . . . of human activity, something man-made. Right, yes. If he is saying anything, what is he saying?

Pupils: [confusion]

J. M.:   Nature is beautiful? How nice it is to ride your bicycle through beautiful places and stop sometimes and look at them? O.K. Good . . . Let's look at . . . That's a beautiful one. [The second card shows a dinghy with furled scarlet sails on Derwentwater. The lake is extremely still, and there are a few wispy clouds above the distant mountains.] Don't show it to us yet, but . . . tell them about it.

Tanya: This photograph looks really attractive and the author . . . Oi! the photographer I think tried here just to depict . . . his own attitude to his favourite, maybe, landscape . . . In the picture you can see a beautiful lake and really beautiful mountains and a boat which is. . . [?] down the lake, and I think that . . .

J. M.:   Sorry, the boat is what, did you say? The boat is . . .

Pupils: Sailing.

J. M.: No, I don't think it's sailing . . . it's still, is it not? It's moored, we might say.

Tanya: The photographer wanted to arouse admiration of nature, because it's really very beautiful and it's painted in bright colours, very bright blue and, er, green, and I think that it's really very picturesque. A very picturesque place.

J. M.: Yes.

Zhenya: In this photograph I can see a boat on a calm water and . . . in that . . . everything around is calm and it seems that it looks gloomy, and I think that the author of this photo wanted . . .

J. M.: [knocks on the desk]

Zhenya: The photographer [wrong stress] wanted . . .

J. M.: Photographer.

Zhenya: to make our mood calm and to . . .

J. M.: Yes, yes, I'm sure you're right, he wanted to make us feel calm. Have you looked at the title? On the back you will find the title, what's it called?

Zhenya: Called 'Red Sails'.

J. M.: Yes, there's a clue there . . . Yes, *alye parusa*, you've read Grin, have you not?[2] . . . Obviously it's the red sails which attracted his attention because they contrast very strongly, do they not with the rest of the picture? Let's have the one . . . [This card is entitled 'Goat in Doorway'.] Yours, a rather interesting one.

Mitya: You see, our picture is not a landscape and it is not an industrial view. We can see only the wall of the house . . . and from the gates of the house a sheep is coming . . .

J. M.: A ship?

Mitya: is coming out.

J. M.: A sheep.

Mitya: I think this is nothing but humour in this picture, because it is only a funny episode. One can see an animal which is carefully coming from the house, and which is looking at the photographer.

J. M.: Yes.

Vanya: I think the photographer, the man who took this picture, is a very skilled photographer, because he saw a very curious episode and make a photo of it and he made that photo . . . good . . . this is a good coloured picture . . .

J. M.: Yes, he made it very well, he took a good photograph. You called it a sheep, actually it isn't a sheep, I thought that, actually it's a goat. It tells you on the back 'Goat in Doorway'. There we are.

So there we think the motive of the photographer was humour. Now then, let's hear about that one. [This photograph is entitled 'Rock Pools'.]

Natasha: You see, I think that this photograph, this photo is really a pleasant to see it, because we can see here a seaside. It is rather rocky and the picture was made during the sunset and it is really very beautiful because the sky, it is blue, white, red and many colours are present here and . . . there on the picture . . . the scene is really calm . . . is really calm and . . . and it is dark, and so I think that the picture is really pleasant to look at.

J. M.: Do you think it's a happy picture?

Natasha: No, I think it is . . . a dull.

J. M.: A dull. . . ? Yes . . . Can I just give you one . . . This is a difficult word, but it's a good word [writes on board]. Do you know it – elegaic? Do you know what an elegy is?

Mitya: Elegiya.

J. M.: *Elegiya*, yes. What is an *elegiya*, what is an elegy?

Pupil: *Grust'*[3]

J. M.: Yes, *grust'*, it's a rather sad poem, isn't it, an elegy? So we may think that the mood of that is elegaic.

Anya II: You see, we can see here a striking contrast between the very dark seaside and the sea and a very bright sky. But we can see that everything in nature is in harmony, and the author, Oi! the photographer wanted to say, it's really attractive and very interesting.

J. M.: Yes, thank you very much, let's show it to everybody. It is rather fine, I think. *Marsianskiy peyzazh*, did you say? What would the English for that be?

Vanya: Marsyan . . .

J. M.: Yes, Martian landscape. Good, yes, you might think it looks like the Moon, or some remote planet . . .

Now then, let's hear about yours now. This is quite a

difficult one. [The picture shows a large wheatfield with a few red poppies growing in it. In the background is a large barn looming before a completely colourless sky.] Someone found a political message in this this morning in the other class.[4] There you are, tell us about it.

Nastya: You see, this is a landscape, and on the ... in this picture we can see an endless wheatfield ... and in the background you can see a very dark house. It's rather small. You see, this picture has rather many feelings. The colour of the wheatfield is not bright, you see, but it's dirty yellow.

J. M.: You're right, it is a dirty yellow.

Nastya: And the colour of the house is dirty greyd.

J. M.: Dirty grey.

Lena: At first, when I looked at this picture I was struck by the fact that there was no sky on it; we can't see the sky in the picture, and er, looking at it, when I first looked at it I thought that it was autumn here but we think of it, we understand that wheat is on the fields only in summer, and I think that there is really something strange in such an autumn-looking summer, if I can say in this way, and I think that looking at this picture we can understand that really all the bright time, such time like summer, comes to its end and I think that the fact that there is no sky means that really ... this will be by all means ... the end of all the bright time ... the gay time will come to its end.

J. M.: What mood do you think there is ... were you going to say something about the mood, Peter?

Peter: The picture is very gloomy and one can feel, I should say, some sort of pessimism looking at it. The absence of sky, I think, means the absence of any prospect, any hope, and ...

J. M.: Yes, it is threatening ... is the adjective, you know what to threaten is? *Grozit'* is to threaten [writes on board], threatening the adjective. You look at that great house, it's dominating, staring at you, then you look at the field of corn, what is it, it's wheat ... What's the meaning of those few poppies, is there a meaning, you see the red flower?

Lena: When I noticed them I understood that there is such a strange thing that here in the foreground we can see really some bright, some flowers, and in the background, so further on, there is no sky and there is a dark house and I think it means that maybe the photographer thought about something, er . . . something bad which is going to happen in future, so now it is a bit better and in future it will be worse.

J. M.:   Good. What does a red poppy mean to an English person or a French person or a Belgian? Do you know what special meaning it has?

Pupils: [in background explaining the meaning of 'poppy' to each other] *Mak, mak.*

Lena: I think it means that somebody perished here . . .

J. M.:   What is the reason for that?
Well, in the first World War the Western Front, the battlefields were fought in Flanders, where there are many, many red poppies. And of course, as you know, there were millions of people killed in the War, and after the War, every November 11th, which is the day on which the Armistice was signed in 1918, everybody goes round in England wearing a red poppy.

Lena: And so it reminds about those people who really had no future.

The lesson continued, but this transcript of twenty-six minutes of it (not including time for preparation) should be sufficient to indicate the standard of spoken English of these pupils. It must be remembered that what is recorded here is spoken language, which often looks odd in print; many things which are acceptable orally – repetition, reconsideration of sentence structure or adjustments to the grammar – do not always look right when written down. If the reader seeks any reassurance on this point, look at my own statements, which are not always couched in literary style, though I am a native speaker of English. The pupils' language is very good indeed, bearing in mind the circumstances: the fact that it is largely unprepared and spontaneous, that the subject matter is fairly sophisticated and the activity quite demanding. It shows, however, in places some over-reliance on learned interjectional phrases: especially 'you see', but also 'to tell the truth', 'I think that' (rather than 'I think'), 'really' (which is almost done to death!) On the other hand 'the thing is' and 'in the first place' are used well. Articles, 'any' and 'some' give slight problems, but not more than would be expected, bearing in mind the pupils' native language. Prepositions too: 'in the same time', 'on the field' and the puzzlement over 'in', 'near' and 'on'. Certain turns of phrase are correct, but un-English: 'which' used when better omitted in the spoken language ('an animal which is coming out of a door'), word order ('there were taken ... photos'; 'we can see here a seaside'), and 'it's rather hard for me to speak about'. It is actually quite hard to find out-and-out errors, but there are some: 'a dying of AIDS man', 'a dull' (meaning 'a dull one', but even I repeated and apparently accepted this one!), sequence of tenses ('not sure we will meet again') and 'it reminds about' (the direct object missing).

What the printed page does not show is the speed of delivery and lack of hesitation on the part of nearly all the pupils. They were ready with ideas, for the most part intelligent ones, and were so concerned to convey meaning that no fear of perpetrating grammatical errors inhibited fluency. Their pronunciation varied a lot, and was in many cases far from perfect, being very thick and Russian. What they all need (or, perhaps, should have had a year or two previously) is some residence in an English-speaking country and a prolonged period of study with a native speaker to complement the undoubtedly excellent work done by the English staff of School 1937. There is a point beyond which *teaching* in a foreign language cannot go. These young people, it seemed to me, had reached that point some little time previously. They would doubtless go on adding to their knowledge of the language, but three weeks living in an English family would have transformed it.

* * *

The previous sentence could almost stand as the principal conclusion of these two chapters on the learning of English in School 1937. A high level of motivation and interest, excellent teaching by dedicated and, for the most part, well qualified staff, hard work and the division of large classes into a manageable group size, which is the main privilege of the subject of English in schools like No. 1937 with an intensified programme, have led to high, but not miraculously high, standards of achievement in English. More suitable and more interesting teaching materials of a higher linguistic standard would bring about more effective learning and, if their content were more reliable and informative, a better all-round level of general education and knowledge and understanding of English-speaking countries. An extension of opportunities to travel would put the finishing touch to a process which already deserves the admiration of foreign language teachers throughout the world.[5]

11 Outside the Classroom
Opportunities for Personal Development

One morning when sitting in a dark corner of Marina's room in an attempt to get over a headache, I was approached by a colleague with something on her mind. It was not the best time for a discussion, but it turned out to be an interesting one. What was the view in Britain, Natasha wanted to know, about out-of-school activities? It had been impressed upon her in training that a good schoolmistress should become involved in the hobbies, interests and leisure-time development of the children, but at School 1937 there were not very many opportunities for such activities in direct connection with the school. The pupils, she said, tended to go elsewhere to find scope for their out-of-school interests. This she could understand, but it did little to sustain any *esprit de corps* within the school. My colleague regretted the relative lack of opportunity for pupils and teachers in this school to get to know each other through sporting, cultural and recreational pursuits.

Countries fall into two distinct types over the reaction of their teachers to this question. In some, the teaching profession sees itself as employed to instruct children in a subject, not to run stamp clubs or hockey teams. The Soviet Union and Britain hold the opposite view. It was true that School 1937 could not, from its own resources, provide a great variety of clubs and societies, but many additional opportunities were available to the pupils from outside agencies. This chapter outlines many of these.

WHAT THE SCHOOL ITSELF OFFERS

At the beginning of the school year the children are offered a choice from thirty-seven approved activities, and when their preferences are known, the eight most viable clubs are set up. The school is allowed to pay staff for running these eight societies in the sense that doing so is considered part of their teaching load. One of the youngest teachers, therefore, whose normal teaching periods would be eigh-

145

teen in a week, teaches fifteen and runs the International Friendship Club, which is considered equivalent to the remaining three. Sometimes an outsider may be paid to run a club. It is possible for parents to subscribe towards paying for a leader to run an activity which would not otherwise be available, and the club would therefore be self-financing. Under *glasnost'* paying for 'extras' has become more common than previously.

One member of staff, Irina Maksimovna, has the special responsibility of seeing to all this: she is entitled 'organiser of out-of-school and extra-curricular upbringing work'. This is an administrative task of some complexity, as it involves liaison with a number of outside agencies. Clubs provided in School 1937 are *Poisk* ('Quest', about which more will be said later), *KID* (abbreviation for International Friendship Club), 'Skilful hands' (a handicraft club run by the labour education teacher), 'Get to know Moscow' (run by parents for primary children), two groups receive swimming training at the car factory sports centre nearby (they have to pay for entry to the baths and for the trainer), *OFP* (general physical training, for the extended-day group – referred to again below), the Shooting Club (run by the military training instructor), art clubs for both senior and junior pupils, chess club for younger pupils (run by parents), and the puppet theatre (for both primary and secondary-age pupils). There is also a *KVN* or *klub veselykh nakhodchikov*, a phrase which defies translation: literally, 'club for merry resourceful people'. Pupils in this are amateur comedians or revue artistes, and put on shows of amusing and satirical songs and sketches, sometimes in formal competition with other schools.

Irina Maksimovna is not responsible for the subject clubs for more senior pupils, but the school does run Russian literature and mathematics circles. In recognition of the work she does in this field, her classroom teaching load is significantly reduced. She became interested in this type of work when she chose a course on the subject at college, and previously to working at School 1937 she was a 'methodologist' in a Pioneer house. These are teachers who organise leisure activities within such institutions (described later), which may in fact be an extension of school study in more relaxing surroundings.

It would be tedious to enter at length into every one of these clubs, so I shall say a little about two of them in particular. Many Soviet schools have International Friendship Clubs and they seem to be popular with pupils up to class 6 or 7, and often even later. Foreign visitors are, of course, often taken to meetings; more exactly, it may be said that when foreign visitors are around the school would be incompetent not to organise a meeting at which their presence could be exploited. My own appearance at the *KID* at School 1937 was one of the more memorable events of my period in the school. I spoke briefly about school life in England, and questions were fired at me about all aspects of Britain for a very long time afterwards. It formed a marked contrast with other such meetings I had attended in other Soviet schools in the past, when the proceedings had sometimes become rather stiff and stereotyped; happily, at School 1937 many of the children knew me by the time of the meeting and had got over any sense of awkwardness at having an Englishman around. One small group even accompanied me to the underground station afterwards to continue to practise their English and to prolong the discussion. There is no doubt that curiosity about foreign countries, especially capitalist ones, is strong among young people in the Soviet Union. The wish to travel abroad, until very recently one most unlikely to be realised, doubtless intensifies interest in *KID*.

Perhaps the most interesting club to an outsider would seem to be 'Quest'. It obviously has a strong element of moral and political education, and it has been referred to in other parts of this book for that reason. It has various purposes and aims: to keep alive among young people interest in the history of the Great Patriotic War, to look after and take an interest in elderly veterans of the battle of Moscow, to mark anniversaries and research the topography of the struggle. So in addition to the moral and political aims referred to above, social service was involved, and the club's activities had some of the fascination of local history studies too. Despite what seems to be a lively subject for pupils' activities, Quest at School 1937 seemed to have run into difficulties, a fact I had picked up from overheard staff conversations. In addition, I may have hit upon an unlucky meeting, for that which I attended was an unfortunate one. Apart from me, there were only ten people present, all women, and they did not seem to include a single present pupil of the school. Two were old ladies living locally who had fought as partisans against the Germans in 1941–43. Some others were teachers and there were one or two former pupils, who had become 'hooked' on the club and still attended. The present pupils had clearly twigged that this was going to be a boring meeting, and they had stayed away. The teacher in charge read aloud at very great length extracts from the minutes of the proceedings of early meetings of the Komsomol in 1918–20; the purpose of this was not in itself clear, but it transpired that she was simply presenting material which might or might not be useful in compiling a commemorative evening of drama, song, poetry and documentary history for the anniversary of the retreat of the Nazis from Moscow. I have to confess that I could not see exactly how the extracts related to this. However, the ferment in the Komsomol at that period was thought to resemble the controversy in the same organisation today; consequently, it might have been meant to show the present younger generation that their forefathers were not so different from the youth of today. Moreover, at another recent meeting, I was told, one of the veteran partisans had bewailed the apathy of the youth of today towards the Komsomol. Unfortunately, as none of the pupils were present, the point could scarcely be made to them.

An important part of the extracurricular arrangements in any urban school is the 'extended day'. In a society in which over 90 per cent of women of working age do in fact go out to work it is obvious that many mothers of young children will not be at home to greet them on their return from lessons at midday or soon after. School lunch, clubs, the pioneer house or whatever else is available become vital agencies for child minding in these circumstances. Many schools in the industrial suburbs of cities make arrangements for children in classes 1 to 6 to stay on the premises; I have visited one in Minsk where the parents of almost every child in this age group take advantage of this. Some schools extend the opportunity up to class 8, age fourteen. School No. 1937 offers it only to years 1 to 3. A hundred children with three teachers participate. The children's homework is supervised, there is extra PE; remedial or at least additional work in English, Russian, mathematics and art is done. The children may stay on the premises until 6 pm, but many are collected by their parents earlier than this.

OUTSIDE ACTIVITIES FOR ALL

In Chapter 7 the official youth organisations have been described particularly from the point of view of their political significance. Here we look at the recreational side of their activities. Visitors to the Soviet Union are often taken to see the 'pioneer palaces' or 'pioneer houses'. The word 'palace' or 'house' is used, one is told, to distinguish the degree of lavishness provided by the establishment. Some 'pioneer houses', however, are as magnificent as other 'palaces'. Their actual title is 'palaces of pioneers and schoolchildren', indicating that they are open to all aged from five to seventeen, both younger and older than the official age range of the pioneers.

Each of the thirty-five boroughs of Moscow has its pioneer palace and there is a much visited central one on the Lenin Hills. I have visited such places in three Soviet cities and have received certain impressions of the work done within them which are relevant here. First, there is a great variety of pursuit for the children to become involved with. Dance, music, art, sport, film, writing, scientific circles, modelling, and handicrafts all figure in the programme. Taking the first of these alone, one can see every variety of dance practised: folk, ballroom, disco, ballet and so on – the point is made to illustrate the variety of opportunity offered. Secondly, when visiting the groups at work it is immediately obvious that much of the teaching or coaching is of very high quality and is carried out with great enthusiasm by the leaders, who may be trained teachers or qualified in other ways professionally. Many of them work part time. Thirdly, it often hits the visitor in the eye that these classes are open to children of all aptitudes. The ballet class will contain the odd future Pavlova or Nureyev as well as a whole range of children down to those with little sense of rhythm or coordination.

There can be no doubt that these places offer splendid opportunities to children and young people to take up and develop an interest in all sorts of hobbies, games, crafts, sciences and arts. Some of the palaces are open 363 days a year at all hours of the day, and the Moscow Central Palace, the biggest and best, claims to offer 968 different activities and to cater for between 3000 and 7000 children every day. Children may register for one or two activities, and usually the groups meet twice a week. What the pioneer houses are not is a sort of youth club or coffee bar where children can merely drop in for purely social purposes. Despite the fact that the Central Palace in Minsk had a corner full of electronic games of the Space Invaders type, it would probably be true to say on the whole that Soviet educators see it as no part of their job to provide purely recreational opportunities to children.

One group of final-year pupils from School 1937 had formed a political song group under the auspices of one of the pioneer palaces, where they received coaching and had a place to meet as well as contact with other like-minded youngsters. A cassette recording of some of their pieces shows that the political message strongly emphasises the 'struggle for peace' and the hoped-for victory of the working classes over the representatives of reaction and property. But, as well as this strong stuff, there are humorous items, and other whimsical numbers made popular by pop groups on which the young people model themselves: Time Machine (*Mashina vremeni*) and Cinema (*Kino*). Some of these sing obliquely of young people's desires to be independent and free. The text of the songs is easy; the subtext sometimes impenetrable to a foreigner.

Another type of institution with comparable aims to the pioneer houses is the 'house of culture', such as that run in connection with the factory which was the 'base enterprise' of School 1937 (and of seventeen other schools). This firm employs 70,000 workpeople, not all of them in one single factory, but a major part of its activity, including the manufacture of motor vehicles, takes place within a few hundred yards of the school. The House of Culture is an absolutely splendid establishment, intended for the work force of the enterprise (whose average age is thirty-five), their spouses and children, pensioners and the whole community. There is a certain superficial similarity to a Butlin's holiday camp. Polished wooden floors, marble halls, pillared entrance and concourse areas, regal staircases – the building has all the elegance and grace of a Moscow underground station, but at the same time it affirms the declared values of Soviet society: culture is important, the worker deserves good recreational and educational facilities. And despite the name 'house of *culture*', which might seem off-putting to a Westerner, it was intended for recreation as well as education. Five hundred people are employed in this building and its two smaller branches. Outside are playing fields for many different sports, including the stadium of a well-known Moscow team, which is sponsored by the factory. The House of Culture offers choirs, dancing, bands, clubs, adult education, drama (there is an excellent theatre, which is supported by several of the nation's best-known actors), counselling for young parents, instruction in domestic skills, arts and crafts, an astronomical observatory, concerts, films and a 'video-salon'. Useful contacts with important concerns in the film and television field mean that sometimes films are on show here even before general release.

Perhaps the most impressive facility offered to the public is the library. There are three major sections to the library, a lending department, a reference section of 60,000 books which subscribes to 260 periodicals, and an excellent children's library. The reading room was quiet and not overcrowded, and one of the people who showed me round commented that she had written a dissertation for a higher education course there, since it was possible to obtain materials on inter-library loan. As the average number of library users was sixty a day, the crush was considerably less than the Lenin Library in central Moscow, where one sometimes has to wait over an hour to leave a coat in the cloakroom before getting anywhere near the books. The children's library was not enormous, but was extremely well and attractively arranged, stocked with school books, additional reading on school subjects and recreational reading. The staff were, of course, specially trained children's librarians and had a sophisticated system for keeping track of the users' reading, encouraging them to extend their ability and range of literature tackled.

One or two chance remarks made during a visit to the House of Culture indicated that these places were not without their problems at the present time. The appetite of the young for rock concerts was mentioned; the establishment was keener to provide cultural and intellectual activities. It is not only in such places that some unease may be detected about the taste, if that is the word, of the Soviet young for international commercial pop to the exclusion of much else. One cannot doubt the quality of what is offered by the House of Culture to young and old, but the staff were open in their expressions of regret that more young people did not take advantage of the facilities. Clearly, all such places have their plans and their norms to fulfil, like anywhere else in the Soviet planned society. The way this was once done was revealed by Irina Maksimovna in a comment made as we left the premises. 'Once', she said, 'they only had to ring the school to tell us they needed thirty children for a folk-dancing group, and we would have to find them. But children today don't see why they should do things they don't want to.'

THE ENCOURAGEMENT OF TALENT

What follows is not to imply that the House of Culture or the Pioneer Palace do not encourage talent, but it is clear that there are other establishments which aim more specifically at fostering the development of the skills of talented children. Pupils at School 1937 spoke of attending classes for athletics, swimming, art and music, where they received special coaching as for potentially gifted performers. One eleven-year-old girl gave me one of her paintings, which certainly demonstrated talent well above the average for a child of her age. I have visited schools for the talented in sport, art and music – and I am speaking of after-hours schools for children who receive their general education in a regular school. There are also establishments, often mainly boarding schools, for the exceptionally highly gifted, such as potential Olympic athletes or professional footballers, future concert soloists and so on; these are not the subject of this section.

It would be tedious to attempt to describe in detail all these establishments, but an idea of the objectives and ethos of such schools may be conveyed by describing a 'children's music school' which I was able to visit. Its primary aim was given as not so much to provide future concert artists, but 'to raise the general level of musical culture in the population', though the director was proud of those former pupils who had made it to conservatoire. The school concerned served an area (of Leningrad, though similar places exist in all cities) with a population of about 50,000 inhabitants, and there were 380 children enrolled, some as young as five to seven in preparatory classes. Seven to ten-year-olds would attend up to three times a week (six hours) and four times (eight and a half hours) after this age. Only two or three hours would be devoted to instrumental teaching, the rest to classes on aural work, musical literacy, theory, choir or ensemble work. Children have to show a certain musical aptitude before being admitted, but the staff insisted that the very highest standards are only demanded from those children who really can meet them; for the rest, the majority, in fact, the requirements are tempered to what they can reasonably achieve. In some cases parents are advised to remove their children and send them to the pioneer house 'where the demands upon the pupils are less stringent'.

The school visited was provided out of the city budget and charged moderate fees, based on the parents' ability to pay, of one rouble fifty a month to 23 roubles (for parents with a salary of 400). The director described it as being situated in a 'rich working-class area', so many were paying reasonable fees. There are parallel institutions working *po samookupaemosti* – at cost, where the fees can be as much as 35 roubles a month. Of the forty-six children's musical schools in Leningrad eleven were of this latter type.

The building was constructed in 1961 for the purpose, and it contained an attractive small concert hall (150 seats) with decent acoustics, a large platform and raked seating. There were many individual sound-proofed small teaching and practice rooms, where lessons were going on at the time of my visit. It was late Saturday afternoon in mid-December, and the feeling of fatigue and holidays coming soon was quite strong, but none the less many of the sixty teachers (who can earn up to 300 roubles a month) were hard at work with children, and some of them would be there until 9.30 that evening. For the most part, the rooms I visited were occupied by teachers with pupils at a relatively early stage of instruction; we heard a variety of music executed (perhaps this is the best word) on pianos, clarinet, bayan (a type of accordion which is extremely popular in Russian folk music) and xylophone. All these players, except one who was having problems which were explained to me, showed good musical sense and aptitude, but I would have thought none were in any way likely to become outstanding performers. In the hall a junior ensemble of six boys and four girls was tackling Purcell's famous Chaconne. It was their first year of orchestral experience, and they were being introduced to four-part string playing through study of a selection of baroque miniatures. Their rhythm, intonation and ensemble were very good, so was their posture and the concentration they brought to the playing; the tone quality was what one expects from inexperienced young players.

It was my strong impression that the school provided a potentially excellent training for able young musicians who might or might not be or become high fliers. In Britain many if not most schools provide instrumental teaching, which can, of course, also be 'bought' privately by parents; local authorities as well as individual primary and secondary schools also often have bands, orchestras, choirs and the like, which children may join. There are not many places, however, which provide up to eight and a half hours a week of systematic music education which is extra to the school curriculum. It may even be thought that this is too much for many children, even quite gifted ones. Yet the single-mindedness with which this work is carried on, the high level of organisation, the degree of standardisation of the curricula, the provision of suitable premises and so on are all impressive. Some may feel that it is in fact better for Johnny to be dragged out in the middle of mathematics to be given his oboe lesson in some dark corner of the school by a demoralised peripatetic teacher who 'does' all the woodwind instruments – and of course there are many peripatetics who are not demoralised and whose teaching is very good. But the Soviet children's musical school system would appear to have certain advantages.[1]

A final point about outside provision for the gifted in the arts or in sport concerns the level of luxury of the resources. The remarks about Butlin's in the section above on the House of Culture should not be taken to mean that the premises are either tawdry, or on the other hand flashy and over-done. In any case, those remarks apply to other types of establishment, where a degree of showiness may be taken to indicate the values of society and the importance attached to the leisure of the workers. However, a feature of the arts and sports coaching centres would seem to be a certain no-nonsense practicality. The facilities are adequate and suitable for the purpose, but are rarely, in my experience, lavish. The music teaching rooms, the painting studio, the gymnasium are all satisfactory, but on the whole they are short on chromium plate, polished panelling or refined decoration. The shower appliances in the changing room, or some of them, may be rusty and falling off the wall, but the Russians know that athletes are made by good training, not by magnificently appointed showers. It would seem to be policy to achieve a level of resourcing which is sufficient without extravagance to allow good work to be done.

* * *

We return to Natasha's question with which this chapter began. The pupils in School 1937 have splendid opportunities to develop their talents and interests outside the classroom, but she is right: the school cannot supply these opportunities from its own resources. The sporting, cultural, social and recreational facilities it can offer are not negligible, but they are very limited. Pupils are best advised to go outside the school, where facilities are extremely good, and this, of course, they do. It is a feature of Soviet education, indeed of Soviet life, to make central provision for needs of all sorts – in fact, this applies to teaching for handicapped and retarded pupils, since 'mainstreaming' is a notion which has not yet caught on in the USSR. But the consequence is undoubtedly what Natasha said: the staff have little opportunity to work, learn or relax with pupils when they are not fully engaged in their professional duties. The professionalisation of out-of-school provision denies the teacher who is an enthusiastic and knowledgeable amateur opportunities to become involved in *school* activities with pupils where this amateur expertise can be useful. At the same time, the teacher is free from a sense of obligation to run such activities and probably therefore has more energy for her fully professional duties. It is a matter of taste and opinion as to whether this, on balance, is a good thing or a bad one.[2]

12 Interview with the Director
The Work of the Headmistress

The head teacher of Moscow School No. 1937 is Yevdokiya Stepanovna. She is in her early sixties and could have retired at fifty-five, but she prefers to continue working. The first part of this chapter reports in her own words how she sees the job she is doing, how she came to obtain it, and what her problems are.

J. M.: I'd like to begin with some facts about the school. What about the staff, first of all?

Y. S.: We have forty-four working teachers, of these thirteen teach English. On 1 September we had 654 pupils.

J. M.: What is your own experience in the teaching profession?

Y. S.: I've been in the profession for thirty-two years, and I've been here since 1971 on 5 March. Before that I was deputy head of an ordinary, not a special English, school, where I'd been Secretary of the Party Organisation and a teacher.

J. M.: How were you chosen or appointed for the headship?

Y. S.: At that time there weren't any elections for headships. The Education Office and the Area Committee of the Communist Party built up a reserve of potential heads. I was sent on a course in an in-service institute to train me for the post of head teacher, and completed it successfully. Often enough in a year or two one could hope to be nominated to fill a vacancy, though that might not happen. What happened to me was that Vera Ivanovna, the head here, retired and the local authority had to appoint a replacement. I was summoned and asked to do it. There were very many seeking the post of head in this school: I was overawed and asked why me? They said – that's our business, do you want the job or not? They persuaded me to take it on the grounds that I'd passed the course, so do it!

J. M.: Were posts advertised in those days?

Y. S.: No, it was all settled locally in the education office.

J. M.: And what happens now?

Y. S.: Now ... In another school the head was promoted to a Ministry job. There were three candidates and the staff of the school chose by secret ballot. Each applicant head drew up her programme, her specific proposals on how she would act, what changes she would make; her concept; her platform for the job. And the staff voted. That's what has been happening since 1986, since reform and restructuring was started. It's what has been happening in industry for a little longer: it happens in schools now too. And that's what will happen here when I retire. Not an appointment, but an election.

J. M.: What does the salary of a head depend on?

Y. S.: On the number of pupils in the school. But the salary of a head used to depend on length of service. But now it doesn't matter how old or how young a head is, the salary will be calculated by the size of the school. Plus extra if we actually take lessons.

J. M.: And do you like this school?

Y. S.: Yes, indeed, but it was very hard at first, in 1971. I didn't know whether the staff would accept me. But when they see a head is prepared to work day and night for the school and put her back into the job, the relationship changes. When they see the head is all for the school, then if I ask them, they'll give their all too. But the first year was dreadful. There were constant complaints and questions. And in the other school, the one I came from, there had been an excellent staff spirit, and I'd been there for ten years. We were one happy family. But we've got a good staff here now.

J. M.: And who appoints staff?

Y. S.: Now that the system is being reformed, I do myself. I interview candidates and appoint or not, depending on whether I like them. I both appoint and dismiss. But before that it was the Education Office that issued the orders.

J. M.: What are the school's problems, if I may ask?

Y. S.: There are an awful lot of problems. Some are connected with restructuring in our society in general. There is the problem of how to motivate children, how to make them want to learn. Dealing with the history of our country and the teaching of it in view of 'restructuring' [*perestroyka*] – that is a problem, 'openness' [*glasnost'*] has appeared, and how do we deal with it and accommodate it? This is very difficult. But another problem is, if the school is to change, what about provision of equipment? We are introducing six-year-olds, a five day week – that means for the first class we need a dormitory for their afternoon nap, we need a play room for the little ones. Consequently, since we haven't the space, we shall have to make the third year work on a second shift – so how can we timetable the teachers so they aren't overworked? But there are other things too: where is our sports hall with all the equipment we ought to have for sports training? It would be nice to have a swimming pool. Then there's the problem of occupying the pupils – keeping them busy at school. Now, they aren't going to extend our school or give us extra buildings. And next year we have to accommodate six-year-olds. The workmen will set up a dormitory and make minor modifications, but they aren't going to extend the buildings. We are merely supposed to take the changes on board by making the third year come in the afternoon on a second shift.

J. M.: And when will the second shift start?

Y. S.: I suppose when other primary classes have finished at 12.20, the two third year classes will start at about 12.30. And if there are four or five lessons, it might go on as late as six o'clock.

J. M.: And why won't they extend the building? Is there no money?

Y. S.: Well, that's true, there isn't any money. But anyway our school isn't all that old when you consider it. It was built in 1956–57, and other schools – the one near the metro station has been standing since 1933! Its roof is falling in in places. So if they can afford a full scale repair job on two schools, it won't be us that gets it, as there are six or seven schools as old as ours in the area. They'll repaint and do minor repairs. We try to do what we can ourselves. We get the children to give it a thorough clean once in a while – it's going on at the moment – but there's no chance of a complete refit for the present. And then there's the question of computer technology. We haven't got the equipment and our children have to go to the UPK [vocational training centre], which is probably better for them anyway because there is a proper computer class-room there.

J. M.: I'd heard they were talking of joining these two schools, this one and the one next door.

Y. S.: I started on this one in 1971 when I arrived. I saw the architect. But we can't build on to the school because the essential services pass the school underground on both sides. There has been a suggestion to build a passage, a covered way between the two school buildings, so that the junior classes would be taught next door, and the senior ones in this building, but the money wasn't available, neither in the twelfth nor the thirteenth five-year plan. It could be that by the year 2000 something might come of it, if people really see the need for it.

J. M.: Now a question about this school as one with intensified instruction in English: a year or so ago the Soviet press was full of criticism of such schools. Of course they aren't the only type of specialised schools. What is the public attitude to them now?

Y. S.: Yes, it's true, especially last year and the year before there were many complaints – the cry was – it was supposed to be élitism, and who were the children who were attending this school? Articles like that did appear in the press. Now, since the February Plenum of the Party, when Ligachev made his speech about reform, the course has changed 180 degrees, so that they've come to the conclusion there should be various types of school. So, if a child has a bent for languages he should go to a school with an intensified programme in English. And now they're opening other schools – mathematics schools. In every area of Moscow higher education institutions are opening their own schools. In this borough MIFI (Moscow Institute of Physics) on a basis of the already existing School No. 704 is opening ninth and tenth classes with intensified maths and physics teaching. And in that school there will be four ninth classes, maybe five, and they've announced competitions – entrance tests – and they'll select five ninth classes for children from the whole of Moscow. It's been on TV, so everyone knows about it, and they're arranging for expert staff. Somewhere else, I've forgotten the number of the school, one of the best language institutes is planning a similarly high-powered school for English. Someone has opened a 'university' school, where the teaching is done by staff of the university or college. There are lectures in university style. The system of assessment is also somewhat different, as well as the teaching methods. So after all the high-level conferences and the Plenum, the conclusion now is that children's abilities need to be developed, and they should follow their interests.

J. M.: Why did the opinion change?

Y. S.: Why? It's hard to say why. But probably they studied the problems of these schools and children, and came to the conclusion that if we force physics and mathematics and what else onto children with a facility for English, the children lose their motivation. I don't know why they decided this, but I can say that this year things have quietened down, and the schools with intensified instruction have been left alone. So in our borough there's a history school, and one for maths also, taking pupils in to the ninth class by competitive examination, and they offer public seminars too. Obviously they've studied the practice and come to the conclusion such schools are a good thing. Whose decision it was, I can't say.

J. M.: What is your relationship with the RONO [local education office] as far as the administration of this school is concerned?

Y. S.: I've worked now with three area education officers over the years. We've never had a 'conflict situation' between the RONO and our staff. Relations have been excellent.

J. M.: And what is their responsibility for you – are they your 'bosses'?

Y. S.: Yes. They are our immediate superiors.[1] Whatever happens we have to first report to them. And they report to the *glavka* [the city education office]. When it comes to inspections, say a 'frontal' (full) inspection, they are the ones who call us to account. If I need a telling off for bad work, it's the RONO's job to give it – they are my immediate superiors. They have never had to sort out trouble among the staff here; we've always had colleagues who work well together.

J. M.:   And who can inspect the work of your school? Is it the RONO only, or is there a city inspectorate or what?

Y. S.:   If a full scale inspection of every aspect of the whole school is to be done, the RONO plan for it.

J. M.:   Does that happen often?

Y. S.:   No. If we're talking about the sort of inspection where they look at absolutely everything, it's about once in five years. Or perhaps four. But 'thematic' inspections happen every year. Maybe this year they'll decide to inspect Russian, and next year maths. English is inspected *only* by the *city* authority, the GUNO, only the *Glavnoe uprav-lenie*. English is not inspected by our RONO. And if we give open lessons, day seminars, on English teaching, we do them for the city, not for the ordinary schools in our area. If the GUNO comes to us to inspect, the method is for five or six people to attend lessons, discuss and analyse them afterwards; then give a report saying what is good and what is bad. We take this into account and try to put things right.

J. M.:   And central inspection? Is there anything higher than the GUNO?

Y. S.:   No. We are inspected by these immediate superiors. If it went any higher it would be the State Committee, as it's called now. We are in a transitional phase at present; the State Committee was formed only a few months ago and some of the functions of the GUNO have been absorbed into it.

J. M.:   Tell me a little about the role of the *profsoyuz*, the teachers' professional association in the school.

Y. S.:   Well now, the *profsoyuz* is a school of Communism, so to speak, it is there to guard the rights of the teachers. If a situation of conflict arises – say, I dismiss a teacher without the assent of the *profsoyuz*, I can't do it. If a teacher feels unjustly treated in such cases, he can appeal to the union and they negotiate on his behalf with me – we have to sort it out together. And such things as being on duty in holiday time, to give another example, I cannot make up a duty roster on my own without consultation. It has to be signed both by me and the president of the union. Allocation of passes to holiday houses and treatment centres is all decided by the union. Sick pay is all arranged through the trade union too.

J. M.: And is one member of the teaching staff the secretary or convener? . . .

Y. S.: We call it the president. The person concerned is elected by open vote. And we elect a professional committe of five or six . . . If it's a big school, they may have a larger committee of eight or nine.

J. M.: Last Saturday the staff were voting for delegates to some conference or other . . .

Y. S.: Yes . . . we were electing delegates to a local conference, the function of which was to elect delegates to the All-Union Congress of Workers in Education, which will be taking place in December. We had the right to recommend one member of our staff as a candidate for election from the local area to the All-Union Congress, and we chose Marina Georgievna. All or most schools in the area will have put someone forward, and at the local conference two delegates will be elected by secret ballot.

J. M.: And what will they discuss at the national Congress? The new 'Conceptions'?

Y. S.: Yes . . . Every candidate will have to state his or her platform; what constructive proposals they have for the reform of education.

J. M.: One last question . . . Supposing you had complete freedom of action to bring about changes in this school or anywhere else, what would you do?

Y. S.: Well, since we are a school with a special programme in English, I would introduce more lessons of English. We carried out an inquiry by questionnaire among the children in the eighth class, and they said they thought four lessons a week in a school that set out to give an intensive programme in English was still not very much. Maybe I would make certain other subjects voluntary. I'd like better equipment and premises. And I would prefer the school to work on a five-day week. There's another very sore point. I have no answer to the attitude in our school towards productive labour. Where is the best place to run

> it, here or in the UPK [*Uchebno-pedagogicheskiy kom-binat*: a labour training centre serving several schools], and what jobs to offer training in ... I have a lot of thinking to do about this, and have no answer yet.

J. M.: Why is that a problem?

Y. S.: Well, they go to the UPK on one day a week, and what do they do? The sort of trade they learn there ... Some of them do metalwork and others work with wood, they learn joinery ... well, that doesn't satisfy our children, they aren't getting a worthwhile professional training. Something needs to be done about it, but what ...

I was able to discuss some of the same issues with a member of the senior management of my Leningrad school, and one or two of her remarks further amplify what Yevdokiya Stepanovna said in this interview. First, I had been able to make Yevdokiya Stepanovna understand exactly what was meant by the question about the way headships were advertised in the past and how potential heads made their interest in a particular post known. It was said by my Leningrad informant that this was not done formally, but simply by finding out about vacancies by jungle telegraph and then ringing up a few people who were likely to know something about the job, or who might be in a position to put in a good word. The many candidates seeking the headship of School 1937 all, apparently, let their interest be known in this entirely unofficial way.

It can, apparently, be difficult to fill vacant headships these days. One Leningrad school had a vacancy for a year before anyone could be found to fill it. The reasons suggested for this were that the salary differential was insignificant: the head's salary would be 350 roubles a month, while a deputy head was getting 317. Many teachers thought they would find the job of head a very responsible and difficult one, and very much less pleasant than teaching in the classroom.

Yevdokiya Stepanovna's problems and the issues worrying her would seem to be very much the major problems of Soviet education today. The resourcing of the school is a symptom of the underfunding of the whole education system which the government is now seeking to remedy by injections of further money. How to cope with six-year-olds is a matter which is referred to several times in this book. Incidentally, the apparently quite favourable staff:pupil ratio and the large number of English teachers are explained by the fact that English in a school with a special profile is taught in small groups of one third of the normal class size. The motivation of the children is a matter related to the curriculum and especially to decisions about allowing some specialisation in the senior classes of secondary school. She was obviously very relieved that some of the heat had gone out of the argument about the supposed élitism of schools like No. 1937, but I was disappointed not to hear a spirited defence of them from her: diplomat that she is, she was simply prepared to say that 'they' have obviously decided that the development of talent is an important task for such schools. As for vocational and labour training in school – it is scarcely surprising that she has no answer, since the whole system has been grappling with this problem off and on since the Revolution of 1917.

TRAINING OF HEADS AND THE JOB THEY TRAIN FOR

Very little has been published in English about the work of a Soviet school principal. In many ways it clearly resembles the job done by the director of schools in other countries. Yevdokiya Stepanovna referred in her interview to training courses for potential head teachers. A summary timetable has to come to hand from one of these courses.[2] It shows no more than the allocation of contact hours to the principal subject areas, but that in itself is interesting. The course lasts for two months, six hours a day and six days a week: education in the Soviet Union never seems to leave much time for reflection! Eighteen hours go on Marxist-Leninist theory and politics, but 190 hours are devoted to problems of school administration (management of classroom work and upbringing, extra-curricular activities, issues relating specifically to the primary phase, assessment of performance, record keeping and documentation, the head's financial responsibilities). There are thirty hours of 'psychology and ethics of school administration' and fourteen of law and administration. Four whole days are spent on practical activities in schools, and twelve hours are given up to 'individual work'. Apart from this, the vast majority of the sessions consists of lectures, and only eighty or so of the total 288 hours go on seminar and workshop activities.

Textbooks for such courses are available,[3] but far more interesting are some handout materials which have come my way. They were used on such courses in another republic (Estonia) a few years ago.[4] They contain over a hundred problematic situations which are intended as material for discussion, role-play and 'in-tray' exercises.

Many of them are very interesting indeed, and they both confirm the assumption that the problems of a head teacher are very similar the world over and illustrate special features of life in the Soviet Union which impinge upon the work of a school. Despite their date of compilation (ten years ago now) and their regional application, they undoubtedly throw light on what goes on in a Soviet headteacher's office.

First comes pupil discipline: truancy, skipping of lessons, detecting thefts from the cloakroom, rebelliousness, bullying, bad language, girls wearing revealing clothing, boys with facial hair, pupils refusing to obey instructions from a teacher and the like. Then there is pupil welfare: provision of free dinners for children from families with low incomes. Conflicts between pupils and teachers figure fairly prominently, and the problems outlined relate to such matters as disciplinary measures which pupils thought to be unfair or marks they considered to be unjustly awarded. Sometimes administrative error complicates these matters as in one case:

> A ninth-class pupil, Alexandrov, has worked badly all year. He was unable to redeem his unsatisfactory marks ['twos'] by the spring quarter; he was given three twos by the teachers' council and it was decided to make him repeat the year. The teacher of Russian did not know of this decision, agreed to test him again, and awarded him three ['satisfactory']. Then the boy's father appealed for the decision to be reconsidered, but the next teachers' council meeting would not be until August. In any case the boy's achievement in mathematics was minimal. What would you do?

Teacher appraisal, discipline and welfare figure prominently among the cases. Sometimes these are connected with the desire of an older teacher to be given more teaching periods before retirement in order to boost the pension. Sometimes they are disciplinary: one of the trickiest is about a teacher discovered to have been drinking with pupils on a school trip; mostly these problems relate to familiar matters like poor timekeeping or late submission of reports. 'Conflict situations', to use Yevdokiya Stepanovna's phrase, between teaching colleagues represent a major preoccupation of the author of these materials.

One or two of these difficult staff issues illustrate the fact that Soviet professionals see it as their duty to meddle in the personal affairs of colleagues in a way which would be unacceptable in the

England, where this one might be more likely to have been picked up by the school governors.

> The relationship between the male and female PE teachers has reached the stage where Kirillina has given birth to a daughter. The spouses of both work in this same school. Markov lives in the same flat as his wife, but they do not cohabit. Kirillina's husband knows nothing about what has been going on, though everyone else in the village is fully aware, and family life continues as usual, and other people have decided, it seems, to keep Kirillin in ignorance for the sake of his own happiness. A group of teachers is demanding to raise the matter in public. What should you do?

There are a number of cases dealing with the wise handling of administrative and caretaking staff; a secretary who takes advantage, arrives late and leaves early, an unsatisfactory caretaker, and an inefficient cleaner: 'You have been fined 20 roubles by the public health authorities for the dirty condition of your school building. It is the fault of a cleaner. What do you do?' Another case states: 'You have sacked the boilerman for drunkenness and it is minus twenty degrees outside. Both the assistant boilermen work only part-time, and cannot, by reason of their other employment, be on duty twenty-four hours a day as is necessary. What do you do?' There are welfare problems for both administrative and teaching staff, such as the allocation of free passes to convalescent homes or of a new flat. A few cases concern anonymous complaints made by disgruntled pupils, parents or staff to the media.

Some rather more special items reveal particular aspects of a Soviet director's work. Two of the cases concern the religious beliefs of pupils or teachers. The Soviet Constitution is supposed to guarantee freedom of belief, but it is well known that this provision (at least until very recently) has been honoured more in the breach than the observance:

> You believe that as a head teacher you know all your staff well. By chance you discover that an older teacher of the primary classes, is a Christian, an active member of a church congregation. In school she keeps herself to herself, but is conscientious and industrious. What ought the head to do?

And:

> The school is preparing for the New Year Fir-Tree Festival. In all

classes there have been lessons about old new year customs and atheistic education. On Christmas Eve the deputy head and the Pioneer leader stand by the door of the local church to prevent [sic!] children from attending the service. The minister [remember, this is Estonia] complains to the Education Department about their unworthy behaviour.

1. Assess the atheistic education of the school. 2. What ought the Education Department to do?

The first assignment here illustrates that rather touching naive faith that many Soviet educationists have in the power of education: namely, that if the atheistic propaganda in the school was properly done, no child would want to go to church.

Relations between the school and the 'base enterprise', the factory or business which is responsible for assisting the school in its polytechnical and labour education, do not figure very prominently among the problems for discussion in these materials, but this item occurs:

> The factory refuses to help the school financially, stating that the profitability of the enterprise is too low. What should the head do to make the factory fulfil its obligations?

Three of the cases involve illegal or doubtful practices, which one hopes are in fact rare in Soviet as in other schools:

> A quantity of white paint has been delivered to the school for redecoration. The painters are issued with 200 kilogrammes, which are locked up in a classroom. A few days later the clerk of the works reports that this white paint has been stolen. Nothing else has been taken. The police are unable to detect the offenders. The next day the clerk of works tells the head that he has reported the theft of 300 kilogrammes of paint and that he has been promised that this amount will be written off. He offers the head 20 kilos of white paint. What should the head do? There is no white paint in the shops. The school bursar has played no part in all this. The head has been in post five years, the bursar two.

Another source of information about the work of a Soviet head-teacher is, of course, the educational press. Articles will most likely deal with particularly difficult problems, so in looking at what is published, it should be remembered that the topics listed here are not meant to be equivalent to a typical day in the life of a head. During

1988 the following subjects were dealt with in a monthly education journal, in the section concerned with the work of school director.[5] Topics included international education, creating a united staff in a school, preventing drug abuse among schoolchildren, relations with the families of pupils, moral training, the induction and development of young teachers (three articles), pastoral matters (several articles), the certification of teachers, the extended day and intersubject links. In the first six months of 1989 the same journal devoted rather less attention to the work of heads, but one article dealt with the continuing education of heads, while two others were examples of good practice in the directors' study.

CONCLUSION: COMPARISON WITH ENGLAND

Comparison with the conditions of employment for head teachers in England at the present time[6] is instructive. English heads, like Yevdokiya Stepanovna, are responsible for the management of staff, liaison with teachers' unions, reviewing the work of the school, appraising, training and developing staff; they have to see to the academic progress of pupils, discipline and pastoral care (in Russian conditions, read 'upbringing work'); they must maintain relations with parents, other educational establishments, outside bodies and authority; they are responsible for the school's resources and premises. Whereas these duties correspond in the two countries, the accepted way of carrying them out differs. Children in England would never be allowed by trade unions such as NUPE and NALGO to clean the school! Heads would be held ultimately responsible for badly maintained premises, but not fined. Afternoon naps for six-year-olds are never thought of in England. Yevdokiya Stepanovna's problem with labour training has something in common with the English secondary head's concern with TVEI (Technical and Vocational Education Initiative) and other such ventures; close links with industry are encouraged, but have not reached the advanced stage which they have in the Soviet Union.

Parallel reforms relating to the financial management of schools will bring the work of directors in both countries closer together, as will the introduction of the national curriculum in England and Wales. Soviet schools do not have governors yet, but there have now been concrete proposals to introduce school councils (see Chapter 6).

The main differences[7] would seem to be, first of all, the fact that nearly all Soviet schools are all-age primary *and* secondary establish-ments, and the head as to be abreast of developments in all sectors of school education. This must considerably affect the nature of the job. Secondly, pre-service training for heads before appointment is vir-tually unknown; there is 'lip-service' to post-appointment training. A third major difference is the mode of appointment both of the head and her (or his) staff. Elections to a headship are entirely foreign to the English system. Whereas doubtless many workers in English schools might think it a very good idea, it seems most unlikely that governors and local authorities would ever relinquish their strangle-hold in this area. Appointment of teachers in England is no longer in the hands of heads alone, if indeed it ever was. Heads' conditions of employment, which have the force of law, give only the duty of *participating* in the appointment of staff. The reader will have noticed that, while Yevdokiya Stepanovna claimed to have the right to hire and fire staff, the right was not entirely unfettered: the trade union had some rights in the matter too.

Exactly what influence does the school director in the Soviet Union have on the development of the educational system, on changes in that system? No-one at present can answer that question. There is an interesting pointer in the interview with Yevdokiya Stepanovna. Most of her concerns were with the day-to-day running of the school; she seemed content also to accept policy decisions from above. It is notable, however, that when asked what she would do if she had complete freedom, she indicated that she would like to change the curriculum, in other words to do that which, on the face of it, the Soviet school director is *least* likely to be able to do. Moreover, though the changes she wished to make were generalised, they had their origin in the specific needs of the children in her particular school. Her wish may not be pure fantasy. For a start, it is possible that in discussion in the many pre-service and inservice training sessions and meetings with each other and with superiors heads create movements in educational opinion which ultimately influence the operation of the system. Moreover, the Provisional Statute (see Chapter 6, note 10) promises local schools new freedoms scarcely dreamed of a year or two ago.

13 The Teachers' Trade Union

The Role of the Professional Association in the Welfare of Education Workers

The term 'trade union' suggests to the Western reader an organisation, the primary function of which is to negotiate wages and salaries with management. In the public mind unions are perhaps associated with strikes or other forms of what has come to be called, by a strange euphemism, 'industrial action'. To the Western worker the union to which he belongs is an agency protecting his interests, to which he can turn if threatened with unfair dismissal or an unjustified cut in salary, which protects his pension interests and is concerned for his welfare, which sees to it that management is not neglectful of his safety at work and that it obeys the law in other ways. A trade union, as do the teaching unions in Britain, may seek to further the development of the industry or profession with which it is concerned in a more general way. The union can be used to promote a political cause which may not be connected with its basic purpose, such as a trade boycott of an unpopular foreign regime.

The traditional Soviet conception of a *profsoyuz* ('professional union') derives from Lenin's phrase, the 'transmission belts running from the vanguard to the mass of the advanced class, and from the latter to the mass of the working people'.[1] The implication of this is that the *profsoyuz* existed to pass the requirements down the line from the Party (the 'vanguard') to the workforce and to maintain labour discipline. In the same speech Lenin calls the trade unions 'a reservoir of the state power'. In a capitalist or mixed economy, on the other hand, the workers see the union as transmitting their demands to the employers. As with so many things in Soviet society, this difference is eroding. Strikes were, of course, known in Soviet industries before the massive industrial relations crises of the summer of 1989, and instigators have in the past been made to suffer by imprisonment or loss of employment, even when the cause has been recognised as in some measure justified. Moreover, memories of union behaviour under Stalin persist, and many still think of the *profsoyuz* as nothing more than another arm of Party or government.

Nevertheless, Western or at least British, trade unions share more than might be expected with their Soviet counterparts, as will be seen from the answers to questions transcribed below. This short chapter aims to illustrate the typical activities of the education workers' union in one school in the USSR. What follows is a transcript of an interview held in the school in Leningrad where I taught after leaving Moscow School No. 1937. The speakers are the present and former presidents of the professional association committee, Irina Zakharovna and Aleksandra Ivanovna.

J. M.:   Do all the teachers in your school belong to the *profsoyuz*?

I. Z.:   Practically all.

J. M.:   And what union is it?

I. Z.:   It is called the Union of Workers in Education, Higher Education, and Scientific Establishments, and membership is open to all who work in such places, whether as teachers, administrators or even cleaners. So the entire workforce within the school belongs to one union.

A. I.:   With the exception, by the way, of the canteen staff. The school dining room is a totally separate institution and is quite a different agency for employment.

J. M.:   What is the reason for virtually 100 per cent membership?

I. Z.:   The main motivation for joining the union is to do with sick pay. Union members receive a higher proportion of their salary, especially early in their years of service, if they are forced by illness to miss work.

J. M.:   What are your duties as president?

I. Z.:   In general, to represent the interests of our members in matters related to the running of the school. We don't plan the timetable or organise the teachers' duties – that's the job of the head and the school administrators – but the timetable and suchlike must be agreed with the union committee. And so must a teacher's workload ... A teacher's salary depends to some extent on the workload. Days off, leave and so on are all our concern.

A. I.:   I can add a few things. Officially the professional committee of the union has five general areas in which it should be active. They are: academic and pastoral work, out-of-school activities, work concerning the interests of the school staff, matters regarding the health of pupils and teachers, and the material and technical resourcing of the school.

J. M.: Now, you have mentioned the union 'professional committee', the *profkom* – presumably you mean the body through which the union works. How many serve on this committee?

I. Z.: Seven. A head or a deputy head cannot serve on it.

A. I.: But they can on a 'commission for industrial disputes'.

J. M.: Presumably that is set up when serious problems arise. Does that happen often?

A. I.: About once a year or less. A commission for disputes is quite separate from the professional committee of the union. If a teacher feels badly done to for some reason, they can ask for one to be set up. If they are not satisfied by its findings, they can ask for the *profkom* to reconsider the matter. If the two bodies disagree, the *profkom* has the last word and can overturn the decision of the commission.

J. M.: What other say do you have in the working of the school?

I. Z.: Our opinion is sought on the allocation of certain resources. The extent of this is limited. We wouldn't be allowed to get rid of a teacher and spend her salary on audio-visual equipment or anything like that, but there is a small amount of money . . .

A. I.: About 500 roubles a year.

I. Z.: And decisions on how to spend it are left to us . . .

A. I.: We're responsible to the *raykom* [The Party regional committee], by the way, for this money.

I. Z.: Yes, and it is for certain specified purposes, such as excursions, visiting speakers and the like. We can use it for what you might call 'welfare' purposes – material help in cases of hardship, death of a member of the family and so on.

A. I.: Returning to day-to-day administrative matters within the school, which teacher has what room may also be something we have to seek agreement about from our members.

J. M.: Some of these seem to be relatively minor concerns. What

	are your major responsibilities?
I. Z.:	One of them concerns the distribution of *putyovki*, free or partly-paid passes to sanatoria, treatment centres or convalescent homes. There are not many of these available, and they aren't distributed on a basis of so many per school, but within the local area. If anyone in our school has a health problem and needs a *putyovka*, we have to be reasonably well organised and put our bid in in good time.
A. I.:	Socialist competition is another duty of the union.
J. M.:	That is a concept I have heard of, but have never been too clear exactly what it means.
A. I.:	You aren't alone in that. Competition in a socialist society is something which might appear contradictory. The purpose of it is to stimulate everyone to better work, and raise the level of performance not just for the 'winner' of the competition, but for everybody.
J. M.:	Who is it that competes, then?
A. I.:	There can be socialist competition between teachers of a subject, between classes or between schools.
J. M.:	How might teachers compete?
A. I.:	It's sometimes hard to persuade them. The professional committee might suggest organising a competition, but if the teacher says 'No', then that's the end of it. But the sort of thing there might be is for the best subject room, for example – the most attractively arranged, the best organised and most educationally useful displays and so on. Or we sometimes have a competition for writing and preparing teaching materials: the best ideas and lesson plans for teaching a particular topic. We also have contests for the most imaginative use of visual aids or technical resources.
J. M.:	How might classes compete – the highest average marks, or something?
I. Z.:	Yes, but we also get them to compete in *vospitannost'*, good behaviour.
J. M.:	Who on earth would decide the winner?
I. Z.:	Oh, there would be a jury of teachers, and it would also depend on analysis of quarterly reports as well as the marks individual pupils received for specific subjects. *Vospitannost'* doesn't just mean good behaviour, but the existence of a nice atmosphere in a class; outings, excur-

sions, picnics and so on do help to create that among a group of pupils.

A. I.:   Another very important duty of the *profsoyuz* is to take an interest in our pensioners.

J. M.:   Retired people connected with the school? I've noticed them occasionally at special school occasions.

A. I.:   Yes, the *profkom* makes a point of seeing they are not forgotten and that they *know* they aren't forgotten. We remember their birthdays, invite them to parties and other school events. And when they get very old and aren't even able to do their own shopping, we make sure that somebody sees to it. Often the young Pioneers or the Komsomol do it as social and community service. The headmistress who was here during the blockade was looked after by colleagues and pupils until the day she died. And if the family cannot afford, or is unable to arrange the funeral – or maybe there is no family – the union sees to it. We receive a sum of money for this from the local committee and we collect the rest from colleagues. So, till the very end, they are members of the collective.

J. M.:   And do they pay a subscription?

I. Z.:   Yes. Five copecks a month!

J. M.:   Does the union committee have any disciplinary power?

A. I.:   None at all.

I. Z.:   That doesn't stop us trying. We can talk to difficult colleagues and reason with them.

A. I.:   That's true. We had a case recently when one teacher in the school was poisoning the atmosphere by extreme rudeness to other staff, sometimes in front of pupils. The effect on the school and on staff relations was appalling. The *profkom* has no right at all to deliver a reprimand, but in this case it gave the teacher concerned a talking to, in the hope that the damage could be limited.

J. M.:   And was it?

A. I.:   Yes, it was highly effective.

I. Z.:   But sometimes it has no effect whatever!

The present state of trade union law and the accepted practices of the unions have been built up over the decades since the Revolution, and it is scarcely necessary to say that they have varied according to the style of leadership of the nation and of the Party at the time. Public opinion – and worker opinion – in the USSR expresses itself in other ways than through 'industrial action'. Dissatisfied employees may write letters to Party agencies or to the press. They may leave their jobs to work elsewhere, they may become poor attenders at their place of employment, their productivity may be unsatisfactory or the quality of the goods they produce may be poor. Soviet management have been held responsible for all of these failings, and unions are expected to rub their noses in it if they make a mess of managing a concern.

A union of education workers probably has a different style of behaviour from a factory-based *profsoyuz*. Nevertheless, the various duties described by the women reported in this chapter conform closely to industrial practices.[2] All unions are concerned with welfare in general, most importantly health, sick pay and the well-being of pensioners. The attention paid in School 1937 to pensioners – former members of staff – was heartwarming. Working conditions are likewise important, and unions are expected to keep management up to the mark in this respect. They are responsible for 'socialist competition' in whatever industry they are active. They have a responsibility for education and upbringing in the broadest sense, which explains why they are obliged to take action if a school head teacher complains to them about the bad behaviour of the child of one of their members, as explained in Chapter 2. In the all-important matter of the resolution of conflict, efficient and determined Soviet trade unions have a very good record in protecting the livelihood of their members: well over half the disputes about dismissals which reached the courts even in the 1960s and 1970s (that is, 'conflict situations' which could not be resolved in the workplace itself) were decided in favour of the dismissed worker.

The staff-room notice-board in School 1937 had one section devoted to trade union matters. When I showed interest in this particular notice, it was explained that the figures mentioned in it were merely a plan, which did not represent reality in every respect! There was a list of 'socialist obligations accepted by the staff of School 1937', which included 'to admit sixty pupils to class 9' [out of seventy-eight in class 8],

> not to permit the selection [*otsev*, 'sifting'] of pupils; to send three pupils to the PTU and six to secondary education [presumably to transfer them to ordinary schools – is this not selection?]; to create

three 'extended day' groups making 105 pupils altogether; to admit 60 pupils to class 1; to generalise and disseminate [*obobshchit' i vnedrit'*] the experience of V. T. Goryachkina; to see to it that all pupils had textbooks, that clubs run, that 100 per cent of pupils had hot dinners; to broaden the pupils' horizons by encouraging them to enter Olympiadas [interschool academic competitions]; to arrange two 'subject weeks'; to give all material assistance and to get reports in on time.

These pious remarks are, it must be admitted, strongly reminiscent of the platitudes of the bad old days, and it is good to know that they are regarded as purely theoretical. They do, however, illustrate the work of the committee as described in the interview above. The most difficult task in view of the facilities at School 1937 is probably to ensure hot dinners for the pupils – at least, seeing to it that they actually are hot. In any case, children cannot be forced to eat the dinners if they do not want to. The figures for what is to happen to children at age 14–15 do not seem to add up, but to lose eighteen out of seventy-eight pupils to other types of establishment would be about average for a school at this stage. The 'obligations accepted' include the necessity to ensure adequate resourcing; just how the *profkom* could do this if textbooks were not available is difficult to see, but then Russians have ways of overcoming problems of that sort which remain mysterious to foreigners. There are elements of 'socialist competition'. The requirement to make known the experience of one particularly gifted teacher (actually of physics) is interesting.

This chapter has briefly illustrated the work of the education workers' union at school level, by simply reporting the remarks of two of the responsible officials in one particular school. Writers on the role of the *profsoyuz* in Soviet society, on the other hand, often refer to the 'democratic centralism' of the system, which means that real power is concentrated at the centre, and that the unions are subservient to the Communist Party. There is disagreement among Western observers as to how weak or strong Soviet unions are. However, a key word in Soviet political and social life is now 'democratisation', and if the devolution of power which this implies really comes to be, Irina Zakharovna and Aleksandra Ivanovna will be leading a higher level of worker participation in management than they are at present.

14 Future Good Men and Women

Moral Teaching in the School of Today

While visiting Soviet schools my opinion has often been sought about *vospitanie*, the 'upbringing' or moral education which schools provide. Could I, as a British educationist, suggest any measures which might improve the performance of Soviet teachers in bringing children up properly? (British pedagogues, restrain your ironic laughter.) This, for the Soviet teacher, is not just a matter of encouraging good behaviour in any trivial sense, of stopping pupils dropping litter or committing acts of minor vandalism, but of instilling moral qualities, the highest possible moral qualities, those worthy of the 'new Soviet person' which it is the aim of the education system to mould. Educators speak of being 'sculptors of personality' and of engaging in the all-round development of character, to use a phrase – perhaps even a cliché – which is heard everywhere in educational discussion. True, under *glasnost'*, questions have been asked even about this sacred cow. None the less, the notion that the school has a duty to instil a set of moral principles is not questioned, nor is it likely to be.

What, it may be asked, should a British educator say when asked how we instil moral values in our schools? It is possible, of course, to comment on the cultural assumptions behind the question. The principal one is that it is possible to carry out moral education in such a way that it can be almost totally successful, and this is, of course, a very Soviet point of view. Since Marxism-Leninism is 'scientific socialism', and can by definition be proved correct scientifically, then science must have the answer to the methodological problem of how to convince children that they ought to think and behave in certain ways, the ways specified by Marxist-Leninist thought. Not all Soviet teachers would put it like that, but many of them seem to accept that the Soviet child would be perfectible, if only they knew how to do it. British teachers, accustomed by centuries of Christian thought, are more receptive to the idea that people, including children and teachers, must be expected to fall drastically short of the ideal, and that success in moral education can only be relative.

It is vital to understand that in the Soviet school the ethical and moral aims of education are taken seriously by the teachers, are not an optional extra, are not an empty formality and are not seen as something divorced from the academic aims of education. This is not the same as saying that children are not resistant to moral education. Teachers subscribe to the idea of the 'unity of instruction and upbringing', by which the teaching of all subjects from mathematics to music has moral as well as academic content. The values the school is to impart are laid down by society; indeed they are included, many of them, in the Soviet Constitution.[1]

The ethical and moral upbringing aims are striven for both in class and outside.[2] The youth organisations, which are dealt with in Chapter 7, namely the Octobrists, Young Pioneers and the Communist League of Youth, play a large part. Extracurricular activities and clubs contribute too. Syllabuses in certain subjects in the curriculum are designed specifically to contribute to the instilling of these attitudes. But the teaching of *every* subject has to emphasise these values through the knowledge it conveys, the passages set for reading, the questions given for discussion and the interpretation of the facts presented. There is no secret about this and it is not a 'hidden' curriculum, but an openly tendentious one; a vast literature exists instructing teachers what to teach and how to teach it.[3] Doubtless many teachers in Britain and the West might fear that to say all this is to admit that the Soviet system of moral upbringing is little more than brainwashing. It is true that only one set of ethical ideals may be taught, and that these are presented as the only acceptable ones for an all-round developed Communist. Nevertheless, in these days of multi-cultural, anti-racist, non-sexist education, it should be remembered that schools in the West are expected to instil certain moral attitudes and would be severely criticised if they taught certain others. Soviet education goes much further, however, in seeking to mould political and philosophical attitudes.

THE QUALITIES OF A SOVIET CITIZEN

A great deal has been written recently[4] about moral education in Soviet schools, which it would be tedious to repeat here in great detail. Let us, however, first look at the characteristics of a 'new

Soviet person' and then see how the presentation of these qualities impinges upon the attention of a visitor to School 1937.

The model product of the moral education in a Soviet school is both a patriot and an internationalist. He or she is supposed to love the Soviet Union because it is the first socialist state in the world and thus embodies the aspirations of the working class universally. To love Russia (or whatever republic the person concerned belongs to) and one's native region is also considered proper and is encouraged by teachers. People should know the culture of their nation and be aware of its scientific achievements. To be an internationalist and to work for peace is also good; one motto of the Communist movement is, after all, 'Workers *of the world* unite'. Another feature of the Soviet citizen is to remember the sacrifices made in order to establish and defend the Soviet Union, most especially in the Revolution and Civil War and later in the Great Patriotic (or Fatherland) War, as the East European theatre of the Second World War is significantly called.

Good Soviet citizens are intended to be sober, incorruptible and conscientious both in study and at work. They should be interested in extending their awareness of all branches of knowledge, and should be educated both aesthetically and scientifically. They are not supposed to be individualistic, but to seek fulfilment working as a member of a team. They should have sound knowledge of the law and of the duties, responsibilities and privileges of citizens. They should know quite a lot about modern industry and about the craft and skills of those who work within it; children should themselves have some experience of such work. Equally important, because it is in the interests of society for them to do so, they are meant to show progressive working attitudes and be technologically minded. Courage and inventiveness are qualities which are regarded with approval. Physical fitness is not merely a fad for a certain type of sports-minded person, but a political obligation – playing games fosters the collective spirit, exercise makes it less likely that the person concerned will have to call upon the health services, and sporting activity induces courageous and adventurous behaviour.

In their personal lives, model Soviet citizens should be disinclined to seek material wealth or to heap up personal possessions. *Potrebitel'stvo*, a Russian word usually rendered somewhat misleadingly as 'consumerism' in official Soviet translations, is regarded as a vice of capitalism. One British scholar has translated the word as 'commodity fetishism', since it means desire for (usually unobtainable) consumer goods.[5] 'New Soviet people' should be well behaved in public; they should be considerate of and show respect for others, a state which not all have attained. They should be in favour of and do their best to maintain stable marriage (which is no longer considered a 'bourgeois' virtue) understanding in their treatment of the opposite sex and solicitous for the raising of the new generation.

More specific political and philosophical attitudes are intended to be part of the Communist personality. People should have a Marxist-Leninist worldview with all which that entails: respect for the Communist Party, a dialectical-materialist and scientific attitude and they should be militantly atheistic. Statements of the required aspects of a Communist personality have traditionally included 'respect for state property and resources', and in recent years a new one has been emphasised: a conservationist attitude to the environment and natural resources.

If it were possible for Soviet teachers to instil these qualities completely, education would be the solution for many, possibly all, of the ills of society. Crime, vandalism and dishonesty would be no more. The Soviet family would be firm as a rock. There would be an end to political disillusionment and social fragmentation, not to mention dissatisfaction with low salaries and the non-availability of consumer goods. Teachers fail in some measure to do this, which would seem to an outsider to be only to be expected, since the aim is unattainable one hundred per cent. This is, however, regarded with dismay by many citizens and with equal dismay and self-critical attitudes by many teachers. Of course, they try very hard. How is the moral upbringing work of School 1937 obvious to the visitor? How is one made aware that the business of turning children into new Soviet people is being taken seriously?

VISIBLE *VOSPITANIE* IN SCHOOL 1937

The moral content of education in the Soviet school is omnipresent. If one reads the statements of aims for the teaching of every subject in the curriculum, it can immediately be recognised that moral and ideological aims are to be found in all of them – even technical drawing. Geography fosters an internationalist attitude, biology a materialist belief in evolution, social studies and history conviction of the correctness of peaceful Soviet policies, and so on. *Vospitanie* goes on in class, in clubs and societies and in the youth organisations. In what ways does it impinge on the consciousness when one is inside School 1937? Here are some examples.

A regular feature of lessons, and here I am thinking mainly of foreign language lessons where I have frequently witnessed this type of work, is the moral assessment of human behaviour. The characters in stories which the children read in their textbooks are often the subject of ethical discussions. Why did he act in this way? Was it right to do so? Was the character loyal and courageous or did he take the easy way? In one sixth-year English lesson, the text was from Enid Blyton's *The Naughtiest Girl in the School*. 'I cannot tell you anything about this author', said the teacher, apparently unaware of the poor reputation Blyton enjoys among British teachers or of her popularity with children. It can nevertheless be confidently asserted that the clear moral attitudes of a Blyton story are very much what Soviet teachers want for children of that age. With older pupils I both witnessed and gave lessons in English where the topic for discussion was the friendship of Engels and Marx. My colleague used the material as a starter for a protracted and very interesting discussion of the nature of friendship, the virtues necessary in a good friend and the weaknesses which lead to the collapse of friendship. The content of this lesson was highly moral; nevertheless, pupils participated with great enthusiasm. My attempt later to emulate the performance with a different group was not a total failure, but was certainly less successful – probably because I felt a little too diffident to handle what seemed to me to be a slightly ticklish topic with the confidence which a Russian teacher would have brought to it. Reading material was obviously chosen with possible ethical discussion in mind, and not only so that the teacher could point out the evils of capitalism, though this would have been possible in the case of two other stories I read with classes, O. Henry's 'No Story' (a short story which could be seen as raising issues of social responsibility under capitalism) and Arthur Hailey's *The Final Diagnosis* (one of his popular novels with a serious side, in this case concerning the duties of the medical profession to patients in the context of a need to be 'accountable' to the notabilities who form the board of management of a hospital). Even the youngest children in Russian language and literature lessons are called upon to comment on the moral characteristics of the personages in fairy stories.

Respect for the revolutionary past of the country is, of course, engendered in lessons of all sorts, especially history and literature, as well as in the Pioneers and Komsomol. Festivals recalling the events

of the past are celebrated at school; a Pioneers' parade was held in
the assembly hall a few days before School 1937 broke up for the 7
November holiday. At the same time of year the tenth class were
reading in English an extract from John Reed's *Ten Days That Shook
The World*, in which the author described the burial on Red Square
of those who died in the Revolution in Moscow. I took this lesson
jointly with the class's regular teacher, who did not stress too
emphatically the political message. Her comment to me afterwards
was, 'I don't know what you think of that passage, but it struck me as
sad that an American journalist could write so optimistically of a new
dawn for the Russian people in 1920 – and we're still waiting for it to
come in 1988.'

Memories of the 1941–45 War are treated very positively in all
schools, not least No. 1937. The work of the club *Poisk* in keeping
alive memories of the War by contacting veterans of the defence of
Moscow has been mentioned in Chapter 11. The school has a
'museum', consisting of several well-maintained display boards in the
concourse area on floor 3, devoted to the battle of Moscow. In my
Leningrad school research into its wartime history had been undertaken with great enterprise and energy, and I was fortunate to be
there when a new museum was opened devoted to the life of the
school and its staff and pupils during the Siege. A number of
fascinating photographs had been unearthed and the recollections of
older people collected. Much of the effort was concentrated on
finding out as much as possible about one particular hero of the
resistance, an undercover agent who appeared to be working for the
Germans while in fact he was organising sabotage against their cause.
This aspect of moral education – the provision of heroes to admire –
is not treated squeamishly in Soviet education. Here at least the cult
of personality is felt to be a good thing.

And what about peace education, you may ask? As Wendy
Rosslyn concludes, 'peace' in the Soviet Union is conceived in social
and political terms, not as a matter of personal relevance or as
referring to the resolution of conflicts within the self; peace education
is also to support Soviet foreign policy.[6] The year begins on 1
September with a 'peace lesson', which is intended to make children
aware of the need to 'struggle for peace', as the Soviet expression has
it. It is no easier for the Soviet teacher to strike the 'correct' balance
between honouring war dead and promoting the cause of peace than
it is for teachers anywhere else. That there is a tension in this matter
is not in dispute, for complaints occasionally reach the press that

peace is stressed in schools at the expense of honouring the fallen. Children sing and even compose songs about peace, they produce poems and paintings on the subject. The International Friendship Club is very popular. To some extent at least, the matter of peace must have caught the imagination of the children.

The International Friendship Club is, of course, also an indication of the fostering of internationalism in the school. Visitors from abroad, by the very nature of things, often find their way to the meetings of such clubs, and it is perhaps difficult to assess whether the excellent attendances at the meetings are due to the presence of real foreigners. The meetings often present the opportunity for the performance of songs and dances from other countries. The style of the meetings is sometimes not unlike an evangelical meeting, being interspersed with community singing of songs rather than hymns ('We shall overcome' is popular) and miscellaneous poetry readings, and having a main item (sermon?) such as a talk by or a discussion with a visitor. It is well for the visitor to know the sort of remarks with which to respond to the little speeches of the pupils; one quickly learns. Bearing in mind that travel abroad is such a rare privilege, the meetings certainly encourage interest in foreign cultures. This is paralleled by a corresponding determination in the school to present the cultural heritage of Russia and of other Soviet peoples. It is not just in the art and music lessons that painting and song play a part; they are used in language teaching (native and foreign) too. Again, this is not an empty jingoism, but an opportunity to teach children to value the art of their own and other countries, both past and present.

In view of the nationwide celebrations of the millennium of the conversion of Russia to Christianity, which took place in 1988, it may be easy to forget that atheistic education is taken very seriously.[7] Party leaders and Church dignitaries appeared on the same platform in the Moscow Kremlin and television current affairs programmes sometimes contain items of Church news presented without hostile comment. But the state is still militantly atheistic. Though Marx and Engels were not unsympathetic to the masses who found religion a necessary 'opium' with which to deaden the pain of backbreaking labour, Lenin was strongly hostile to religion, and especially to those intelligent modern priests who could make Christianity acceptable to the educated and defend its propositions intellectually. Religion in the USSR is not only a matter of Christianity, of course, and in residually Christian areas Orthodoxy is not the only denomination, although traditionally it is the Russian Church, and before the

Revolution it was in fact illegal for any Orthodox Christian to renounce his Church and join another. One fairly hostile, but interesting, critique of Orthodoxy was published in the millennial year of 1988,[8] and the author commented upon the Church's desire to present itself as the guardian of national tradition and to arouse interest among 'that part of the population which does not possess sufficient political maturity and atheistic conviction'. Pointing to 'sound progress in undermining the spread of religion', he comments that the Church is in a 'contradictory' condition, in which there is a hiatus between the sophisticated level of contemporary Orthodox theology and the low intellectual level of many believers.

Head-on attacks on religion are no longer felt to be appropriate in Soviet society or in the schools. The sort of attempted coercion of children by head teachers and their deputies referred to in Chapter 12 is now probably less common than it once was. Young atheist clubs exist in some places (not in School 1937, as it happens). Youth organisations have a programme of anti-religious activity. Syllabuses still contain much material which is or is believed to be atheistic in tendency. Apart from this, I have to say that I encountered little direct evidence in School 1937 of what actually went on in this field, and I did not seek to raise the issue myself. It was once raised with me by some pupils: how, they wanted to know, did British children relate to religion? One of these girls bewailed the difficulty of persuading her grandmother that God did not exist. 'I've proved it to her scientifically, but she gets angry and starts shouting at me!' On another occasion my own church connections had come up casually in conversation with a colleague, though I did not pursue the matter. However, a few days later, during one of the breaks, Marina was gazing out of the window at children playing outside. 'Tamara tells me you asked whether any of our children believed in God', she commented. I certainly had not asked this question, but indicated that I would be interested to know the answer. 'Well, there is one boy who does. That's him down there playing football.' She clearly believed she had the answer to my imagined question exactly.

Success in inculcating the work-ethic must vary considerably from school to school; in School 1937 it was, on the surface, very good. The children were for the most part highly achievement-oriented and ambitious, they sought good marks and were punctual for lessons – the lessons they attended, that is. There was certainly a problem of skipping lessons, those which the senior pupils did not think were important to them. Here we have the crux of the matter: motivation to attend and work hard was probably not due to any ideological assent to the need to develop one's personality all round, but to a perception of what was essential to achieve future goals. The same can be said about the labour education: was it really achieving moral aims of inducing respect for the craft of the artisan, knowledge of modern industrial processes and developing a taste for cooperative working? The workshops as they were in School 1937 would not develop knowledge of modern anything, and sessions at the inter-school production centre where more advanced training went on were felt by some senior pupils to be an activity which could be dropped when academic pressure was strong.

The more specifically political education of School 1937 has been dealt with in Chapter 7. Mention of the physical fitness of the children may seem like an irrelevant footnote to a chapter on moral upbringing, but this is not so. We have already seen the importance of what the Soviets call 'physical culture' to society, and it is the duty of the new Soviet person to keep fit and therefore healthy, to be therefore ready to do a good day's work and, if necessary, defend the State against attack and avoid being a drag on the health services. School 1937 was scarcely equipped to foster a high degree of physical achievement in the pupils. As we have seen, the gym was small and unsatisfactory, and the outdoor sports area almost non-existent. I enquired about the national system for the improvement of physical fitness known as the GTO (the initials stand for *gotov k trudu i oborone*, 'Prepared for Labour and Defence'). This series of standards is incorporated into school physical culture programmes, but none of the pupils I asked showed the least interest in gaining the certificates: 'They are not very important to us.' Maybe the difficulty of achieving anything in the conditions of that particular school acted as a disincentive.

IS THE MORAL UPBRINGING IN SCHOOL 1937 A SUCCESS?

Readers may consider this analysis of the many components of Soviet moral education to be an inherent absurdity. We do not judge a man morally by saying, 'He is nice to his grandmother, but not very good at running the hundred yards or preaching atheism.' It seems unlikely that they do this even in the Soviet Union. We are much more likely to make a global judgement on a person's character, awarding something between an overall alpha and a gamma minus, and perhaps afterwards being specific about particular aspects of personality. Though I did not set out in this chapter to make such specific judgements in the case of School 1937, it will be obvious from some of the above remarks what they are likely to be. What about the overall assessment? It must have an alpha in it at the very least. It is impossible to know how completely the pupils assimilate official political values – which are in a state of flux at present anyway. However, their ability to relate in a mature manner to adults without losing their independence, the good humour of the place, the general attitude to work, the feeling of belonging to a team – all of these outweigh any insufficiencies which may be detected in the carrying out of official programmes of moral education, or misdemeanours committed by individual pupils. For this, the staff must be largely responsible, and they must have the support of parents. The children are, on the whole, a credit to both parties.

In Conclusion

The purpose of this book has been to describe and discuss School No. 1937, not primarily to sustain an argument about the entire system of education. The portrait must stand on its own. Either it is convincing to the reader, or it is not. In these concluding lines I shall make one or two points which relate to the entire experience of teaching in the School. I intend also to look at what people (including myself) were writing about Soviet schools a few years ago, to see whether we must revise our opinions in view of recent developments.

Teaching at School 1937 was an immensely enjoyable experience, because of the excellent spirit on the staff and the warmth and enthusiasm of the boys and girls. A great strength of the Soviet system, which it is easy to think of as little more than administrative detail, is the fact that primary and secondary education have not been as rigidly separated from each other as they have in Britain. Indeed, in England the division may go even further: schools are organised for children aged five to eleven, next eleven to sixteen, and then sixteen to eighteen, not to mention the various schemes for middle schools which hack up the school life of the child into quite separate pieces. This then creates a new educational industry dealing with the 'problems' of primary-secondary transfer. In the Soviet Union, there doubtless are problems caused by the change of teaching style at the age of ten, but at least the child still goes to the same familiar building and sees his or her former teachers around the place. The primary and secondary staff know and work with each other, they overlap to some extent and work in both sectors, the school director and her or his deputies have to be proficient in both, hostility and suspicion arising out of ignorance of the other's job are minimised.

The 'feminised' atmosphere, which is due to the almost totally female staff, dedicated and expert though the teachers undoubtedly are, is something of a drawback. Children and adolescents need to work with adults of both sexes, and they should learn to relate to both men and women at school. It is a shame that Soviet men, or Russian men at least, regard the teaching profession as a job for women; this reflects badly upon the attitudes which have got abroad in society. It cannot be good for the female teachers to work almost exclusively with other women, nor for the men to be so isolated in what appears to be a woman's world. Those who seek to break down sex-role stereotyping have a virgin forest to fell in the USSR.

Throughout this book I have referred to the poor building and inadequate resources of School 1937 and said more than once that it deserves much better. How important is this, and does it really matter? When I was a young teacher thirty years ago, we did not have the technological aids in foreign language teaching which exist today – tape recorders, video, projectors, visual aids and glossy textbooks. We got on as best we could in bare classrooms with nothing but the book, the chalk and the board. (In teaching Russian, moreover, the book was very likely to be most unsuitable.) We managed quite well in the educational context of the time; knowing nothing else, we made do and made progress. I would, however, not make too much of a virtue out of this. *Of course* a teacher alone without technological aids in front of a class in a simple teaching room can do excellent work. But in the modern age, when so many better things can be available, it is a pity when good teachers are having to make do for decades on end with poor rooms, poor equipment and a limited choice of books, which in some cases so bore the pupils that they are disinclined to read them. The opportunities offered to a teacher by good teaching materials and conditions are worth every extra copeck.

Like Natasha, the colleague who consulted me as described at the beginning of Chapter 11, I have always believed that a good school has a lot to offer pupils outside the classroom, and that a good schoolmaster or schoolmistress becomes involved with the cultural, recreational or sporting activities of pupils. It was a matter of regret to me that School 1937 seemed to have relatively few clubs and societies of its own. Most of those the school had did appear to be enjoyed and supported by pupils. The logic of concentrating sports coaching in outside centres and gathering interested musicians and artists in the Pioneer Houses (and talented ones in the musical and arts schools) makes sense in one way, but in another it removes an important dimension from the life of the school itself, which is regrettable. More contact with the pupils in activities of this kind would surely make easier and more effective the task of *vospitanie*, which is held so important in the Soviet school.

The curriculum of School 1937 has an odd feature with some unexpected consequences. Here is a school of over 600 pupils, dedicated to the teaching of English as a priority – *everyone* makes a special study of English. There is no comparable stress on any other subject in the school, and hardly any opportunity to use the few periods set aside for optional subjects to develop an interest in any

other curriculum area. Yet in all three top classes only *one* pupil
wants to go on to study English at college. Any English teacher of
older classes would imagine this to be a recipe for absolute disaster
and would expect to see disaffection, complaints, truancy and
wholesale transfer of pupils to other institutions where they got a
'better' deal. Now, it has been noted that older young people in the
school are apt to become rather selective in the lessons they attend,
labour and military training being particular targets of displeasure.
Some pupils transfer to other schools at fifteen if they are not getting
on well with their English, but not many. None the less, the complete
uniformity of the academic curriculum is, surprisingly, not a subject
of bitter complaint. The pupils recognise the language qualification as
a valuable adjunct to their eventual careers. They do not feel
deprived in regard to the subjects they want to study at university,
probably because of the fact that there is a fresh start at age
seventeen in higher education: no-one expects them to come to
university after a specialist (in English terms 'sixth-form') education
in two or three major subjects. How this will change if and when the
curriculum is differentiated in the last years of secondary education
remains to be seen.

* * *

One of the great attractions of the study of the education system of a
vigorous society is to observe constant change and development, the
ebb and flow of controversy. It is not much good waiting until the
schools 'settle down' before writing a book; one would wait for ever.
My lectures, especially those on British schooling to foreign students
of comparative education have to be rewritten extensively every year.
Looking at what has been published in recent years about Soviet
education, it is interesting to see which of the developments mentioned in Chapter 6 were anticipated and which not expected.[1] In
1978 John Dunstan[2] reported the vigour of the egalitarian tradition in
Soviet education, but wisely warned against underestimating the
'resilience of the trend' towards differentiated schooling, which at
that time accounted for less than 2.7 per cent of the schools by his
own estimate. In 1989, having weathered an outburst of hostility
towards schools with special profiles, we are now seeing the vindica-
tion of these schools.

    None of us foresaw present moves towards decentralisation.
Mervyn Matthews[3] believed education would probably continue to

be dictated from on high. Nigel Grant[4] scarcely considered the possibility, but was of the opinion that decentralisation would only lead to greater discrepancies in the standards of schooling. I would have shared their view, and confess I am still sceptical as to how far local and institutional autonomy will be allowed to get, despite what is promised, since the notion of central authority seems so deeply engrained in the Soviet consciousness. Nevertheless, national unrest in some of the republics and the desire of the centre to appease the complainants may well strengthen the elements of republican autonomy which already exist in the educational system. Just as Scottish and Welsh nationalism in the United Kingdom tends to lead to cries for more autonomy from some of the English regions, areas of Russia too may establish their claim for more freedom of action in the schools. It will be pointed out that in England and Wales education is moving away from regional autonomy at present. This is true, but England would have to move very much further in that direction before it met Russia coming the other way.

The same could be said about differentiation in the curriculum of the general school. England has traditionally had a very high degree of specialisation in the last two years of school, allowing the universities to achieve high standards in relatively short, usually three-year, courses. Scotland has traditionally opted for a broader curriculum. Russia has eschewed specialisation at school, and its university courses are staggeringly high in content hours and broad in curriculum. Now England, after decades of false starts and fierce resistance in certain quarters, is talking of broadening curricula, while the Soviet Union speaks of 'profound differentiation'. The two countries in this instance too are moving in opposite directions from the two extremes – but will they meet in the middle? I think not. In both countries the force of tradition will be hard to resist. Dora Shturman's book, written by a former school director who emigrated to Israel, illustrates through her own personality how strong the force of Soviet tradition can be. While cautiously accepting notions of freedom in education, she clearly dreads its turning into 'chaos', and it seems doubtful that the educational philosophy of many Soviet teachers could easily accept present moves in the Soviet Union.[5]

Several writers have cast doubt on the effectiveness of the political education or indoctrination delivered to young people. Ten years ago Grant reported that some Marxist-Leninist educators were critical of the success of the dogmatism of their colleagues and were being thoroughly castigated for their opinion.[6] Matthews found them 'not very successful' in inculcating acceptable values.[7] I have been critical of the notion that children could be taught to think for themselves and at the same time necessarily assent to correct ideological attitudes,[8] and I was fairly sure in my own mind that the latter would prevail. What I saw in School 1937 was encouraging and suggests I was wrong. There were, it is true, some traces of old attitudes appearing in a new form – a pupil being corrected for not producing views reflecting the 'new' way of thinking. Nevertheless, while there was no ideological unorthodoxy, there was what I believed to be a new spirit of honesty and frankness in many of the teachers – well, the only word for it is openness, *glasnost*'! I saw much less evidence than ever before of a teacher 'settling' a discussion by presenting the official view, and frequent evidence that Soviet education in that school was moving into an era when teachers genuinely desire to teach children to think for themselves.[9]

* * *

Two months is not a very long time to work in a school and to build up relationships with young people. Yet, how easy it was to get through to the pupils in School 1937! The warmheartedness of the Russian people is one of their most endearing features. When I left the school, I was given a trunk-load of farewell presents from classes and individuals. These included little articles the children had made themselves, postcards with friendly messages, one or two scrolls inscribed in comic mock Old Russian, albums containing photos of the members of a class, an enormous red flag with hammer and sickle and covered with expressions of good will, a tape of songs recorded by the school folk group, posters inscribed 'To Sir With Love' and 'From Russia With Love' (how they knew about James Bond I do not know), and several beautiful books, many of them bearing quite touching inscriptions. I treasure them all, but one gift in particular both impressed and surprised me. It was a school notebook containing eight translations (by seven different pupils – one boy had made two versions) into Russian of eight lines of Shakespeare, beginning,

> He that is thy friend indeed
> He will help thee in the need.

This is from *Sonnets to Sundry Notes of Music VI*, the poem which begins: 'As it fell upon a day . . .' The pupils were in the eighth class, aged fourteen or so. It was amazing to me that seven out of the twelve in the group had been sufficiently interested to attempt such a translation. They were all in different forms; one of the most striking had kept Shakespeare's metre and rendered the meaning of each couplet in Russian that, to my ears, is not without 'punch' and distinction. It is greatly to the credit of the teacher that she could inspire them to attempt the difficult task of translation. The little book was the final piece of evidence which convinced me, if I needed convincing, of the intellectual liveliness, artistic values and seriousness of academic purpose of School 1937.

Notes and References

1 Day of the Teacher

1. *Pravda* for 7 February 1987, quoted by Wilson, A. and Bachkatov, N., *Living with Glasnost* (London: Penguin, 1988), pp. 80 and 239, stated that 30 per cent of the pensioners in Moscow continued to work after the normal retirement age.
2. Though even the second of the following works in English recommended here is slightly out of date and the former is very much so, both contain useful information about the subject: Adams, A. E., 'The Role, Status and Training of Teachers in the USSR', in King, E. J. (ed.), *Communist Education* (London: Methuen, 1963), pp. 97–123; Grant, N., 'Communist Countries' in Goodings, R. *et al.* (eds), *Changing Priorities in Teacher Education* (London: Croom Helm, 1982), pp. 44–64.
3. See 'The CPSU: the guiding force in Soviet Society', ch. 4 of Smith, Gordon B., *Soviet Politics* (London: Macmillan, 1988), 54–91, esp. p. 63.
4. Smith, p. 62.
5. 'From the CPSU Council of Ministers', *Soviet Education*, v. 28, no. 1, 1985–86, pp. 33–42.
6. Gosudarstvennyy komitet SSSR po statistike, *Narodnoe khozyaystvo SSSR za 70 let. Yubileynyy statisticheskiy ezhegodnik*, (Moscow: Finansy i statistika, 1987).
7. Lane, D. and O'Dell, F., *The Soviet Industrial Worker. Social Class, Education and Control* (Oxford: M. Robertson, 1978), pp. 73–7.
8. 'From the CPSU . . .' (see note 5 above), p. 39.
9. The Soviet educational press describes teachers as possessing various titles, some of which are outlined in Denisova, M. A., *Lingvostranovedcheskiy slovar'. Narodnoe obrazovanie v SSSR*, (Moscow: Russkiy yazyk, 1978).

2 The Children

1. An account of Soviet press coverage of the controversy is available in English: 'Special schools cater to élite's children', *Current Digest of the Soviet Press*, vol. 39, no. 8, 1987, pp. 1–5, 14 and 20.
2. Smith, H., *The Russians* (London: Sphere Books, 1976), pp. 187–8.
3. Petrovskiy, N. A., *Slovar' russkikh lichnykh imen* (Moscow: Sovetskaya entsiklopediya, 1966).
4. Interestingly enough, these strictures apply to some extent to Deana Levin, author of *Children in Soviet Russia* (London: Faber, 1942), who was, of course, not Soviet, but who seemed on the evidence of her book to have absorbed 1930s Soviet ways of doing things. See pp. 18–37 in particular.

3 The Premises

1. During 1987 criticism in the press of schools with a special profile was rampant. The matter is referred to in greater detail elsewhere in this book, especially in Chapter 12. See also note 1 to Chapter 2.
2. The second week of my stint at School 1937 coincided with the visit to the Soviet Union of the then Secretary of State for Education and Science, Kenneth Baker. Mr Baker gave a lesson in English poetry in the flagship of the 'English' schools, School No. 31. David Gow of the *Guardian* visited both this and School 1937. In the issue of 5 October 1988 he wrote: School 1937 'stands drab and bedraggled . . . It lacks the equipment School 31 takes for granted'. Though he commented, probably correctly, that 'both . . . are supposedly neighbourhood schools; both are élitist in their own way', his interesting piece underlined the fact that the resourcing of schools of the same type, even within the capital city, varies considerably.
3. For example, *Uchebno-material'naya baza obshcheobrazovatel'noy shkoly. Sbornik dokumentov* (Moscow: Prosveshchenie, 1984). This handbook contains dozens of pages of lists of essential furniture and teaching equipment as well as the official orders and instructions relating to them.
4. 'Finansirovanie: problemy ostayutsya', *Narodnoe obrazovanie*, no. 4, 1989, pp. 173–4.

4 The Story So Far

1. There have been a number of works in English which contain a general description of the Soviet system of schooling. In view of the present ferment in Soviet education (see Chapter 6), all of these are out of date in matters of detail, but still contain useful information. See in particular Grant, N., *Soviet Education*, 4th edn (Harmondsworth: Penguin, 1979); Tomiak, J. J., *Soviet Education in the 1980s* (London: Croom Helm, 1983); a Soviet textbook by a former education minister is Prokof'ev, M. A., *Narodnoe obrazovanie v SSSR* (Moscow: Pedagogika, 1985).
2. Henze, J. (ed.), *Halbjahresbericht zur Bildungspolitik und pädagogischen Entwicklung in der DDR, der UdSSR, der VR Polen, der CSSR und der VR China, 2. Halbjahr 1986* (Bochum: Ruhr-Universität, 1987), p. 36.
3. 'The Family', *Current Digest of the Soviet Press*, vol. 39, no. 12, 1987, p. 15.
4. I am indebted for some of these insights to members of a group of experienced primary school teachers from more than one country with whom I visited Soviet schools in 1987.
5. A recent very full and reliable report in English on the schools with intensified instruction is Dunstan, J., 'Gifted Youngsters and Special Schools', in Riordan, J. (ed.), *Soviet Education: the Gifted and the Handicapped* (London: Routledge, 1988), pp. 29–69.
6. See Rosslyn, W., 'Peace Education in the Soviet Union' in Avis, G.,

The Making of the Soviet Citizen (London: Croom Helm, 1987), pp. 161–83.

7.   'Tipovaya instruktsiya ob ekzamenakh', *Narodnoe obrazovanie* no. 2, 1986, pp. 100–2.
8.   See, for example, the official translation of the 1984 'Guidelines for Reform of General and Vocational Schools', in *USSR: New Frontiers of Social Progress*, (Moscow: Novosti Press Agency, 1984), pp. 50–78: 'Teachers . . . must help [pupils] to think independently' (p. 60).

5   The Curriculum

1.   The theory of the Soviet curriculum is dealt with in much greater detail in 'The Content of Education: What and Why', ch. 2 of Muckle, J., *A Guide to the Soviet Curriculum* (Beckenham: Croom Helm, 1988), pp. 22–33. Full details of all subject syllabuses are to be found in that book.
2.   Information on schooling for children with special educational needs may be found in Riordan, J. (ed.), *Soviet Education: the Gifted and the Handicapped* (London: Routledge, 1988).
3.   The evidence is presented in a report by J. Henze: see Chapter 4, note 2.
4.   An account in English of methods for teaching reading to Russian-speaking children may be read in Downing, J., 'Reading Research and Instruction in the USSR', *Reading Teacher*, vol. 37, no. 7, 1984, pp. 598–604.
5.   The evidence for this statement may be found in Zverev, I. D. and Kashin, M. P., *Sovershenstvovanie soderzhaniya obrazovaniya v shkole* (Moscow: Prosveshchenie, 1985), pp. 62–3.
6.   I have visited an 'English school' (not in Moscow) where the head stated quite openly that a test was administered for this purpose.
7.   The Marxian idea of 'polytechnical education' has caused difficulty for Soviet educators at different times in Soviet history. A recent brief account in English of the present interpretation appears in Muckle, *A Guide to the Soviet Curriculum*, pp. 34–44. See also Smart, K. F., 'The Polytechnical Principle' in King, E. J. (ed.), *Communist Education* (London: Methuen, 1963), pp. 153–76.

6   Glasnost', Perestroyka and the School

1.   Private communication.
2.   'Guidelines for Reform of General and Vocational Schools', in *USSR: New Frontiers of Social Progress* (Moscow: Novosti Press Agency, 1984), pp. 50–78.
3.   One of the best treatments of the 'Guidelines' is Dunstan, J., 'Soviet Education Beyond 1984: a Commentary on the Reform Guidelines', in *Compare*, vol. 15, no. 2, 1985, pp. 161–87. Dunstan's article is complemented by another well-informed commentary: Szekely, B. B., 'The New Soviet Educational Reform', *Comparative Education Review*, vol. 30, no. 3, 1986, pp. 321–43.
4.   Rutkevich, M., 'Is the School Reform Another "Mistake"?', *Current*

Digest of the Soviet Press, vol. 38, no. 47, 1986, translated from *Sovetskaya Rossiya*, 24 October 1986.

5. Ligachev, E. K., 'O khode perestroyki sredney i vysshey shkoly i zadachakh Partii po ee osushchestvleniyu', *Pravda*, 18 February 1988, pp. 1–4.
6. The first is entitled *Zdravstvuyte, deti!* (Moscow: Prosveshchenie, 1983), and the second *Kak zhivete, deti?* (Moscow: Prosveshchenie, 1986).
7. Two useful articles on this fluid period in Soviet education appeared in the *Soviet Education Study Bulletin*, vol. 7, no. 1, 1989: Suddaby, A., 'Perestroika in Soviet Education', pp. 14–21, and Sutherland, J., 'Soviet Education Since 1984, the School Reform, the Innovators, and the APN', pp. 21–33.
8. 'Proekt. Kontseptsiya obshchego srednego obrazovaniya kak bazovo-go v edinoy sisteme nepreryvnogo obrazovaniya (tezisy)', in *Uchitel'skaya gazeta*, 25 August 1988, p. 2.
9. Gosudarstvennyy komitet po narodnomu obrazovaniyu, Vremennyy nauchno-issledovatel'skiy kollektiv 'Shkola', *Proekt. Kontseptsiya obshchego srednego obrazovaniya*, mimeographed typescript in book-let form (Moscow: *Uchitel'skaya gazeta*, 1988).
10. 'Vremennoe polozhenie o sredney obshcheobrazovatel'noy shkole SSSR (primernoe)', *Uchitel'skaya gazeta*, no. 85, 18 July 1989, pp. 1–2.
11. 'Ne stroit' novoy ‹piramidy›', *Uchitel'skaya gazeta*, no. 94, 8 August 1989, p. 1.
12. 'G. Yagodin: za uspekh nado srazhat'sya', *Uchitel'skaya gazeta*, no. 84, 15 July 1989, p. 2.

7 Political Activity in the School

1. A handbook for lecturers delivering these courses gives hints on how to handle passive and indifferent, perhaps even hostile, students: see Razin, V. I., *Obshchaya metodika prepodavaniya filosofii v vuzakh* (Moscow: Vysshaya shkola, 1977), pp. 31–9.
2. On the Komsomol, see Pankov, Yu. N., *Communists and the Youth* [sic!], (Moscow: Progress, 1984), for the traditional official viewpoint. In Russian, standard textbooks for teacher trainees and others include treatment of the youth organisations: see, for example Prokof'ev, M. A., *Narodnoe obrazovanie v SSSR* (Moscow: Pedagogika, 1985), pp. 267–80. Smith, G. B., *Soviet Politics* (London: Macmillan, 1988), esp. pp. 47–8, outlines the Komsomol. A mildly rapturous picture is given in Weaver, K., *Russia's Future* (New York: Praeger, 1981). For the present 'crisis' in the Young Communist League, see Riordan, J., 'The Komsomol', ch. 2 of Riordan, J. (ed.), *Soviet Youth Culture* (London: Macmillan, 1989).
3. On the meaning of 'socialist competition', see Chapter 13.
4. Hill, R. J. and Frank, P., *The Soviet Communist Party*, 2 edn (London: Allen and Unwin, 1983), pp. 37–8, 43 and 65, underline the imbalance between women and men.

5.   'Politiker sollten ihre Worte wägen', *Der Spiegel*, vol. 42, no. 43, 24 October 1988, pp. 20–1.
6.   Lebedeva, S. M. *et al.*, *Izuchaem vtoroy inostrannyy yazyk* (Moscow: Vysshaya shkola, 1986). The extract is even more surprising in view of the relatively recent date of publication of the book.
7.   On 20 October 1988 Soviet Television broadcast a programme for 16-year-olds, in which teenagers were invited to comment on paintings in an exhibition. One picture, entitled 'Has everyone voted?' showed a vast assembly voting unanimously. A young boy commented that it made him realise the dangers of the Stalin and Brezhnev eras, when everyone went along with decisions from above and no one ever spoke out.

8 Learning in Class

1.   The issue attracted wide public attention in England after the publication of S. N. Bennett, *Teaching Styles and Pupil Progress* (London: Open Books, 1976). This work encouraged a mass of discussion, criticism and further studies.
2.   Some of the material used in this chapter is derived from observation of teachers at work, reports of which appeared in Muckle, J., 'Classroom Interactions in Some Soviet and English Schools', *Comparative Education*, vol. 20, no. 2, 1984, pp. 237–51.
3.   Reported in S. A. Gerasimov (ed.), *Sistema esteticheskogo vospitaniya shkol'nikov* (Moscow: Pedagogika, 1983), pp. 80–1.
4.   See Chapter 4, note 6.
5.   The unwillingness of so many Soviet teachers of most subjects to organise their lessons in any other way than as chalk, talk and questions, is illustrated by many orthodox handbooks for teachers. I mention one only; it is a guide for beginning teachers and deals purely with the 'frontal' type of lesson: N. M. Yakovlev *et al.*, *Metodika i tekhnika uroka v shkole* (Moscow: Prosveshchenie, 1985).
6.   The article referred to is that cited in note 10 below. The Soviet version of it appeared as Makl, Dzh. [Muckle, J.], 'Dmitriy Kabalevskiy i ‹tri kita›' in *Muzyka v shkole*, no. 1, 1988, pp. 72–8.
7.   '*Glasnost* in the Communist Curriculum', *Times Educational Supplement*, 30 September 1988, p. 29.
8.   Department of Education and Science/Welsh Office, *English in the National Curriculum* (London: HMSO, 1989).
9.   Zverev, I. D. and Kashin, M. P. (eds), *Sovershenstvovanie soderzhaniya obrazovaniya v shkole* (Moscow: Pedagogika, 1985), p. 62.
10.   Dmitriy Kabalevsky's collection of articles on music education, *Vospitanie uma i serdtse* (Moscow: Prosveshchenie, 1981 and 1984) has appeared in English under the title *Music and Education* (London: Kingsley/UNESCO, 1988). An analysis of his innovative work is contained in Muckle, J., 'Dmitriy Kabalevsky and the Three Whales. Recent Developments in Music Education in the Soviet General Education School', *British Journal of Music Education*, vol. 4, no. 1, 1987, pp. 53–70.

11. Nemensky's work is not so well documented in English as Kabalevsky's. A short article in Russian gives the flavour of his innovations: Nemensky, B., 'Mudrost' krasoty', *Kultura i zhizn'*, no. 6, 1982, pp. 21–2.

9 English Lessons I

1. Monk, Bruce W., English Language Teaching in the USSR with Particular Reference to the Specialised Language Schools. Unpublished M. Phil. thesis, Birkbeck College, University of London, 1988.
2. Those who read Russian may keep abreast of current trends in English teaching through the journal *Inostrannye yazyki v shkole*, published six times a year in Moscow. Some recent articles in English include: Monk, B., 'Some Aspects of the Teaching of Oral Skills in Soviet Schools', *Modern Languages*, vol. 17, no. 2, 1989, pp. 80–7; the same writer's 'Foreign Language Teaching in the Soviet Union: Continuing the Trend', *Journal of Russian Studies*, vol. 50, 1986, pp. 28–37; Muckle, J., 'The Foreign Language Lesson in the Soviet Union', *Modern Languages*, vol. 42, no. 3, 1981, pp. 153–63; and Muckle, J., 'Modern Language Teaching in the Soviet Union', *Perspectives*, vol. 12, 1983, pp. 65–80.
3. For example, Khrustaleva, L. V. and Bogoroditskaya, V. N., *English VI. Uchebnik angliyskogo yazyka dlya VI klassa shkol s uglublennym izucheniem angliyskogo yazyka* (Moscow: Prosveshchenie, 1988).
4. *Ministerstvo prosveshcheniya RSFSR. Programmy sredney shkoly 'Inostrannye yazyki' (dlya shkol s prepodavaniem ryada predmetov na inostrannom yazyke)* (Moscow: Prosveshchenie, 1983).
5. Bogoroditskaya, V. N., *Kniga dlya uchitelya k uchebniku angliyskogo yazyka dlya V klassa . . .* (Moscow: Prosveshchenie, 1985).

10 English Lessons II

1. Divinskaya, E. A. and Vinogradova, E. A., *English X. Uchebnik angliyskogo yazyka*, 5th edn, Moscow (Prosveshchenie) 1984.
2. I refer to Alexander Grin (1880–1932), Russian novelist and story writer. *Scarlet Sails*, a novel set in the author's fantasy country of 'Grinlandia', is probably the best known of his works. It appears in English (with the title curiously translated by Fainna Glagoleva as 'Crimson Sails' [!] in Grin, A., *The Seeker of Adventure* (Moscow: Progress, 1978).
3. The Russian word for 'sadness'.
4. The pupil concerned actually said: 'I can see a political meaning in this picture. The field is full of wheat, but the building in which it is kept [I provided the word 'barn'] seems to have no roof. This is significant for our country today. We have many rich resources, but we cannot organize our affairs correctly.' She had picked up the message of *glasnost'*, it would seem.
5. It is good to be able to add to these remarks that in early 1989 fifteen of the ninth-year pupils and two teachers spent six weeks in America on a

school exchange. This was the first time such a thing had ever happened in that school.

11 Outside the Classroom

1. Such schools as this one here described work according to official statutes. I am grateful to the director for supplying a copy of that which refers to both music and art schools: Ministerstvo kul'tury SSSR, *Polozhenie o detskoy muzykal'noy shkoly i shkole iskusstv sistemy Ministerstva kul'tury SSSR* (Moscow, 1978). It is described on p. 1 as 'Annexe to order no. 515 issued by the Ministry of Culture of the USSR, 17 July 1978'. Note that the schools are run by the *Culture* Ministry, not any of the Education ministries.

2. Documentation specifically on extracurricular activities is not easy to provide, and the reader with no Russian will be hard pressed to find substantial studies of the subject. See, however, Morton, M., *The Arts and the Soviet Child* (New York and London: Free Press, 1972), which contains much valuable information from this date about the musical schools like the one described in this chapter (of which Morton says there are 3500 in the USSR), amateur activities in the arts, libraries, children's theatre and other such matters. The children's and young people's sports schools are described by Riordan, J., in *Soviet Sport* (Oxford: Blackwell, 1980), pp. 59–64.

    In Russian, standard textbooks for trainee teachers often contain sections on extracurricular activities, e.g. Savin, N. V., *Pedagogika* (Moscow: Prosveshchenie, 1978), esp. pp. 280ff., 289ff., 292ff. On extracurricular work with primary children, see for example Bolotina, L. P., *Metodika vneklassnoy vospitatel'noy raboty v nachal'nykh klassakh* (Moscow: Prosveshchenie, 1978).

12 Interview with the Director

1. There is no publication in English which goes in any detail into the administration of education in the USSR. In Russian, see Panachin, F. G., *Upravlenie prosveshchenie v SSSR* (Moscow: Prosveshchenie, 1977).

2. For this information I am indebted to an unpublished source, Lynch, J., *et al.*, 'Report of a Visit by an Educational Delegation from the United Kingdom to the Soviet Union in September 1983', which was presented to the British Council in October 1983. The programme of study described appears on pp. 13–14.

3. Such as Panachin, F. G., *Shkola i obshchestvennyy progress* (Moscow: Prosveshchenie, 1983).

4. Tyurnpuu, L. A., *Problemnye zadachi dlya rukovoditeley shkol*, 2 mimeographed booklets 32 and 25 pp. (Tallin, 1979).

5. *Narodnoe obrazovanie*, 1988, nos 1–12, and 1989, nos 3, 4, and 5.

6. 'Conditions of Employment of Head Teachers', in Department of Education and Science, *School Teachers' Pay and Conditions Document 1989* (London: HMSO, 1989), pp. 20–3.

7. For some of the insights in this paragraph I am indebted to Mrs P. Partington, a headteacher and official of the National Association of Head Teachers.

13 The Teachers' Trade Union

1. Lenin, V. I., *Collected Works* (London: Lawrence and Wishart, 1965), vol. 32, p. 20.
2. For a very brief outline in English of the Soviet trade union movement, see Smith, G. B., *Soviet Politics, Continuity and Contradiction*, (London: Macmillan, 1988), pp. 204–8. A fuller account appears in Ruble, B., *Soviet Trade Unions* (Cambridge: Cambridge University Press, 1981). Documents relating to trade union legislation are contained in Alekseev, G. P. *et al.*, *O pravakh profsoyuzov. Sbornik zakonodatel'stva SSSR* (Moscow: Profizdat, 1983).

14 Future Good Men and Women

1. See Articles 60 to 69 in ch. 7 of the USSR Constitution of 1977.
2. The classic Western study of upbringing in the Soviet family and in pre-school education is Bronfenbrenner, U., *Two Worlds of Childhood. US and USSR* (New York: Simon and Schuster, 1972).
3. It would be impossible to begin to present a representative list of such works here. However, one little handbook for class tutors must have proved invaluable to many a Soviet teacher: Oliferenko, L. Ya. (ed.), *Sputnik klassnogo rukovoditelya 1988/89* (Moscow: Prosveshchenie, 1988). It contains a host of short articles on such topics as the youth organisations and their role in upbringing work, the duties of a class tutor, the lives of famous people whose jubilees occur during the year and the 'peace lesson' on 1 September (referred to later in the text of this chapter). Each month of the school year is taken separately; there is a list of festivals and anniversaries which may or must be celebrated and suggestions for topics of tutorial discussions – alcohol abuse, ecological matters, AIDS, patriotic education, Lenin, 'non-traditional religions' and their dangers to young people, artistic matters, and many, many others.
4. A full treatment has recently appeared in English, covering moral, political, atheistic, peace, gender and multi-cultural aspects of the subject: Avis, G., *The Making of the Soviet Citizen* (Beckenham: Croom Helm, 1987).
5. Riordan, J., 'Youth Organisations in the Soviet School', in Avis (see note 4 above), p. 153.
6. 'Peace Education in the Soviet Union' in Avis, pp. 161–83, esp. p. 179.
7. Dunstan, J., 'Atheistic Education in the USSR', in Avis, pp. 50–79.
8. Gordienko, N. S., *Sovremennoe russkoe pravoslavie* (Leningrad: Lenizdat, 1988).

In Conclusion

1. I have used the following works in this discussion: Dunstan, J., *Paths to Excellence and the Soviet School* (Windsor: NFER, 1978); Grant, N., *Soviet Education*, 4th edn (Harmondsworth: Penguin, 1979); Matthews, M., *Education in the Soviet Union: Policies and Institutions Since Stalin* (London: Allen and Unwin, 1972); Muckle, J., *A Guide to the Soviet Curriculum* (London: Croom Helm, 1988); and Shturman, D., *The Soviet Secondary School* (London: Routledge, 1988).
2. Dunstan, pp. 250–1.
3. Matthews, P. 205.
4. Grant, p. 179.
5. Shturman, p. 303.
6. Grant, pp. 176–7.
7. Matthews, p. 202.
8. Muckle, pp. 105–6.
9. Muckle, pp. 188–9.

Index